CAREER OPPORTUNITIES IN TRAVEL AND TOURISM

CAREER OPPORTUNITIES IN TRAVEL AND TOURISM

JOHN K. HAWKS

Facts On File®

AN INFOBASE HOLDINGS COMPANY

Career Opportunities in Travel and Tourism

Facts On File, Inc.
460 Park Avenue South
New York NY 10016

Library of Congress Cataloging-in-Publication Data

Hawks, John K.
　　Career opportunities in travel and tourism / John K. Hawks.
　　　　p.　cm. — (Career opportunities series)
　　Includes bibliographical references and index.
　　ISBN 0-8160-3036-7 (hardcover)
　　　　0-8160-3037-5 (paperback)
　　1.　Tourist trade—vocational guidance.　I. Title.　II. Series.
　G155.5H39　1995
　338.4'791023—dc20　　　　　　　　　　　　　　　94-39981

Facts On File books are available at special discounts when purchased in
bulk quantities for businesses, associations, institutions or sales promotions.
Please call our Special Sales Department in New York at 212/683–2244 or
800/322–8755.

Jacket design by Amy Beth Gonzalez

This book is printed on acid-free paper.

Printed in the United States of America

VB FOF 10 9 8 7 6 5 4 3 2 1

Other Books in Facts On File's Career Opportunities Series:

Career Opportunities in Theater and the Performing Arts
Career Opportunities in the Sports Industry
Career Opportunities in the Music Industry
Career Opportunities for Writers

Other Facts On File Books by John K. Hawks:

Youth Exchanges: The Complete Guide to the Homestay Experience Abroad

For my brother Billy

CONTENTS

ACKNOWLEDGMENTS

This book would not have been possible without the patient help and exhaustive research provided by the following travel industry colleagues: Dick Knodt and Nancy Gravatt at the American Society of Travel Agents; W. James Host, Hank Phillips, Lisa Carey, Lisa Simon, Kim Griffin, S. Burkett "Doc" Milner, and Bob Hoelscher at the National Tour Association; Ed Griffin at Meeting Professionals International; Richard Newman and Stephen Carey at the International Association of Convention and Visitors Bureaus; Ken Hine and Chuck Timanus at the American Hotel and Motel Association; Bill Fisher and Wendy Webster at the National Restaurant Association; Bill Jackman at the Air Transport Association of America; Jan Armstrong at the American Car Rental Association; George Snyder and Susan Perry at the American Bus Association; Steve Sprague at the United Bus Owners of America; Jim Godsman at the Cruise Lines International Association; John Severini and Valerie Gadway at Royal Cruise Lines; John Stachnik and Mary Stachnik at Mayflower Tours; Woody Peek at Opryland USA; Eugene Dilbeck at the Denver Convention and Visitors Bureau; Ed Hall at the Greater Houston Convention and Visitors Bureau; Mac Lacy and Herb Sparrow at *The Group Travel Leader*; Dinah Spritzer at *Travel Weekly*; Mikki Dorsey at *Travel Agent*; Dee Minic at the Tourism Works For America Council; Patti Hubbard at the National Council of State Travel Directors; Cheryl Hargrove at the National Trust for Historic Preservation; Keith Howard and Karen Lucas at the National Tour Foundation; Ned Book, Russell Lee, Dexter Koehl, and Tom Berrigan at the Travel Industry Association of America; Karen Peterson at Davidson–Peterson Associates; and Al Anolik of Alexander Anolik Professional Law.

These professionals answered my initial questions about their segments of the vast travel industry, gathered research reports and other objective data, and (in many cases) reviewed the final entries in the book. I thank them for giving their time and talents cheerfully in this project.

I want to extend my gratitude also to Michelle Fellner, my editor at Facts On File, for her infinite patience as I completed the manuscript in the midst of launching a new business.

Finally, my writing career would not be possible without the faith and devotion of my agent Anita Diamant.

FOREWORD

As one who has been a part of the travel industry for more than 40 years, there are two points that my tenure suggests: I am probably older than the person who is going to read this book; and second, I like this industry.

There's not much to comment on the first point. About the second? Indeed, I do like travel and tourism, and I hope that you will find a career path in the industry that will provide you with as much challenge, excitement, and satisfaction as it has brought me.

Opportunity abounds in the travel industry. It is the third largest business in the nation and the second largest employer—only the health care industry employs more people—and it should continue to grow.

But know this: As large as the travel industry is, and as much as it contributes to the economy, culture, and social fabric of the country, the challenges it faces in the years ahead will test its health and vitality and could dim the bright vision of opportunity it should present to you.

Here are brief descriptions of three challenges that stand out, and what they mean to you.

First, recent tax legislation shows that the federal government seems to be taxing the very industry that is growing the fastest and providing jobs and income at a rate unmatched in our nation's economy. Not only that, few of the taxes affecting the travel industry are returned to pay for programs that would support the industry.

This means that you should not think that travel is an apolitical industry. Whatever your politics are—and you don't have to wear them on your sleeve—we're going to have to stick together and make sure the industry's agenda is heard and heeded.

Second, if the field is going to continue to grow—especially in terms of international tourism—someone is going to have to pay for all of the infrastructure needs this entails. This includes new roads. Airport expansion. Additional customs facilities and personnel. And on and on.

Due to this—and related to the first point—we in the industry have got to work to make sure that governments and kindred industries work with us to find funding sources for our very real infrastructure needs.

Finally, you are going to have to continue to educate yourself as the industry grows; growth means technology will get smarter and more complex in order to deal with the processing needs that expansion warrants. Think of it. Only 20 years ago, most airline ticket reservations were done by hand and over the telephone. Today's computer reservation systems in all parts of the industry mandate that even entry-level employees must be not merely literate but computer literate.

For you, this means that you're going to have to work hard just to stay in place. If you want to get ahead, you're going to have to work even harder. Expand your capabilities and grow with the industry.

With all of these challenges, I am pleased that *Career Opportunities in Travel and Tourism* is available. It makes choices easier by making things clear and easy to understand. It is the first step in mustering the energy and commitment that you will need to help yourself and this industry meet the challenges that lie ahead.

So, as you're told often these days, go for it!

And good luck.

Edward R. Book, Former President
Travel Industry Association of America

AGENTS, PACKAGERS, AND PLANNERS

OWNER/MANAGER, TRAVEL AGENCY

CAREER PROFILE

Duties: Manages the operations and customer service functions in a travel agency; trains and supervises the agency's personnel; prospects and develops new clients

Alternate Title(s): None

Salary Range: $21,000 to $45,000

Employment Prospects: Very good to excellent

Best Geographic Location: Most regions of the country offer management and ownership possibilities.

Prerequisites:

Education and Training—High school diploma required, with math, business, and geography courses helpful; college degree desirable, with computer science, business, and geography courses helpful; completion of a travel agent program in a recognized travel academy; completion of a recognized professional certification program

Experience—Work experience in customer relations or direct sales; business management experience; work experience in a travel agency and/or other segments of the travel industry (e.g., hotel, tour company)

Special Skills and Personality Traits—Sales ability; attention to detail; organization; problem-solving ability; supervising employees; business planning; strong oral and written communication skills; interpersonal skills

CAREER LADDER

```
┌─────────────────────────────────────┐
│                                      │
│    Manager or Owner, Travel Agency   │
│                                      │
└─────────────────────────────────────┘

┌─────────────────────────────────────┐
│                                      │
│            Travel Agent              │
│                                      │
└─────────────────────────────────────┘

┌─────────────────────────────────────┐
│                                      │
│          Clerk, Travel Agency        │
│                                      │
└─────────────────────────────────────┘
```

Position Description

The owner or manager of a travel agency assumes the ultimate responsibility for the agency's success. The owner must deal with the financial, operational, legal, and customer service functions that arise in the course of running the average agency.

As a first step, the owner must receive the approval of various industry conferences—organizations of airlines or other travel suppliers—in order for the agency to claim commissions on its bookings. For example, before airline commissions are paid the owner may have to prove that the agency is currently in operation, that it is financially sound, and that it employs at least one experienced travel agent who can handle reservations properly. Because conference approvals can be delayed for a year or more in some cases, the manager must have a sufficient amount of working capital to operate the

agency in the first year before these additional profits are earned. (Typically, commissions on hotel rooms and tours can be requested without conference approvals.)

Also, the owner must learn about the current licensing, bonding, and registration requirements in the state or states in which the agency operates. For example, Hawaii requires agencies to register with the state and demonstrate that they have adequate insurance coverage. (Such insurance includes errors and omissions insurance, which protects the owner against mistakes such as the wrong price being printed in an agency brochure.)

Because travel agents actually sell services on behalf of travel suppliers, the manager must train and maintain a professional staff who can handle detailed reservations under stressful conditions. The manager will be responsible for designing training programs and scheduling "familiarization" trips (low-cost tours taken by travel agents to learn more about different destinations).

In today's competitive marketplace, the agency manager will have to implement aggressive marketing and promotion plans to entice more leisure travelers to rely on the agency's services. To capture business travelers, the manager will be the primary salesperson contacting corporations and businesses to become new clients.

Beyond dispensing advice to their clients, agents play a critical role in confirming arrangements for a trip. They secure the necessary documents for segments of the trip (airline tickets, hotel reservations, etc.) and transfer payment to the corresponding suppliers, who then issue commissions (ranging from 5 to 15 percent or more) to the agency. Therefore, the owner must have the financial acumen and organizational skills to track these activities and to resolve paperwork or payment problems.

Given the industry's strong focus on personal sales guidance, a travel agency must develop a reputation for excellent customer service. Therefore, the owner will be charged with resolving disputes raised by customers, ranging from inferior accommodations on a tour to lower prices offered by competing agencies. The agency actually may bear legal liability in some cases, so the manager must be aware of current laws and display sensitivity in working with customers.

The owner must develop strategic plans for the future direction of the agency. Most agencies tend to handle all types of clients, both corporate and leisure. However, the owner may choose to specialize in one of several areas: group sales, corporate travel accounts, or "FITs" (Frequent Independent Travelers). Also, managers may concentrate their efforts on a particular mode of traveling (e.g., cruises, rail travel) or on specific destinations (e.g., United States, Caribbean, South Pacific).

Salaries

Travel agency managers with one to five years of experience may earn $21,000 or more, depending on the agency's customer base and structure. Managers with more experience can advance to salaries of $45,000 or more.

While they may not draw large salaries when they launch their agencies, owners have greater earning potential once the business is established, largely as the result of retained earnings in the agency.

In terms of benefits, most owners and managers have health and life insurance, and many of them enjoy travel perks (such as reduced fares and incentive gifts) at travel industry events and on familiarization tours.

Employment Prospects

Most areas in the United States offer very strong management and business opportunities for qualified owners and managers, depending on the level of competition in a given location and the experience and financial resources of the manager.

Several trends point toward continued growth for travel agencies in the 1990s and beyond. Improving business conditions will support steady corporate travel patterns. More consumers (particularly aging baby boomers) will invest in vacations to enjoy their leisure time and to expose their children to new experiences.

Because new owners must demonstrate that at least one employee has the necessary experience and skills to handle reservations in order to gain conference approvals, prospective owners and managers should have several years of experience in a travel agency, particularly in using computerized reservations systems.

Some new owners begin their agencies independently, relying solely on their working experience in the industry. Other owners decide to join existing travel agency alliances and consortia such as American Express, gaining expertise and support services (such as preferred supplier agreements, which give the owners greater commissions for selling the travel packages of certain cruise lines or tour operators); in return, the owners pay royalty fees, advertising fees, or similar charges to the alliances or consortia. To avoid a prolonged start-up period, some owners may purchase an existing agency, so that they can rely on its cash flow and its conference appointments immediately.

(Given the low average salaries for travel agents, starting or purchasing an agency requires a great deal of advance planning and, in many cases, loans or outside investors to make the deal work.)

Advancement Prospects

Within a single agency, becoming owner or manager is the top step in terms of advancement. However, owners and managers can expand the company, and thus increase the scope of the position, by opening or purchasing other agencies, by increasing their specialization in popular types of travel, or by offering their own package tours or other travel "sideline" businesses.

Education and Training

Within the industry, the primary avenue for advanced training is the Certified Travel Counselor program offered by the Institute of Certified Travel Agents.

Also, owners and managers may opt for the Destination Specialist programs, to increase their knowledge about the Caribbean, South Pacific, or North America.

In certain sales areas, owners and managers will seek specialized certifications (e.g., the Certified Tour Professional program for group sales offered by the National Tour Association).

Additional training in sales skills, computer operations, and geography will be helpful.

Experience, Skills, and Personality Traits

The most important skills for an owner or manager will be motivating and managing employees and prospecting and securing new clients. Increasingly, the manager will need computer skills and financial acumen to operate the agency in today's very competitive environment.

Unions and Associations

Travel agency owners and managers generally do not belong to a national union. Two major national associations exist for travel agents in general: the American Society of Travel Agents (ASTA), located in Alexandria, Virginia, and the Association of Retail Agents (ARTA), located in Harrisburg, Pennsylvania. Both groups offer seminars, government representation, and marketing assistance to travel agents, managers, and owners.

Tips for Entry

1. Consider entering a travel agent training program (which lasts one month to one year or longer) offered by a recognized travel academy, college, or university. You will need the specific skills offered in this type of program, particularly if you plan to launch your own agency.

2. Gain experience working with customers in a travel agency. Beyond the actual skills you will develop in planning trips for these clients and serving their needs, you will learn firsthand whether owning or managing an agency is for you.

3. Develop your sales abilities, accounting skills, and computer knowledge through advanced training or additional work experience.

4. Increase your understanding of the world's geography, until you have a working knowledge of the location of major nations and cities. Also, consider developing a base of experience and knowledge in a certain area of the world or in one type of traveling (e.g., cruising).

5. Write major travel agency franchisors or consortia to request information about their requirements for membership. You will be able to plan ahead in terms of the financing or years of experience required.

6. If you launch your own agency, plan on a tight cash flow for at least the first full year, as you apply for conference approvals.

TRAVEL AGENT

CAREER PROFILE

Duties: Counsels clients, recommending destinations and specific travel services; confirms details of a trip for clients; serves current clients and solicits new ones

Alternate Title(s): Travel counselor

Salary Range: $17,900 to $26,100

Employment Prospects: Excellent

Best Geographic Location: Most regions of the country offer job possibilities.

Prerequisites:

Education and Training—High school diploma required, with math and geography courses helpful; additional training in computer systems; completion of a travel agent program in a recognized travel academy

Experience—Direct sales; customer relations; work experience in another segment of the travel industry (e.g., hotel, tour operator)

Special Skills and Personality Traits—Sales ability; attention to detail; organization; problem-solving ability; strong oral and written communication skills; interpersonal skills

CAREER LADDER

```
┌─────────────────────────────────────┐
│                                      │
│   Manager or Owner, Travel Agency    │
│                                      │
└─────────────────────────────────────┘

┌─────────────────────────────────────┐
│                                      │
│             Travel Agent             │
│                                      │
└─────────────────────────────────────┘

┌─────────────────────────────────────┐
│                                      │
│         Clerk, Travel Agency         │
│                                      │
└─────────────────────────────────────┘
```

Position Description

Travel agents deal directly with prospective travelers to select and confirm the various components of their trips: transportation, accommodations, meals, admissions to attractions, and other details. Although agents serve legally as sales representatives for travel suppliers, who pay commissions based on the agents' sales of their services, travel agents actually work for the traveler by making objective recommendations about specific destinations and travel services.

Essentially, travel agents serve as a source of information for travelers. Through the agency's inventory of brochures and their own travel experiences, agents provide travelers with the necessary background for making critical decisions about their upcoming trips. In this role, agents guide their clients in planning where to go, how to get there, and what to do once they arrive.

In recent years, however, agents have assumed more responsibility for initiating and closing sales with consumers, rather than simply dispensing advice and taking orders. Successful agents develop a base of clients who

receive regular advice on potential trips, special supplier rates, and other information designed to encourage these travelers to take additional trips.

Given the industry's strong focus on personal sales guidance, agents must practice excellent customer service habits.

In many agencies, agents spend most of the time serving the needs of existing clients. However, working with the agency owner or manager, agents may be involved in soliciting and making presentations to prospective clients.

Beginning agents tend to handle all types of clients, both corporate and leisure. However, agents with more experience may choose to specialize in one of several areas: group sales, corporate travel accounts, or "FITs" (Frequent Independent Travelers). Also, agents may concentrate their efforts on a particular mode of traveling (e.g., cruises, rail travel) or on specific destinations (e.g., United States, Caribbean, South Pacific).

Beyond dispensing advice to their clients, agents play a critical role in confirming arrangements for the trip.

They secure the necessary documents for segments of the trip (airline tickets, hotel reservations, etc.) and transfer payment to the corresponding suppliers, who then issue commissions (ranging from 5 to 15 percent or more) to the agency. Beyond the electronic reservations made via computer, agents must deal with a complex amount of paperwork, from client itineraries to confirmation notices, making clerical skills and an eye for accuracy very important.

With any number of new trips being planned daily, combined with the amount of time needed to confirm every segment of a proposed trip, the average day in an agency can be very hectic. Successful agents exhibit very strong organizational skills to track this activity, so that clients receive satisfactory service every time.

If clients encounter problems during their trips, or if they return with complaints, agents are the primary persons responsible for resolving the problems and satisfying the clients. Therefore, agents must have strong problem-solving skills, such as the ability to identify the proper managers in a hotel or other travel supplier who can remedy the situation, and they must possess the public relations sense to turn each complaint into a positive experience for the client.

There is an increasing trend for agents to be paid on commission, rather than strictly a base salary, which can lead to enormous stress at times. Agents need to be able to handle such pressure and derive satisfaction from helping travelers plan and complete their journeys.

Salaries

Travel agents with less than five years' experience earn salaries averaging $17,900, while those with six to 10 years' experience average $20,800. The pay level increases to an average of $26,100 for travel counselors with more than 21 years of experience. Agents who wish to increase their earnings more significantly must consider moving into agency management or ownership.

Nearly half of all agents earn, on the average, an additional $1,320 per year from commissions, bonuses, or incentives.

In terms of benefits, three out of five agents receive paid days for participating in travel industry events or familiarization tours. They usually can arrange discounted personal vacations in addition to these familiarization tours. Half of all agencies provide health, life, and dental insurance.

Employment Prospects

Most areas in the United States offer very strong job opportunities for qualified travel counselors, especially agents with advanced training such as the Certified Travel Counselor program or Destination Specialist programs offered by the Institute of Certified Travel Agents.

Several trends point toward continued growth for travel agencies in the 1990s and beyond. Improving business conditions will support steady corporate travel patterns. More consumers (particularly aging baby boomers) will invest in vacations to enjoy their leisure time and to expose their children to new experiences.

Because travel agencies depend heavily on the use of computer reservation systems, agents familiar with one or more national systems will have the freedom to seek employment throughout the country.

Advancement Prospects

Travel agents seeking to advance in their careers face two possible options. They can move into management positions within their agency by gaining additional years of experience or by completing advanced training programs. Another way many agents choose to advance is to establish their own agency (as an independent location, as an affiliate in a travel agency consortium, or as a franchised agency).

Education and Training

Within the industry, the primary avenue for advanced training is the Certified Travel Counselor program offered by the Institute of Certified Travel Agents.

Also, agents may opt for the Destination Specialist programs, increasing their knowledge about the Caribbean, South Pacific, or North America.

In certain sales areas, agents will seek specialized certifications (e.g., the Certified Tour Professional program for group sales offered by the National Tour Association).

Additional training in sales skills, computer operations, and geography will be helpful.

Experience, Skills, and Personality Traits

The most important skills for a travel agents are a keen sense of organization and attention to detail to plan the complex itineraries of clients and strong communication abilities to relate well with clients and coworkers in a stressful, hectic environment. Increasingly, agents will need direct sales training and computer skills to cope with the more demanding business climate.

Unions and Associations

Travel agents generally do not belong to a national union. Two major national associations exist for travel agents: the American Society of Travel Agents (ASTA), located in Alexandria, Virginia, and the Association of Retail Agents (ARTA), located in Harrisburg, Pennsylvania. Both groups offer seminars, government representation, and marketing assistance to travel agents, managers, and owners.

Tips for Entry

1.   Consider entering a travel agent training program (which lasts one month to one year or longer) offered by a recognized travel academy, college, or university.

2.   Develop your sales abilities and computer skills through advanced training or additional work experience.

3.   Increase your understanding of the world's geography, until you have a working knowledge of the location of major nations and cities.

4.   As you interview with agencies, highlight any past experience working with travel suppliers or public-sector tourism organizations, especially if the work included direct sales experience.

5.   To discover whether you would enjoy being an agent, offer to intern at a local agency, as an office clerk or administrative assistant. Many successful agents have followed this path—even without pay—in order to gain valuable work experience.

OUTSIDE SALES AGENT, TRAVEL AGENCY

CAREER PROFILE

Duties: Serves as a counselor to clients, recommending destinations and specific travel services; confirms details of a client's trip; develops independent bases of clients

Alternate Title(s): Independent agent

Salary Range: $15,000 to $35,000+

Employment Prospects: Very good

Best Geographic Location: Most regions of the country offer job possibilities.

Prerequisites:

Education and Training—High school diploma required, with math and geography courses helpful; additional training in computer systems; completion of a travel agent program in a recognized travel academy

Experience—Direct sales; customer relations; work experience in another segment of the travel industry (e.g., hotel, tour operator); managing an independent business

Special Skills and Personality Traits—Sales ability; attention to detail; organization; ability to work alone; problem-solving ability; strong oral and written communication skills; interpersonal skills

CAREER LADDER

```
┌─────────────────────────────────────┐
│                                      │
│   Manager or Owner, Travel Agency    │
│                                      │
└─────────────────────────────────────┘

┌─────────────────────────────────────┐
│                                      │
│  Outside Travel Agent, Travel Agency │
│                                      │
└─────────────────────────────────────┘
```

Position Description

Outside sales agents deal directly with prospective travelers to select and confirm the various components of their trips: transportation, accommodations, meals, admissions to attractions, and other details. However, while the average travel agent is a full-time employee of the travel agency, an outside sales agent serves as an independent contractor.

Outside sales agents develop their own clients, through their reputation as excellent travel planners or their affiliation with special-interest groups (e.g., senior citizens' centers, employee associations, civic clubs). They set their own hours and can work out of their homes. Once they have made a sale, they normally will contact the travel agency with which they are working, so that a full-time agent can make the necessary reservations.

Like average travel agents, outside sales agents serve as a source of information for travelers. Through the agency's inventory of brochures and their own travel experiences, outside sales agents provide travelers with the necessary background for making critical decisions about their upcoming trips. In this role, outside sales agents guide their clients in planning where to go, how to get there, and what to do once they arrive.

To cement their relationship with their base of clients, outside sales agents may offer regular advice on potential trips, special supplier rates, newsletters, and other information designed to encourage these travelers to take additional trips.

Outside sales agents must have excellent interpersonal skills, since they must rely on both an extensive network of regular clients and the staffers in the travel agency to make their independent arrangement work.

Unlike agents employed in a travel agency who may deal with many different types of travel arrangements, most outside sales agents choose to specialize in one of several areas: group sales, corporate travel accounts, or "FITs" (Frequent Independent Travelers). Also, they may concentrate their efforts on a particular mode of traveling (e.g., cruises, rail travel) or on specific destinations (e.g., United States, Caribbean, South Pacific).

Because they are independent contractors, outside sales agents do not receive a set salary. Instead, they keep 25 to 75 percent of the commission that the travel agency receives from the bookings they generate, depending on their agreement. The commission amounts received by outside sales agents usually vary proportionally to the volume of business generated. In many cases, outside sales agents also receive an allowance to cover a portion of basic business expenses (e.g., postage, telephone calls).

Successful outside sales agents must exhibit very strong organizational skills to track numerous new trips being planned daily as well as confirmation of every segment of a proposed trip.

Salaries

Because the earnings of outside sales agents are based entirely upon their sales productivity—most outside agents work on 100 percent commission, with no base salary and a share of their expenses to absorb—beginning outside agents can expect to earn $15,000 or more in their first year. As they expand their clientele and gather repeat business, their earnings can grow to $35,000 or more. In most instances, however, they must pay for fringe benefits such as life and health insurance.

Employment Prospects

Most areas in the United States offer very strong job opportunities for qualified outside sales agents, especially agents with advanced training such as the Certified Travel Counselor program or Destination Specialist programs offered by the Institute of Certified Travel Agents.

While their status as independent contractors allows outside sales agents greater mobility in moving to another part of the country, their success in a new location will depend greatly on existing client contacts and their ability to generate new clients on their own.

Advancement Prospects

Outside sales agents may advance their careers by continuing to expand their client bases, even to the point of generating sufficient volume to open a new agency. If they prefer, they can move into an agency as a full-time employee, bringing their clients with them.

Education and Training

Within the industry, the primary avenue for advanced training is the Certified Travel Counselor program offered by the Institute of Certified Travel Agents.

Also, outside sales agents may opt for the Destination Specialist programs, increasing their knowledge about the Caribbean, South Pacific, or North America.

In certain sales areas, outside sales agents will seek specialized certifications (e.g., the Certified Tour Professional program for group sales offered by the National Tour Association).

Additional training in sales skills, computer operations, and geography will be helpful.

Experience, Skills, and Personality Traits

Outside sales agents must have a high level of motivation and sales ability, to generate the number of independent customers needed to support themselves. Also, they must be organized and pay attention to details so that they can keep track of the reservations made for their clients.

Unions and Associations

Outside sales agents generally do not belong to a national union. Two major national associations exist for travel agents: the American Society of Travel Agents (ASTA), located in Alexandria, Virginia, and the Association of Retail Agents (ARTA), located in Harrisburg, Pennsylvania. Both groups offer seminars, government representation, and marketing assistance to outside sales agents, travel agents, managers, and owners.

Tips for Entry

1. Consider entering a travel agent training program (which lasts one month to one year or longer) offered by a recognized travel academy, college, or university.

2. Develop your business management and sales skills in another position—particularly within a travel agency—before you go out on your own.

3. Check recent changes in independent contractor rules before you sign an agreement with a travel agency. For example, the Internal Revenue Service now enforces a strict list of 20 conditions that independent contractors must meet; otherwise, the travel agency becomes liable for certain employment taxes.

4. Consider your possible client bases carefully. Do you have contacts and friends in local clubs or companies who would book travel through you? You will need a fairly substantial base of clients to generate enough cash flow to support yourself as an independent agent.

5. As you interview with agencies, highlight any past experience working in travel agencies or other travel companies. Be ready to prove your worth to an agency by listing your potential base of clients.

6. Make plans to publicize your services extensively. In fact, map out a full marketing plan that you can share with prospective travel agencies.

CORPORATE TRAVEL MANAGER

CAREER PROFILE

Duties: Plans and confirms travel arrangements for a company's employees, customers, or suppliers; manages travel and entertainment expenses to meet budgets; negotiates favorable travel agreements and fares; plans and coordinates the company's meetings and (in some cases) conventions

Alternate Title(s): Business travel manager

Salary Range: $22,500 to $50,300+

Employment Prospects: Good

Best Geographic Location: Most corporate travel managers will be employed in medium-size and large companies. Therefore, most job opportunities will be found in major metropolitan areas or suburban corporate centers.

Prerequisites:

Education and Training—High school diploma required; college degree generally required, with courses in business management, finance, and travel and tourism helpful; completion of a travel agent program in a recognized travel academy helpful; professional certification from a travel industry association; graduate degree in business management helpful for advancement

Experience—Work experience in a travel agency (especially dealing with business travelers) or another travel company; financial management; computer operations; human resources programs

Special Skills and Personality Traits—Attention to detail; problem-solving ability; organization; strong oral and written communications skills; interpersonal skills; negotiating skills

CAREER LADDER

```
┌─────────────────────────────────┐
│                                 │
│  Vice President, Human Resources │
│         or Finance              │
│                                 │
└─────────────────────────────────┘

┌─────────────────────────────────┐
│                                 │
│    Corporate Travel Manager     │
│                                 │
└─────────────────────────────────┘

┌─────────────────────────────────┐
│                                 │
│  Clerk, Corporate Travel Department │
│                                 │
└─────────────────────────────────┘
```

Position Description

Because travel and entertainment costs have become one of the largest categories of expenses for many U.S. corporations, corporate travel managers have become critical experts in the finance and administrative departments of these companies.

Their primary responsibility is to construct a travel management program that allows the company's workers to serve customers and expand the business without exceeding acceptable limits on travel and entertainment expenses. Will travel decisions be centralized in the company's headquarters, or decentralized throughout every branch office? How do these policies compare with those of similar corporations around the country? The corporate travel manager must consider these and many other questions in structuring the company's travel management program.

To insure that the company's employees understand and support the overall program, corporate travel managers must design and communicate specific travel policies. These policies range from the instances in which first-class air travel will be allowed to the number of times an employee must remain in a city through Saturday night in order to receive discounted weekend airfares. Because these policies may favor the company's need to save money over the employee's personal preferences, corporate travel managers must be skilled communicators and firm authorities to insure that both budgets and morale are preserved.

In many cases, the company needs the services of a travel agency or travel management company to organize travel plans and coordinate reservations. Corporate travel managers must assess the company's needs, select the appropriate travel management company, and supervise the daily operations and reservations work. When activity and expense reports are needed from the agency, or when problems arise between employees and the agency, the corporate travel managers must negotiate solutions.

Today many travel agencies and suppliers employ advanced corporate travel technology to serve their clients. For example, instead of delivering airline tickets by hand to the company's headquarters and branch offices, the agency may install an electronic ticket delivery network, so that airline tickets can be printed within each branch office. Corporate travel managers must make decisions regarding the types of technology needed (and the fees involved) and train employees in using the devices.

Managing meetings falls into the arena of corporate travel managers. They must decide which meetings are necessary (i.e., whether they are worth the cost and time involved, or whether the business could be conducted via other means such as telephone conference calls). Then they must reserve hotel rooms and facilities, plan special events, coordinate airline and car rental reservations, and handle other details of the meetings.

To keep travel costs in line, corporate travel managers must negotiate favorable rates for their company with major travel suppliers such as airlines, hotels, and car rental companies. Also, they will supervise the use of corporate credit cards for travel expenses; in some cases, they will review the actual expense reports filed by employees to insure that all travel policies are being followed.

Salaries

Despite recent cost-cutting and downsizing efforts by U.S. corporations, the salaries of corporate travel managers have kept track with inflation. Like other workers in the finance and administrative departments, beginning corporate travel managers will earn salaries from $22,500. The average salary after eight to 10 years in the travel management field ranges from $39,100 to $50,100.

Employment Prospects

Most corporate travel managers work in companies with a significant number of employees or branch offices. Therefore, the best prospects for work in this field will surface in major metropolitan areas or suburban corporate centers where these large companies can be found.

Because many companies continue to be concerned with cutting costs, many travel managers with experience in travel operations will find opportunities in other firms (especially if they can demonstrate the worth of their recommendations to the company's bottom line).

However, this field may be restricted to some extent by a continuing corporate emphasis on downsizing and on outsourcing (hiring independent firms to handle the tasks normally assigned to corporate travel managers). Also, positions in this field tend to be static, so mobility may be limited.

Advancement Prospects

Corporate travel managers develop key management skills—communication, problem solving, and negotiating—that make them excellent candidates for the upper echelons of management. They will be promoted primarily to higher positions overseeing the company's other administrative services or financial services.

Also, some corporate travel managers opt to transfer to positions with travel agencies or suppliers, parlaying their experience from the client side into a higher assignment.

Education and Training

For most travel management positions, the essential requirement is a college degree with an emphasis in business management, finance, or travel and tourism. To position themselves for future promotions, many managers opt for a graduate degree in business management or finance.

They also may complete a travel agent program in a recognized travel academy.

Additional training in negotiating skills and human resources would be helpful.

Experience, Skills, and Personality Traits

Corporate travel managers must have exceptional skills in oral and written communications, so that they can design effective travel policies and programs and persuade employees to honor them. Given the complex nature of making travel reservations for large numbers of employees, travel managers should develop problem-solving skills to work through the inevitable disagreements and errors that will arise. Negotiating skills will help corporate travel managers strike effective agreements with travel agencies and suppliers.

Unions and Associations

Corporate travel managers generally do not belong to a national union. The major national trade associations for corporate travel managers are the National Business Travel Association (NBTA), located in Alexandria, Virginia, and the Association of Corporate Travel Executives (ACTE), located in Springfield, New Jersey. Both groups offer seminars, government representation, publications, and career planning assistance to corporate travel managers.

Tips for Entry

1.   Consider gaining work experience within a travel agency that specializes in corporate travel. By doing so you will gain a better understanding of corporate travel management from the operations side, before you attempt to secure a job with a company.

2.   Prepare for an extensive job search, since corporate travel management is a relatively new and somewhat limited field. In fact, you should not overlook sources such as recruiters, who place many candidates in corporate travel management positions.

3.   Develop your sales and presentation skills. You will spend much of your time in this field communicating policies and procedures to employees; if you can demonstrate experience in these areas, you will have an advantage in securing that first job.

4.   Remain flexible regarding your desired assignments. Diversify your talents, and work beyond your job description. Your willingness to tackle duties related to corporate travel management will help you when you are considered for promotions.

5.   Take advantage of every opportunity to demonstrate the worth of your work to the company's bottom line. Corporate travel managers should take time to prove their worth in cutting and controlling travel and entertainment expenses.

DIRECTOR OF SALES AND MARKETING, TOUR COMPANY

CAREER PROFILE

Duties: Prepares marketing plans to satisfy current clients and secure new clients for the tour company; schedules presentations and makes sales calls on individual customers and groups; confirms reservations and travel plans as well as payment arrangements

Alternate Title(s): Sales manager

Salary Range: $18,500 to $32,500

Employment Prospects: Fair

Best Geographic Location: Most regions of the country offer job possibilities, especially with smaller tour companies

Prerequisites:

Education and Training—High school diploma required, with courses in business management and geography helpful; additional training in direct sales; college degree helpful, with courses in business management and sales

Experience—Direct sales; customer relations; work experience in a tour company, travel agency, or a travel supplier (e.g., hotel, airline)

Special Skills and Personality Traits—Sales ability; business management skills; strong oral and written communication skills; interpersonal skills; group presentation skills

CAREER LADDER

```
┌─────────────────────────────────┐
│                                 │
│     President, Tour Company      │
│                                 │
└─────────────────────────────────┘

┌─────────────────────────────────┐
│                                 │
│  Director of Sales, Tour Company │
│                                 │
└─────────────────────────────────┘

┌─────────────────────────────────┐
│                                 │
│    Salesperson, Tour Company     │
│                                 │
└─────────────────────────────────┘

┌─────────────────────────────────┐
│                                 │
│   Clerk or Escort, Tour Company  │
│                                 │
└─────────────────────────────────┘
```

Position Description

Tour companies offer exciting destinations and creative itineraries, and it is the job of directors of sales and marketing to bring customers onto these tours. Directors plan, coordinate, and execute all sales and marketing activities for the tour company.

Ideally, establishing the strategic marketing plan for the company is one primary responsibility of directors. This process begins when the tours are actually planned, as directors work closely with directors of operations and other staffers to choose the destinations, routes, modes of transportation, sightseeing excursions, and other facets of each tour that will appeal to potential customers.

Then directors identify potential markets for the tour company's trips. Today many tour companies rely on a number of different market segments to support their offerings. Acting as retailers, they may sell trips to individual travelers (such tours are called "independent tours" or "per-capita tours") or to civic clubs and other special-interest groups (known as "preformed groups"). Acting as wholesalers, they market trips to travel agents, who in turn sell trips to consumers.

As the product types and market segments are being determined, directors also must decide on the tour operator's positioning in the marketplace compared to other companies. For example, will the company become known for deluxe tours or budget tours? Should the operator specialize in the United States or offer tours around the world?

Once these basic decisions have been made, directors will begin identifying prospective customers and soliciting their business. For large-volume customers such as preformed groups, schools, and companies, directors likely follow up direct-mail letters and catalogs and telemarketing calls with personal presentations to the group or selected decision makers. Therefore, directors need to be adept at speaking in front of groups and planning creative presentations to sell the tours.

For the most part, however, directors will rely on standard marketing techniques such as advertising, public relations, and direct-mail brochures. Directors must design and plan the advertisements for the tour operator, choose the media involved, and make the final placement decisions. Directors will usually coordinate press releases and serve as spokespeople for the company to journalists. Using in-house staffers or an outside firm, directors will design and supervise the production of the company's catalogs and brochures; once these pieces are printed, directors will decide strategies for sending them to prospective travelers.

To gauge the effectiveness of these marketing efforts, directors must research the targeted market segments and conduct research that tracks the number of customers who purchase a tour and their satisfaction with the tour. In many companies, this market research includes focus groups and evaluation forms given to tour passengers at the end of the trip.

Salaries

Salaries in tour companies range widely, depending on the size of the company, its position in the marketplace, and other factors. Among smaller tour companies, the director of sales and marketing may be the only sales employee (in fact, the owner assumes these duties in the smallest firms), with salaries beginning at $15,000. Larger companies with strong niche markets or national reputations will pay $50,000 and more for a qualified director.

Employment Prospects

Almost every region in the United States boasts several strong tour operators. However, the entire industry is limited in terms of employment prospects; for example, the National Tour Association includes only 600 tour company members. Nationwide, it is estimated that there are only about 3,000 tour operators in business.

Employment prospects will depend heavily on the director's ability to network with tour operators in search of job leads. Directors who can prove a track record of successful sales efforts in the travel industry—

even in other segments such as travel agencies, hotels, or airlines—will stand the best chances of being hired.

Advancement Prospects

Given the limited number of competitive openings, directors of sales and marketing who wish to advance have few options. They might apply for positions at larger tour companies, but many decide to open their own tour companies or switch to another segment of the travel industry.

Education and Training

Within the tour industry, the primary avenue for advanced training is the Certified Tour Professional program offered by the National Tour Association.

Some directors with travel agency backgrounds also opt for the Certified Travel Counselor program or the Destination Specialist programs offered by the Institute of Certified Travel Agents.

Additional training in sales management, business administration, and marketing will be helpful.

Experience, Skills, and Personality Traits

Directors of sales and marketing for tour companies must have direct sales training and sales management abilities to function effectively in this competitive environment. While high school and college courses will be helpful, most tour operators will value on-the-job experience more highly.

Also, they must have strong communication skills and leadership abilities to motivate their staffers and other professionals involved in the sales and marketing activities.

Unions and Associations

There are no unions for directors of sales and marketing. Their primary trade associations are the Association of Travel Marketing Executives, located in Washington, D.C., and the Association of Group Travel Executives, located in New York City.

However, the most active associations for these directors are two national organizations that accept tour companies as members: the National Tour Association in Lexington, Kentucky, and the U.S. Tour Operators Association in New York City. These groups sponsor annual conventions and trade shows at which directors of sales and marketing meet travel suppliers and learn about new destinations and attractions.

Tips for Entry

1.   Develop your sales and marketing skills, through courses or experience as a salesperson in another industry.

2.   Learn about the tour business by working full or part time as an assistant, clerk, or escort in a tour company. In fact, most tour operators prefer to promote from within.

3.   Build a network of contacts in tour companies by writing tour operators for career advice, by working part time in a tour company, or by serving as an intern in a tour company.

4.   Gain a broad knowledge of the travel industry by reading trade publications for hotels, restaurants, travel agencies, and other travel businesses. Tour companies deal with many different segments of travel, so you will need to be familiar with them in order to understand the demands of a tour company.

5.   If you can demonstrate your expertise in a hobby or special interest that would attract group business, that specialty may help you in getting your foot in the door at some tour companies. For example, if you have a background in classical music, you could apply to tour operators who target music lovers for concert hall tours in Europe.

DIRECTOR OF OPERATIONS, TOUR COMPANY

CAREER PROFILE

Duties: Researches and plans itineraries for tours; selects travel suppliers and sets prices; coordinates reservations and other arrangements for tours; prepares drivers and escorts for each trip

Alternate Title(s): Senior tour planner

Salary Range: $15,000 to $32,500

Employment Prospects: Fair

Best Geographic Location: Most regions of the United States offer job possibilities, especially among smaller operators.

Prerequisites:

Education and Training—High school diploma required, with courses in business management, travel and tourism, and geography helpful; college degree helpful, with courses in business management and sales helpful

Experience—Tour planning, escorting, and operations; customer relations; work experience in a tour company, travel agency, or a travel supplier (e.g., hotel, airline)

Special Skills and Personality Traits—Strong organizational skills; business management skills; strong oral and written communication skills; interpersonal skills; negotiating skills

CAREER LADDER

```
┌──────────────────────────────┐
│                              │
│   President, Tour Company    │
│                              │
└──────────────────────────────┘

┌──────────────────────────────┐
│                              │
│   Director of Operations,    │
│       Tour Company           │
│                              │
└──────────────────────────────┘

┌──────────────────────────────┐
│                              │
│  Tour Planner, Tour Company  │
│                              │
└──────────────────────────────┘

┌──────────────────────────────┐
│                              │
│  Clerk or Escort, Tour Company │
│                              │
└──────────────────────────────┘
```

Position Description

While the average family vacation requires some planning—from reserving rooms at the hotel to purchasing airline tickets—a package tour multiplies the difficulty by involving travel plans for an entire group of 40 or more passengers. A tour operator's director of operations shoulders the responsibility for researching, planning, routing, and scheduling each tour offered by the company throughout the year.

Working with the director of sales and marketing and other staffers, directors of operations begin the process by researching the anticipated demand for new tours and destinations. Relying on previous sales figures, announcements by travel suppliers of new services and locations, comments from customers, and personal site inspections by tour company staffers, directors will decide the direction and focus of each tour for the coming year.

Once the foundation has been set, directors proceed to research the attractions, hotels, restaurants, sightseeing operators, and other travel suppliers in that region. Directors also plot a tentative route for the tour—along interstates and highways for motorcoach tours, or among airports, terminals, and ports for trips involving airlines, railroads, and cruise ships.

With the tentative itinerary in hand, directors contact prospective suppliers to request availability and price quotes. Directors also may investigate the amenities and service record of these suppliers, to select the best ones. Using these data, directors will combine the quoted prices in a formula (adding the company's overhead and profit margins) to calculate the price of the tour. Depending on this price, directors may renegotiate prices with certain suppliers or choose different ones to reach an acceptable price level. Given the very competitive nature of the tour business, directors of operations must be savvy in negotiating techniques to confirm the best prices for the company's tours.

As the tours are marketed to customers, directors of operations oversee the recording of reservations for each tour. At a predetermined date before the tour departs, directors will make the necessary deposits or cancel reserved space with each supplier in the tour. Also, directors will forward tentative and final rooming lists and passenger numbers to suppliers, so that they can prepare for each group's arrival.

If the tour is escorted, directors of operations will prepare background manuals and other materials to support the escort who will accompany the group on the tour. Using evaluations from the escorts and passengers, directors of operations will consider changes in the tour for upcoming seasons.

Salaries

Salaries in tour companies range widely, depending on the size of the company, its position in the marketplace, and other factors. Among smaller tour companies, the director of operations may be the only tour planner (in fact, the owner assumes these duties in the smallest firms), with salaries beginning at $15,000. Larger companies with strong niche markets or national reputations will pay $50,000 and more for a qualified director.

Employment Prospects

Almost every region in the United States boasts several strong tour operators. However, the entire industry is limited in terms of employment prospects; for example, the National Tour Association includes only 600 tour company members. Nationwide, it is estimated that there are only about 3,000 tour operators in business.

Employment prospects will depend heavily on the director's ability to network with tour operators in search of job leads. Directors who can prove a track record of successful reservations work or planning in the travel industry—even in other segments such as travel agencies, hotels, or airlines—will stand the best chances of being hired.

Advancement Prospects

Given the limited number of competitive openings, directors of operations who wish to advance have few options. They might apply for positions at larger tour companies, but many decide to open their own tour companies or switch to another segment of the travel industry.

Education and Training

Within the tour industry, the primary avenue for advanced training is the Certified Tour Professional program offered by the National Tour Association.

Some directors with travel agency backgrounds also opt for the Certified Travel Counselor program or the Destination Specialist programs offered by the Institute of Certified Travel Agents.

Additional training in negotiating, business administration, and geography will be helpful.

Experience, Skills, and Personality Traits

Directors of operations for tour companies must have very strong organizational and planning skills to handle the many different facets of each tour. The average tour company, for example, might have 20 to 30 different tour programs each year, with one or more departures of each program in different months. While high school and college courses will be helpful, most tour operators will value on-the-job experience more highly.

Also, they must have strong communication skills and negotiating skills to coordinate arrangements with travel suppliers and to achieve the best prices.

Unions and Associations

There are no unions for directors of operations. However, the most active associations for these directors are two national organizations that accept tour companies as members: the National Tour Association in Lexington, Kentucky, and the U.S. Tour Operators Association in New York City. These groups sponsor annual conventions and trade shows at which directors of operations meet travel suppliers and learn about new destinations and attractions.

Tips for Entry

1. Develop your negotiating and planning skills, through courses or experience as a salesperson in another industry.

2. Learn about the tour business by working full or part time as an assistant, clerk, or escort in a tour company. In fact, most tour companies prefer to promote from within.

3. Build a network of contacts in tour companies by writing tour operators for career advice, by working part time in a tour company, or by serving as an intern in a tour company.

4. Gain a broad knowledge of the travel industry by reading trade publications for hotels, restaurants,

travel agencies, and other travel businesses. Tour companies deal with many different segments of travel, so you will need to be familiar with them in order to understand the demands of a tour company.

5. If you can demonstrate your expertise in a hobby or special interest that would attract group business, that specialty may help you in getting your foot in the door at some tour companies. For example, if you have a background in art history, you could apply to tour companies specializing in offering tours of the great museums in Europe.

6. Collect brochures from different tour operators, and examine each itinerary. Try to list the steps that the company's director of operations followed to prepare that tour.

ESCORT, TOUR COMPANY

CAREER PROFILE

Duties: Serves as the primary contact person for passengers during a tour; arranges and oversees all aspects of the tour during the actual trip; provides commentary on the different sites visited; helps passengers with sightseeing excursions, currency exchanges, and other needs

Alternate Title(s):   Tour manager

Salary Range: $12,000 to $35,000

Employment Prospects: Good

Best Geographic Location: Most regions of the United States offer job possibilities, especially among smaller operators

Prerequisites:

Education and Training—High school diploma required, with courses in public speaking, travel and tourism, foreign languages, and geography helpful; completion of a tour management program in a recognized travel academy; college degree, with courses in public speaking, foreign languages, and geography helpful

Experience—Travel planning and operations; customer relations; work experience in a tour company, travel agency, or travel supplier (e.g., hotel, airline); experience as a museum or city guide; public speaking

Special Skills and Personality Traits—Strong oral and written communication skills; interpersonal skills; public speaking skills; foreign language fluency

CAREER LADDER

```
┌─────────────────────────────────────┐
│                                       │
│      President, Tour Company          │
│                                       │
└─────────────────────────────────────┘

┌─────────────────────────────────────┐
│                                       │
│  Director of Operations or Director of│
│  Sales and Marketing, Tour Company    │
│                                       │
└─────────────────────────────────────┘

┌─────────────────────────────────────┐
│                                       │
│   Tour Planner or Salesperson,        │
│          Tour Company                 │
│                                       │
└─────────────────────────────────────┘

┌─────────────────────────────────────┐
│                                       │
│      Escort, Tour Company             │
│                                       │
└─────────────────────────────────────┘
```

Position Description

While other employees in a tour company will have invested many hours of work in each trip before the group departs, escorts shoulder the basic responsibility for insuring that the tour is a successful, enjoyable experience for the passengers. Escorts are the primary contact for the passengers during the tour.

Once the operations department has planned the itinerary for a tour—which may last a single day or several weeks—the company assigns an escort to each departure. (In many tour companies, the same itinerary will be repeated throughout the year by different groups of passengers departing at different times.) Escorts will review the company's materials—destination bro-

chures, visitors guides, videos, reports from the operations department, even evaluations from previous tours—to learn as much as possible about the trip.

When passengers assemble for the trip, escorts greet each person and check him or her onto the tour. Final payments may be collected and release forms and other travel documents distributed before the group leaves. Through the activities on the first day or at a welcome dinner or reception, escorts arrange introductions among the passengers.

Each day of the tour, escorts are responsible for keeping the group on time and following the itinerary as closely as possible. Escorts handle payments for meals included in the tour package, distribute room keys at each hotel stop, and set up admissions at attractions or sightseeing tours that are part of the tour package. The escort's basic goal is to handle the administrative and logistical details of the trip so that the passengers can concentrate on enjoying the tour and the destination.

During the tour, escorts will provide commentary on famous sights and scenes along the way, the history of the region, and other topics of interest to the group. While the company and state or local tourism offices will provide the bulk of this information, escorts may have to read on their own to round out their knowledge of an area. In fact, some escorts prefer to specialize in accompanying tours to a particular region year after year.

Because the passengers view the escort as the tour operator's primary representative during the trip, they may call on him or her for personal assistance, ranging from mailing postcards to exchanging currency. In rare instances, escorts may be required to enforce tour company rules or local laws (e.g., smoking is not allowed on most standard tours) or to arrange emergency medical care. Therefore, escorts must possess the presence of mind to handle unexpected situations that may arise on any tour.

At the end of the trip, escorts distribute evaluation forms for the passengers to complete and arrange or confirm return transportation once the tour ends.

While the lure of traveling for a living attracts many new escorts, they should consider the pressures of extensive travel schedules on their families and friends.

Salaries

Salaries in tour companies range widely, depending on the size of the company, its position in the marketplace, and other factors. However, tour escorts typically rank as the lowest paid employees in the company, primarily due to the part-time nature of the work involved and the status of escorts as entry-level employees. Also, most escorts serve as independent contractors, not full-fledged employees, limiting their benefits.

Escorts in smaller companies may earn $300 to $500 per trip, plus gratuities. Escorts who work with nationwide tour operators or specialty tour operators (e.g., adventure tours or deluxe special-interest tours) can earn substantially more money.

Employment Prospects

Almost every region in the United States boasts several strong tour operators. However, the entire industry is limited in terms of employment prospects; for example, the National Tour Association includes only 600 tour company members. Nationwide, it is estimated that there are only about 3,000 tour operators in business.

Employment prospects will depend heavily on an escort's ability to network with tour operators in search of job leads. Escorts who can accept a very flexible work schedule or who offer additional skills (e.g., foreign languages) will stand the best chances of being hired.

Advancement Prospects

Because escorting traditionally is seen as the "ground-floor opportunity" for tour operators, escorts who succeed at working with groups and who seem willing to accept additional responsibilities have excellent chances of moving into tour operations or sales and marketing. Successful escorts set up as independent contractors may opt to work for more than one tour company (provided that the companies do not compete directly) or to launch their own tour companies.

Education and Training

A number of travel academies and colleges around the country offer tour management and tour escorting curricula (which last one month to one year) that grant certificates and diplomas to graduates. Before enrolling in a program, an escort should check its reputation among tour companies and, as graduation approaches, ask about placement assistance.

Within the tour industry, the primary avenue for advanced training is the Certified Tour Professional program offered by the National Tour Association.

Additional training in foreign languages, public speaking, and geography will be helpful.

Experience, Skills, and Personality Traits

Escorts must have strong oral communication skills and public speaking experience to adopt a confident pose and assume direction of a large group of passengers. Also, they need organizational skills to keep track of their specific tasks at each stop along the tour.

Interpersonal skills will be critical, as escorts deal with the many different personalities found in the average tour group, and they must handle any problems that arise on the tour.

Unions and Associations

There are no unions for tour escorts. The most active associations in the tour industry are two national organizations that accept tour companies as members: the National Tour Association in Lexington, Kentucky, and the U.S. Tour Operators Association in New York City. These groups sponsor educational seminars and publications that tour operators use to train new escorts.

Tips for Entry

1. Develop your public speaking and organizational skills, through courses or direct working experience. Tour operators value these abilities highly.

2. Learn about the tour business by taking a tour offered by a local operator—or by tour companies that you plan to target in your job search. Your cover letter and resume will carry more weight if you can include details and procedures that you observed as a passenger.

3. Build a network of contacts in tour companies by writing tour operators for career advice, by working part time in a tour company, or by serving as an intern in a tour company.

4. Gain a broad knowledge of the travel industry by reading trade publications for hotels, restaurants, travel agencies, and other travel businesses. Tour companies deal with many different segments of travel, so you will need to be familiar with them in order to understand the demands of a tour company.

5. If you can demonstrate your expertise in a hobby or special interest that would attract group business, that specialty may help you in getting your foot in the door at some tour companies. For example, if you have a background in environmental science (or if you enjoy camping or backpacking as a hobby), you might apply to tour companies that offer trips through the national parks in the western United States.

6. If you want to specialize in a particular region, take courses or read books dealing with that area's history and culture. Become fluent in the language, if English is not the primary language.

OWNER/MANAGER, RECEPTIVE TOUR COMPANY

CAREER PROFILE

Duties: Researches and plans itineraries for tours in a specific region; selects travel suppliers and sets prices; coordinates reservations and other arrangements for tours; markets trips to tour operators, travel agents, group travel planners, and individual consumers

Alternate Title(s): Sightseeing operator; inbound tour operator

Salary Range: $15,000 to $45,000

Employment Prospects: Good

Best Geographic Location: Most regions of the United States offer job possibilities, depending on the amount of competition from existing receptive operators in a given region.

Prerequisites:

Education and Training—High school diploma required, with courses in business management; completion of a tour management program in a recognized travel academy; courses in travel and tourism and geography helpful; college degree, with courses in business management and sales helpful

Experience—Tour planning, escorting, and operations; customer relations; work experience in a tour company, travel agency, or a travel supplier (e.g., hotel, airline); direct sales

Special Skills and Personality Traits—Strong organizational skills; business management skills; sales and marketing abilities; strong oral and written communication skills; interpersonal skills; negotiating skills

CAREER LADDER

```
┌─────────────────────────────────────┐
│   Owner/Manager, Receptive           │
│   Tour Company                       │
└─────────────────────────────────────┘

┌─────────────────────────────────────┐
│   Director of Sales and Marketing or │
│   Director of Operations, Receptive  │
│   Tour Company                       │
└─────────────────────────────────────┘

┌─────────────────────────────────────┐
│   Clerk or Escort, Receptive         │
│   Tour Company                       │
└─────────────────────────────────────┘
```

Position Description

While most tour companies sell trips that will take customers from home to faraway destinations, receptive tour operators specialize in bringing groups into a particular destination. Rather than concentrating on learning about and promoting attractions in many different parts of the United States and the world, receptive operators focus their attention on becoming experts in one or more cities, states, regions, or countries.

Receptive operators select their specialties for many reasons: being born or living in an area for a long time, the desire to relocate to that area, the anticipated boom in demand for an area. Whatever the reason, receptive operators must research the area thoroughly before they begin marketing themselves as specialists. By taking courses, reading books, or other means, they have to learn the area's history, culture, vital statistics, and language (if other than English).

Beyond those general preparations, receptive operators have a greater need to become familiar with, and judge the relative quality of, the major travel suppliers in the region. They must visit suppliers personally, forge relationships with the sales directors and managers of different attractions and properties, and gauge the attractiveness of each supplier to prospective visitors. This firsthand knowledge of the region and its suppliers gives receptive operators a competitive advantage compared to other tour operators.

Then receptive operators must plan, price, and schedule package tours into the region. These tours will be customized to fit the specific needs of the receptive operators' market segments. For example, school groups might visit the historic forts and museums in a city, while senior citizen groups might opt instead for factory outlet centers and historic gardens. Receptive operators must know which sites and suppliers in the region will appeal most to different types of visitors.

Once the region has been researched and several standard packages have been assembled, receptive operators must market their expertise and services to potential clients. Though some receptive operators target individual travelers (e.g., international travelers coming to a country to tour on their own), many of them concentrate on soliciting groups. Their primary targets are tour operators, travel agents, meeting planners, group travel planners, and any others who make travel decisions on behalf of groups.

Receptive operators design advertising campaigns (particularly in the travel trade press), public relations programs, brochures and catalogs, and other marketing efforts to promote themselves. They exhibit their programs at travel trade shows and make direct sales calls on prospective clients.

When a customer signs up, receptive operators confirm arrangements for the tour, from reserving the proper number of hotel rooms at each stop to prepaying admissions fees at different attractions. If requested, receptive operators provide an escort or guide to accompany the group. In most cases, receptive operators run their tours as "private label" packages; in other words, the name of the client tour company or group travel planner—not the receptive operator—is used throughout the tour.

Salaries

Because most receptive operators run their own companies or act as independent contractors, salaries in this specialized field depend greatly on the demand for a particular region or the number of tours coordinated by the receptive operator. Salaries range from $15,000 for independent contractors with a small number of clients to $50,000 or more for receptive operators in lucrative niches, such as international inbound tours.

Employment Prospects

Receptive tour operators can be found in almost every major city and state in the United States. However, the entire industry is limited in terms of employment prospects; while no reliable statistics exist for receptive operators, observers believe that only a few thousand exist currently.

Employment prospects will depend heavily on the receptive operator's ability to network with tour operators, travel agents, group travel planners, and other potential clients in search of leads. To survive independently, receptive operators need several years of experience in marketing and operating tours, usually within a standard tour company.

Advancement Prospects

To expand their business, receptive operators must encourage more clients to use their services or try their specialty destinations. Other options include extending their number of geographic specialties or adding new niches, such as international inbound tours.

Education and Training

Within the tour industry, the primary avenue for advanced training is the Certified Tour Professional program offered by the National Tour Association.

Some receptive operators with travel agency backgrounds also opt for the Certified Travel Counselor program or the Destination Specialist programs offered by the Institute of Certified Travel Agents.

Additional training in sales and marketing, business administration, and geography will be helpful.

Experience, Skills, and Personality Traits

Receptive operators must have very strong organizational and planning skills to deal with the different varieties of tours that they will be running. While many tours will be built around a standard package or schedule, each trip will be customized to some extent to meet the specific needs of different clients.

Also, they must have strong communication skills and negotiating skills to coordinate arrangements with travel suppliers, to achieve the best prices, and to promote their destinations and services to potential clients.

Unions and Associations

There are no unions for receptive operators. However, the most active associations for receptive operators are two national organizations that accept tour companies as members: the National Tour Association in Lexington, Kentucky, and the U.S. Tour Operators Association in New York City. These groups sponsor annual conventions and trade shows at which receptive operators meet tour operators and participate in educational conferences to continue their professional training.

Tips for Entry

1. Develop your negotiating and planning skills, through courses or experience as a salesperson in another industry.

2. Learn about the tour business by working full or part-time as an assistant, clerk, or escort in a tour company. In fact, most receptive operators began as travel agents or tour operators.

3. Build a network of contacts in tour companies by writing tour operators for career advice, by working part-time in a tour company, or by serving as an intern in a tour company.

4. Gain a broad knowledge of the travel industry by reading trade publications for hotels, restaurants, travel agencies, and other travel businesses. Receptive operators deal with many different segments of travel, so you will need to be familiar with them in order to understand the demands of your business.

5. Collect brochures from different tour operators who run tours into your region. Try to list the steps that the company's director of operations followed to prepare that tour, so that you can begin planning ways to organize the tour differently.

6. If you have already selected your area, begin taking courses and reading books to learn as much as possible about the area's history, culture, and language (if other than English).

7. Assess the popular demand for your chosen region. If you plan to start your own receptive operator company, make sure that you select a destination that will generate enough business to support you.

INCENTIVE TRAVEL SPECIALIST

CAREER PROFILE

Duties: Designs incentive trips for corporate clients; recommends destinations and specific travel services; confirms details of a trip for clients; serves current clients and solicits new ones

Alternate Title(s): None

Salary Range: $17,900 to $45,000

Employment Prospects: Good

Best Geographic Location: Most incentive travel specialists will depend on medium-size and large companies as clients. Therefore, most job opportunities will be found in major metropolitan areas or suburban corporate centers.

Prerequisites:

Education and Training—High school diploma required, with math and geography courses helpful; completion of a travel agent program in a recognized travel academy; college degree helpful, with courses in sales, business management and geography

Experience—Direct sales; customer relations; work experience in another segment of the travel industry (e.g., hotel, tour operator)

Special Skills and Personality Traits—Sales ability; attention to detail; organization; problemsolving ability; strong oral and written communication skills; interpersonal skills

CAREER LADDER

```
┌─────────────────────────────┐
│                             │
│  Manager or Owner, Incentive │
│      Travel Agency          │
│                             │
└─────────────────────────────┘

┌─────────────────────────────┐
│                             │
│  Incentive Travel Specialist │
│                             │
└─────────────────────────────┘

┌─────────────────────────────┐
│                             │
│  Clerk, Incentive Travel Agency │
│                             │
└─────────────────────────────┘
```

Position Description

To motivate employees and customers and reward them for superior performance—from achieving perfect attendance or reaching sales goals to purchasing a certain amount of goods and services—many companies give them free or greatly discounted trips. Incentive travel specialists serve these companies by designing incentive programs and planning the trips.

When a company wants to begin an incentive program, incentive travel specialists will research the types of behavior that the company wants to recognize. They design the criteria that recipients must meet to qualify for the awards, the different levels and types of trips in the program, and the actual procedures for administering the program.

Once incentive travel specialists have designed the mechanics of the award program, the next step is researching potential destinations and trips that will serve as prizes. For example, agriculture instructors who complete a training program for a farming equipment supplier might be eligible for a tour of Wisconsin's dairy region, while computer dealers who sell a minimum number of systems would be given vacations in Hawaii. Incentive travel specialists must determine the destinations and types of trips that will appeal most to the employees or customers targeted by each client company.

Because incentive travel programs are part of a company's overall promotions or sales and marketing budget, incentive travel specialists must be concerned with arranging trips that stay within the amounts budgeted for these programs. They must review quotes from travel suppliers (hotels, airlines, restaurants, etc.) and select the ones that offer the highest quality for the best prices. They plan the itinerary for the trip, including optional excursions that travelers may choose.

Beyond dispensing this advice to their clients, incentive travel specialists play a critical role in confirming arrangements for the trip. They secure the necessary documents for segments of the trip (airline tickets, hotel reservations, etc.) and transfer payment to the corresponding suppliers; these suppliers may pay commissions to the incentive travel agency or to the company. In certain cases, incentive travel specialists will arrange escorts for the trip or even accompany the group personally.

With any number of new trips being planned each week, combined with the amount of time needed to confirm every segment of a proposed trip, the average day in an incentive travel agency can be very hectic. Successful incentive travel specialists exhibit very strong organizational skills to track this activity, so that clients receive satisfactory service every time.

Given the strong focus on these trips as rewards for performance or sales achievements, incentive travel specialists must practice excellent customer service habits. They must anticipate and avoid problems that would reflect badly on the corporation (and, ultimately, on the agency).

Beginning incentive travel specialists tend to handle all types of clients. However, those with more experience may choose to specialize in serving certain types of customers, organizing incentives to a certain destination, or planning one type of trip (e.g., cruises).

Salaries

Incentive travel specialists with less than five years' experience earn salaries averaging $17,900, while those with six to 10 years' experience average $20,800. The pay level increases to an average of $26,100 for specialists with more than 21 years of experience. Those who wish to increase their earnings more significantly must consider moving into agency management or ownership.

Employment Prospects

Given the fact that incentive travel agencies rely heavily on corporate clients for the bulk of their business, most job opportunities will be found in large metropolitan areas or nearby suburban corporate centers. However, some agencies have thrived in more remote areas by linking themselves to clients via electronic networks.

Because travel agencies depend heavily on the use of computer reservation systems, an incentive travel specialist familiar with one or more national systems will have more freedom to seek employment throughout the country.

Advancement Prospects

Incentive travel specialists seeking to advance in their careers face two possible options. First, they can move into management positions within their agency by gaining additional years of experience or by completing advanced training programs. On the other hand, some specialists choose to establish their own agency.

Education and Training

Within the industry, the primary avenue for advanced training is the Certified Travel Counselor program offered by the Institute of Certified Travel Agents.

Also, agents may opt for the Destination Specialist programs, increasing their knowledge about the Caribbean, South Pacific, or North America.

In certain sales areas, agents will seek specialized certifications (e.g., the Certified Tour Professional program for group sales offered by the National Tour Association).

Additional training in sales skills, computer operations, and geography will be helpful.

Experience, Skills, and Personality Traits

The most important skills for an incentive travel specialist are a keen sense of organization and attention to detail to plan the complex itineraries of clients and strong communication abilities to relate well with clients and coworkers in a stressful, hectic environment. Increasingly, incentive travel specialists will need direct sales training and computer skills to cope with the more demanding business climate.

Unions and Associations

Like travel agents, incentive travel specialists generally do not belong to a national union. Their primary trade group is the Society for Incentive Travel Executives (SITE), located in New York City. SITE offers publications, seminars, and other professional assistance.

They identify also with the national organizations for travel agents: the American Society of Travel Agents (ASTA), located in Alexandria, Virginia, and the Association of Retail Agents (ARTA), located in Harrisburg, Pennsylvania. Both groups offer seminars, government representation, and marketing assistance to travel agents, managers, and owners.

Tips for Entry

1. Consider entering a travel agent training program (which lasts one month to one year or longer) offered by a recognized travel academy, college, or university.

2. Develop your sales abilities and computer skills through advanced training or additional work experience.

3. Increase your understanding of the world's geography, until you have a working knowledge of the location of major nations and cities.

4. As you interview with agencies, highlight any past experience working with travel suppliers or public sector tourism organizations, especially if the work included direct sales experience.

5. To discover whether you would enjoy being an incentive travel specialist, approach local agencies with the offer of interning as an office clerk or administrative assistant. Many successful specialists have followed this path—even without pay—in order to gain valuable work experience.

MEETING PLANNER

CAREER PROFILE

Duties: Plans and organizes meetings, conventions, and trade shows for clients; researches destinations and suppliers to host the meetings; makes arrangements and negotiates rates for housing, food, meeting facilities, and other requirements; supervises work of suppliers and vendors at the meeting

Alternate Title(s): Convention planner; conference planner

Salary Range: $15,000 to $85,000

Employment Prospects: Very good

Best Geographic Location: Most regions of the country offer job possibilities.

Prerequisites:

Education and Training—College degree helpful, with courses in marketing, business management, travel and tourism, and communication; completion of a professional continuing education course

Experience—Customer relations; work experience in another segment of the travel industry, especially a hotel, restaurant or convention center; business management

Special Skills and Personality Traits—Attention to detail; organization; strong oral and written communication skills; negotiating skills; interpersonal skills

CAREER LADDER

```
┌─────────────────────────────┐
│                             │
│      Meeting Planner        │
│                             │
└─────────────────────────────┘
```

Position Description

Meeting planners organize and manage the full range of meetings, conferences, and conventions, from local family reunions to international association membership congresses. They may work directly for the companies or associations sponsoring the meetings, or they may serve several clients in an independent meeting planning firm.

Before they reserve the first hotel room, meeting planners typically research the parameters of an individual meeting: its purpose, the expected number of attendees, the budget, the activities and speakers involved, and the timeline for planning before the meeting takes place.

After preparing an extensive budget for the meeting, with estimates for every anticipated expense item, meeting planners select the site of the meeting and the facilities (e.g., hotels, convention centers) involved. The selection process normally involves a site visit, during which meeting planners walk through the facility, checking capacity and equipment. In discussions with facility representatives and managers, meeting planners negotiate favorable rates for meeting rooms and accommodations. Later, meeting planners negotiate rates with transportation suppliers, such as airlines and shuttle bus companies.

Incorporating the educational and business goals of the client, meeting planners will then develop the meeting program and agenda. This phase includes reserving "breakout" rooms and seminar rooms, scheduling meals and breaks, confirming speakers and presenters, confirming entertainers, planning menus and other food and beverage functions, organizing an exhibit hall and soliciting exhibitors, printing programs and other support materials, and coordinating reservations from meeting attendees. Because the budget is set by the client or by the employer, meeting planners must be able to project expenses, track actual expenditures, and develop creative solutions as problems arise, to insure that each meeting stays on or under budget.

Once the preparations have been made, the major remaining duty of meeting planners is managing the meeting on site once it begins. While a board of directors meeting may be relatively calm, with few surprises expected, a full-scale convention or trade show involving thousands of delegates means days and weeks of non-stop decision making and last-minute changes in the plans. Meeting planners must be capable of dealing with enormous amounts of stress and anxiety.

Salaries

Entry-level meeting planners working in corporations and associations can expect average salaries from $15,000 to $19,000. After two to five years of experience, salaries can range beyond $30,000. Planners for major national associations or Fortune 500 companies may command salaries beyond $75,000.

Employment Prospects

Most areas in the United States offer strong job possibilities, since even the smallest states have their own associations in major industries. However, the most visible positions will be found in major metropolitan areas and suburban corporate centers (for businesses) and in Washington, D.C., and New York City (for associations).

Advancement Prospects

Meeting planners seeking to advance in their careers can apply for positions in larger companies or associations or launch their own independent meeting planning firms. In many cases, however, they may have to extend themselves into additional administrative services (e.g., purchasing, corporate travel management) or demonstrate the ability to keep meetings under budget and on schedule, if they hope to approach the top layers of management.

Education and Training

Although several associations offer continuing education programs, the primary avenue for advanced train-

ing is the Certified Meeting Professional program offered by Meeting Professionals International.

Additional courses in marketing, communications, and negotiating skills will be helpful.

Experience, Skills, and Personality Traits

Meeting planners must have very strong oral and written communication skills as well as organizational skills to juggle the many different demands of this career field. The success of each meeting will depend on the coordinated efforts of tens or hundreds of suppliers and workers, all of whom must be directed and supervised by the meeting planner.

Also critical are negotiating skills to confirm the best possible rates and prices from suppliers and the ability to make quick decisions during the most hectic times of the meeting.

Unions and Associations

Meeting planners do not belong to a union. Their primary national organization is Meeting Planners International (MPI) in Dallas, Texas. MPI offers publications, seminars, and government representation to meeting planners as well as the Certified Meeting Professional program.

Tips for Entry

1. Locate a meeting planner who will agree to serve as your mentor. At the least, find one who will allow you to serve an internship (paid or unpaid), so that you can see firsthand whether you like the work.

2. Work part time in a hotel or convention center that hosts many meetings and conferences.

3. Volunteer to organize meetings for civic clubs, churches, and nonprofit organizations in your town.

4. Network your way to finding job leads by writing meeting planners for advice, and read meeting trade magazines to learn the latest trends in the industry.

5. Try to land a clerical position in a company or association from which you could move into planning meetings.

DIRECTOR OF SALES, CONVENTION CENTER

CAREER PROFILE

Duties: Prepares marketing plans to encourage the use of convention center space; schedules presentations and makes sales calls on individual customers and groups; confirms reservations and meetings plans as well as payment arrangements

Alternate Title(s): Sales manager

Salary Range: $18,500 to $65,000

Employment Prospects: Fair

Best Geographic Location: Cities with convention centers and hotels with extensive convention space will offer the best job opportunities.

Prerequisites:

Education and Training—High school diploma required, with courses in business management and communication helpful; additional training in direct sales; college degree helpful, with courses in business management and sales

Experience—Direct sales; customer relations; work experience as a meeting planner, travel agent, or travel supplier

Special Skills and Personality Traits—Sales ability; business management skills; strong oral and written communication skills; interpersonal skills; group presentation skills; negotiating skills

CAREER LADDER

```
┌─────────────────────────────┐
│     Executive Director,     │
│      Convention Center      │
└─────────────────────────────┘

┌─────────────────────────────┐
│ Director of Sales, Convention Center │
└─────────────────────────────┘

┌─────────────────────────────┐
│      Account Executive,     │
│      Convention Center      │
└─────────────────────────────┘

┌─────────────────────────────┐
│  Sales Clerk, Convention Center │
└─────────────────────────────┘
```

Position Description

Though they vary greatly in size and function, from small facilities that host the state Rotary convention to metropolitan complexes that host international trade shows, convention centers rely on directors of sales to solicit and confirm clients who will rent and use the center's rooms and meeting halls. Directors plan, coordinate, and execute all sales and marketing activities for the convention center.

Before embarking on these activities, directors should establish a strategic marketing plan for the convention center. The elements of this plan depend largely on the features of the center itself: the amount of exhibit and meeting space available, the number of individual meeting rooms, the catering and other support services available. By assessing the capabilities of the center, directors of sales decide what types of clients would be interested in reserving space.

Then directors identify potential markets for the center to pursue. What types of local, regional, national, and international clients—mainly associations and companies—would be attracted to the city? Will the features of the center automatically rule out certain types of clients? In the past, have efforts to attract certain types of companies, associations, and expositions succeeded more often than others?

Once these basic decisions have been made, directors will begin identifying prospective customers and soliciting their business. Directors will coordinate direct-mail and telemarketing campaigns to promote the center to businesses, associations, meeting planners, and trade show organizers. Directors must design and plan advertisements for the center, choose the magazines and newspapers that will be read by potential clients (e.g., travel agents, meeting planners, corporate travel managers, and association executives), and make the final placement decisions. Directors usually will coordinate press releases and serve as spokespeople for the center to journalists. Using in-house staffers or an outside firm, directors will design and supervise the production of the center's promotional brochures; once these pieces are printed, directors will decide strategies for sending them to prospective clients.

To make direct contact with customers, directors will attend destination showcases and meetings expositions, usually with brochures and display booths, and schedule appointments during the shows with prospective clients. For larger convention prospects, directors will travel to board meetings and headquarters offices to make direct presentations to decision makers.

Therefore, directors need to be adept at speaking in front of groups and planning creative presentations to sell the center. Also critical are direct marketing techniques and experience in managing advertising and public relations programs.

Salaries

In smaller cities, the director of sales may start under $20,000; in fact, the director also may serve as the general manager for the facility. With several years of experience in the field, salaries can range up to $65,000, depending on the size of the city and its attractiveness as a destination for conventions and trade shows.

Employment Prospects

Almost every city in the United States has a convention center or lies within driving distance of a regional convention center. However, even with that number of centers, the industry tends to offer a limited amount of new positions each year.

Therefore, employment prospects will depend heavily on the director's ability to network with convention center directors in search of job leads. Directors who can prove a track record of successful sales efforts in the travel industry—even in other segments such as travel agencies, hotels, or airlines—will stand the best chances of being hired.

Advancement Prospects

Given the limited number of competitive openings, directors of sales and marketing who wish to advance

have few options. They might apply for positions at larger tour companies, but many decide to open their own tour companies or switch to another segment of the travel industry.

Education and Training

There is no national continuing education program at this time for directors of sales for convention centers. If the director has been hired as an employee of the convention and visitors bureau, then he or she might opt for training offered by the International Association of Convention and Visitors Bureaus in Washington, D.C.

Additional training in sales management, business administration, and marketing will be helpful.

Experience, Skills, and Personality Traits

Directors of sales for convention centers must have direct sales training and sales management abilities to function effectively in this extremely competitive environment. While high school and college courses will be helpful, most convention center governing boards will value on-the-job experience more highly.

Also, they must have strong communication skills and leadership abilities to motivate their staffers and other professionals involved in the sales and marketing activities.

Unions and Associations

There are no unions for directors of sales for convention centers. Their primary trade association is the International Association of Convention and Visitors Bureaus (IACVB), located in Washington, D.C.

Tips for Entry

1. Develop your sales and marketing skills, through courses or experience as a salesperson in another industry.

2. Learn about convention centers by working full or part time as an assistant or clerk in a convention center.

3. Build a network of contacts among convention center staffers by writing them for career advice, by working part time in a center, or by serving as an intern.

4. Gain a broad knowledge of the travel industry by reading trade publications for hotels, restaurants, travel agencies, and other travel businesses. Convention centers deal with many different segments of travel, so you will need to be familiar with them in order to understand the demands of your job.

DIRECTOR OF EVENT SERVICES, CONVENTION CENTER

CAREER PROFILE

Duties: Supervises operations of the convention center for clients; coordinates staffing and equipment needs and room reservations for clients; supervises food and beverage preparation and meal service for clients; serves as liaison between clients and convention center employees

Alternate Title(s): Sales manager

Salary Range: $18,500 to $45,000

Employment Prospects: Fair

Best Geographic Location: Cities with convention centers and hotels with extensive convention space will offer the best job opportunities.

Prerequisites:

Education and Training—High school diploma required, with courses in business management and communication helpful; additional training in hospitality services or travel and tourism; college degree required, with courses in business management and hospitality management helpful

Experience—Hospitality and restaurant management; customer relations; work experience in a hotel or restaurant

Special Skills and Personality Traits—Supervisory skills; business management skills; strong oral and written communication skills; interpersonal skills; negotiating skills

CAREER LADDER

```
┌─────────────────────────────┐
│    Executive Director,       │
│    Convention Center         │
└─────────────────────────────┘

┌─────────────────────────────┐
│   Director of Event Services,│
│    Convention Center         │
└─────────────────────────────┘

┌─────────────────────────────┐
│    Events Coordinator,       │
│    Convention Center         │
└─────────────────────────────┘

┌─────────────────────────────┐
│  Chef or Waiter, Convention Center │
└─────────────────────────────┘
```

Position Description

When the director of sales for a convention center books a client into the center for a convention or trade show, thousands of decisions will follow regarding the meeting schedule, meeting rooms, food service, exhibit space, safety precautions, shuttle transportation, and other elements required to produce a successful show.

Directors of event services plan, coordinate, and execute these services for the center's clients.

As the first step in this process, directors will meet with clients to define their basic needs. They must agree on the scheduling of the meeting or show, the amount of convention center space needed for major functions and exhibit booths, the size and number of meeting rooms and seminar rooms, the timing and content of meals, and other details.

In terms of meeting space, directors will reserve the necessary halls, auditoriums, and rooms for the event and direct convention center employees in setting up each area, including aligning tables and chairs, installing lighting and electrical outlets, arranging audiovisual equipment, and making other adjustments to meet the client's specifications.

For the meals, directors will work with catering staffers to plan menus and schedule food preparation for each meal. Directors will supervise wait staffers in serving the meals and clearing tables at the end of each function.

Working with local authorities and companies, directors may arrange security for the event and shuttle transportation for meeting participants to return to their hotels.

Directors will serve as the primary liaison for clients after contracts have been signed with the convention center. Therefore, directors must be adept at making quick decisions, solving problems, and dealing with difficult situations (e.g., disagreements with union locals whose members work in the center).

Salaries

In smaller cities, the director of event services may start under $20,000; in fact, the director also may serve as the general manager for the facility. With several years of experience in the field, salaries can range up to $45,000, depending on the size of the city and its attractiveness as a destination for conventions and trade shows.

Employment Prospects

Almost every city in the United States has a convention center or lies within driving distance of a regional convention center. However, even with that number of centers, the industry tends to offer a limited number of new positions each year.

Therefore, employment prospects will depend heavily on the director's ability to network with convention center directors in search of job leads. Directors who can prove a track record of managing hotels, restaurants, or other companies in the travel industry—even in other segments such as travel agencies or airlines—will stand the best chances of being hired.

Advancement Prospects

Given the limited number of competitive openings, directors of event services who wish to advance have several options. They might apply for positions at larger convention centers, switch to other segments of the travel industry, or become meeting planners for businesses.

Education and Training

There is no national continuing education program at this time for directors of event services for convention centers. If the director has been hired as an employee of the convention and visitors bureau, then he or she might opt for training offered by the International Association of Convention and Visitors Bureaus in Washington, D.C.

Additional training in hospitality management, business administration, and labor relations will be helpful.

Experience, Skills, and Personality Traits

Directors of event services for convention centers should have experience in hospitality management, meeting planning, or restaurant management as well as personnel management abilities to function effectively in this extremely competitive environment. While high school and college courses will be helpful, most convention center governing boards will value on-the-job experience more highly.

Also, directors of event services must have strong communication skills and leadership abilities to motivate their staffers and other professionals involved in serving the needs of clients.

Unions and Associations

There are no unions for directors of event services for convention centers. Their primary trade association is the International Association of Convention and Visitors Bureaus (IACVB), located in Washington, D.C.

Tips for Entry

1. Develop your hospitality and restaurant management skills, through courses or experience in a hotel or restaurant.

2. Learn about convention centers by working full or part time as an assistant or clerk in a convention center.

3. Build a network of contacts among convention center staffers by writing them for career advice, by working part time in a center, or by serving as an intern.

4. Gain a broad knowledge of the travel industry by reading trade publications for hotels, restaurants, travel agencies, and other travel businesses. Convention centers deal with many different segments of travel, so you will need to be familiar with them in order to understand the demands of your job.

EVENTS COORDINATOR, CONVENTION CENTER

CAREER PROFILE

Duties: Manages operations of the convention center for clients; serves as shift supervisor in charge of staffing and equipment needs and room reservations for clients; serves as shift supervisor in charge of food and beverage preparation and meal service for clients; serves as liaison between clients and convention center employees

Alternate Title(s): None

Salary Range: $15,000 to $32,000

Employment Prospects: Fair

Best Geographic Location: Cities with convention centers and hotels with extensive convention space will offer the best job opportunities.

Prerequisites:

    Education and Training—High school diploma required, with courses in business management and communication helpful; additional training in hospitality services or travel and tourism; college degree helpful, with courses in business management and hospitality management

    Experience—Hospitality and restaurant management; customer relations; work experience in a hotel or restaurant

    Special Skills and Personality Traits—Supervisory skills; business management skills; strong oral and written communication skills; interpersonal skills; negotiating skills

CAREER LADDER

```
┌─────────────────────────────┐
│   Executive Director,        │
│   Convention Center          │
└─────────────────────────────┘

┌─────────────────────────────┐
│   Director of Event Services,│
│   Convention Center          │
└─────────────────────────────┘

┌─────────────────────────────┐
│   Events Coordinator,        │
│   Convention Center          │
└─────────────────────────────┘

┌─────────────────────────────┐
│   Chef or Waiter, Convention Center │
└─────────────────────────────┘
```

Position Description

When a client books a convention or meeting in the convention center, and the basic requirements of the meeting have been discussed with the director of event services, an events coordinator will be assigned to begin preparations for that meeting. The events coordinator will be the primary day-to-day supervisor working with center employees to plan and execute those arrangements.

When the events coordinator is assigned to a convention, the director of event services will outline the requirements for the show: the scheduling of the meeting or show, the amount of convention center space needed for major functions and exhibit booths, the size and number of meeting rooms and seminar rooms, the timing and content of meals, and other details of the event.

In terms of meeting space, events coordinators will directly supervise the setup of each hall, auditorium, or room. Coordinators will order the proper number of tables and chairs or other furnishings and direct crews of workers in outfitting the room to match the floor plans submitted by the client. Under coordinators' supervision, electricians will install extra outlets or run cables as needed, banners and signs will be hung, head tables and speaker podiums will be set, and audiovisual equipment (from microphones to large video screens) will be installed.

Working with catering staffers, coordinators will insure that the menus selected by the client will be prepared fully and on time. They will schedule teams of wait staffers to serve the meals and clear tables.

If the client has requested additional support, events coordinators will go to great lengths to satisfy those needs. For example, if the client needs extra security at the entrances to the exhibit hall, coordinators will contact local security companies and instruct officers in their duties when they arrive. Since large conventions usually require shuttle transportation for delegates to arrive from and return to their hotels, coordinators may solicit bids from local bus companies, work out the best routes between the hotels and the center, and schedule bus runs during the convention.

When the event begins, coordinators will be on duty (rotating perhaps with other coordinators) during the entire event. If a problem arises, coordinators will handle complaints from clients and make decisions on the spot to correct any problems.

Therefore, events coordinators must be adept at making quick decisions, solving problems, and dealing with difficult situations (e.g., disagreements with union locals whose members work in the center).

Salaries

In smaller cities, the events coordinator may start under $15,000. With several years of experience in the field, salaries can range up to $32,000, depending on the size of the city and its attractiveness as a destination for conventions and trade shows.

Employment Prospects

Almost every city in the United States has a convention center or lies within driving distance of a regional convention center. However, even with that number of centers, the industry tends to offer a limited number of new positions each year.

Therefore, employment prospects will depend heavily on the coordinator's management experience. Coordinators who can prove a track record of managing hotels, restaurants, or other companies in the travel industry—even in other segments such as travel agencies or airlines—will stand the best chances of being hired. In many cases, events coordinators begin their career as chefs, wait staffers, or clerks in a convention center.

Advancement Prospects

Given the limited number of competitive openings, events coordinators will have to display a positive record of accomplishments in order to proceed to higher positions. They might succeed their supervising director

of event services, apply for jobs at larger convention centers, switch to other segments of the travel industry, or become meeting planners.

Education and Training

There is no national continuing education program at this time for events coordinators for convention centers. If the coordinator has been hired as an employee of the convention and visitors bureau, then he or she might opt for training offered by the International Association of Convention and Visitors Bureaus in Washington, D.C.

Additional training in hospitality management, business administration, and labor relations will be helpful.

Experience, Skills, and Personality Traits

Events coordinators for convention centers must have some experience in hospitality or restaurant management as well as personnel management abilities to function effectively in this extremely competitive environment. While high school and college courses will be helpful, most directors of event services will value on-the-job experience more highly.

Also, events coordinators must have strong communication skills and leadership abilities to motivate their staffers and other professionals involved in serving the needs of clients.

Unions and Associations

There are no unions for events coordinators for convention centers, although some may retain their membership in restaurant or hotel unions if they were promoted into their current position. Their primary trade association is the International Association of Convention and Visitors Bureaus (IACVB), located in Washington, D.C.

Tips for Entry

1. Develop your hospitality and restaurant management skills, through courses or experience in a hotel or restaurant.

2. Learn about convention centers by working full or part time as an assistant or clerk in a convention center.

3. Build a network of contacts among convention center staffers by writing them for career advice, by working part time in a center, or by serving as an intern.

4. Gain a broad knowledge of the travel industry by reading trade publications for hotels, restaurants, travel agencies, and other travel businesses. Convention centers deal with many different segments of travel, so you will need to be familiar with them in order to understand the demands of your job.

TRAVEL SUPPLIERS

GENERAL MANAGER, HOTEL

Duties: Manages the overall operations of a hotel; supervises staffers in various departments of the hotel; sets rates and guest policies

Alternate Title(s): None

Salary Range: $21,900 to $86,500

Employment Prospects: Very good

Best Geographic Location: Most regions of the United States offer job possibilities.

Prerequisites:

Education and Training—High school diploma required, with courses in business management helpful; college degree usually required, with a major in business management, hospitality management, or travel and tourism; graduate degree in business management, hospitality management, or travel and tourism helpful for advancement

Experience—Work experience in a hotel; work experience in another segment of the travel industry; business management

Special Skills and Personality Traits—Supervisory skills; strong oral and written communication skills; interpersonal skills; financial management skills

```
┌─────────────────────────────────────┐
│                                      │
│   Vice President or President, Hotel │
│          Chain or Company            │
│                                      │
└─────────────────────────────────────┘

┌─────────────────────────────────────┐
│                                      │
│      Regional Manager, Hotel         │
│          Chain or Company            │
│                                      │
└─────────────────────────────────────┘

┌─────────────────────────────────────┐
│                                      │
│        General Manager, Hotel        │
│                                      │
└─────────────────────────────────────┘

┌─────────────────────────────────────┐
│                                      │
│        Resident Manager, Hotel       │
│                                      │
└─────────────────────────────────────┘
```

Position Description

Millions of travelers depend daily on the services of hotels for lodging, meals, and meeting space. The final responsibility for providing these services falls upon general managers, who supervise hotel employees and allocate resources so that guests will be satisfied and the hotel will realize a profit on its operations.

General managers exert authority over every facet of the hotel's operations. This process begins in the front office, where they approve the different rates charged to guests (e.g., corporate, tour operator, discount rates such as AAA and AARP), the check-in procedures by which guests register and receive their keys, and the billing procedures by which guest charges are recorded and payments collected.

Working with hotel engineers and the executive housekeeper, general managers supervise the mainte-nance and appearance of the hotel grounds and interior, from the types of shrubs planted along walkways to the color schemes used in renovating hotel guest rooms. They approve the custodial schedules and practices that the executive housekeeper follows in maintaining the hotel's appearance.

To attract guests to the hotel, general managers review the plans set by the director of sales and marketing. These plans normally include advertisements in magazines and newspapers, public relations campaigns to draw media attention, and (for large clients) personal sales calls and group presentations in which the general managers may participate.

As individual and group clients decide to stay at the hotel, general managers oversee the handling of reservation requests and confirmations. Because computers play an increasingly important role in this process, general managers should understand basic principles of automated reservation systems and computer systems.

Salaries

In smaller properties, the general manager will handle many aspects of hotel operations personally, such as the sales and marketing functions. Entry-level salaries will begin at $21,000. By progressing to larger properties or to management positions in hotel companies, a general manager can boost salary levels to $65,000 and beyond.

Employment Prospects

Any region in the United States should offer the full range of hotel properties, from all-inclusive, deluxe inns to budget motels. Therefore, qualified general managers with demonstrable experience in hospitality management should find available openings around the country.

They can improve their chances if they have a relevant graduate degree, a proven track record in efficient operations and profit levels, or additional skills such as foreign language fluency or real estate management training.

Advancement Prospects

The primary track for promotions in this field is moving to the general manager's position at larger properties, within the same company or within another hotel management firm or chain. Sometimes general managers can advance in terms of salary by switching to another segment of the travel industry or by opening or purchasing their own properties.

Education and Training

Within the hospitality industry, the primary route for continuing education is the Certified Hotel Administrator (CHA) program offered by the American Hotel & Motel Association in Washington, D.C.

General managers who have a special interest in sales and marketing may opt for the Certified Hotel Sales Executive designation offered by the Hotel Sales and Marketing Association International in Washington, D.C.

In certain cases, general managers whose properties depend greatly on tour operator business will complete the Certified Tour Professional (CTP) program of the National Tour Association in Lexington, Kentucky.

Additional courses in foreign languages, financial management, and human resources management will be helpful.

Experience, Skills, and Personality Traits

General managers must demonstrate the interpersonal skills, oral and written communication skills, and supervisory skills to manage large numbers of employees and keep them motivated to do a good job. Because many hotel employees supervised by general managers must provide high levels of customer service for relatively low wages, managers must be able to find ways to retain these employees and keep them motivated to do a good job.

Increasingly, general managers will need computer skills to manage their activities efficiently.

Unions and Associations

As hotel executives, general managers generally do not belong to a national union. Their primary national trade organization is the American Hotel and Motel Association (AHMA), located in Washington, D.C. AHMA offers seminars, conventions, trade shows, publications, and training programs for front-line employees that general managers can use at their properties.

Tips for Entry

1. Strengthen your skills in business management, accounting, and human resources management through courses or direct work experience.

2. Begin your exposure to the hotel industry by working part time as a desk clerk, bellman, concierge, night auditor, or a similar position. Most hotels prefer to promote from within; in fact, several hotel company CEOs trace their careers back to a part-time position.

3. Broaden your knowledge of current hospitality issues by reading AHMA publications such as *Lodging*, the AHMA membership magazine, and other trade magazines.

4. Consider whether your interpersonal skills—especially your ability to supervise and relate to entry-level employees—are strong enough for a people-intensive position in hotel management.

5. Write hotel companies for information about internships and on-the-job management training programs. Many large hotel chains and management companies offer such tracks for liberal arts college graduates, so that these new trainees can learn the hospitality business from their employers.

RESIDENT MANAGER, HOTEL

CAREER PROFILE

Duties: Serves as the primary live-in manager of a hotel; supervises staffers in various departments of the hotel, primarily the front office; serves "on call" in shifts as the primary contact for hotel staffers

Alternate Title(s): Assistant manager

Salary Range: $21,000 to $46,000

Employment Prospects: Very good

Best Geographic Location: Most regions of the United States offer job possibilities.

Prerequisites:

Education and Training—High school diploma required, with courses in business management helpful; college degree usually required, with a major in business management, hospitality management, or travel and tourism; graduate degree in business management, hospitality management, or travel and tourism helpful for advancement

Experience—Work experience in a hotel; work experience in another segment of the travel industry; business management

Special Skills and Personality Traits—Supervisory skills; strong oral and written communication skills; interpersonal skills; financial management skills

CAREER LADDER

```
┌─────────────────────────────────┐
│     Regional Manager, Hotel      │
│       Chain or Company           │
└─────────────────────────────────┘

┌─────────────────────────────────┐
│     General Manager, Hotel       │
└─────────────────────────────────┘

┌─────────────────────────────────┐
│     Resident Manager, Hotel      │
└─────────────────────────────────┘

┌─────────────────────────────────┐
│   Front Office Manager, Hotel    │
└─────────────────────────────────┘
```

Position Description

While general managers hold the primary responsibility for a hotel's condition and financial performance, they rely on one or more resident managers who oversee the day-to-day operations of the hotel. Although some general managers may occupy rooms in the hotel as well, the distinguishing characteristic of resident managers is that they live in the hotel and remain on call, usually even after their eight-hour work shift ends.

During their standard shift, resident managers serve as "hands-on" managers in the hotel. They have wide latitude to make operating decisions in most areas of the hotel, from discount rate requests at the front desk to custodial emergencies. If hotel employees have questions or problems, they turn first to the resident manager before involving the general manager.

If a hotel employs several resident managers who split shifts among themselves, each resident manager may choose to specialize in a certain area (e.g., front office operations, sales, and marketing) while still supervising the operations of other departments during his or her shift.

After their shift ends, resident managers literally never go off duty, because they live in a room or suite on the property. While they do not have to check in with the front desk or actively monitor hotel operations, they will be called by subordinate managers if a major decision or emergency arises. For example, if a guest needs medical attention, the supervising maid may contact the resident manager for additional instructions, once a doctor has been summoned.

Because this position requires intensive amounts of concentration and attention, even when the "work day" ends, resident managers must be able to make quick decisions and to handle significant amounts of stress in order to function effectively.

Salaries

In smaller properties, resident managers will handle many aspect of hotel operations personally; in fact, the general manager also may serve as the resident manager. Entry-level salaries will begin at $21,000. By progressing to larger properties or to general manager positions in hotel companies, a resident manager can boost salary levels to $46,000 and beyond.

In many cases, salaries will be supplemented by the fact that the resident manager receives free room and board during the time he or she she is on duty in the hotel.

Employment Prospects

Any region in the United States should offer the full range of hotel properties, from all-inclusive, deluxe inns to budget motels. Therefore, qualified resident managers with demonstrable experience in hospitality management should find available openings around the country.

Resident managers can improve their chances if they have a graduate degree, a proven track record in efficient operations and profit levels, or additional skills such as foreign language fluency or real estate management training.

Advancement Prospects

The primary track for promotions in this field is moving to the general manager's position at the same hotel or at larger properties, within the same company or within another hotel management firm or chain. Sometimes resident managers can advance in terms of salary by switching to another segment of the travel industry or by opening or purchasing their own properties.

Education and Training

Within the hospitality industry, the primary route for continuing education is the Certified Hotel Administrator (CHA) program offered by the American Hotel & Motel Association in Washington, D.C.

Resident managers who have a special interest in sales and marketing may opt for the Certified Hotel Sales Executive designation offered by the Hotel Sales and Marketing Association International in Washington, D.C.

In certain cases, resident managers whose properties depend greatly on tour operator business will complete the Certified Tour Professional (CTP) program of the National Tour Association in Lexington, Kentucky.

Additional courses in foreign languages, financial management, and human resources management will be helpful.

Experience, Skills, and Personality Traits

Resident managers must demonstrate the interpersonal skills, oral and written communication skills, and supervisory skills to manage large numbers of employees and keep them motivated to do a good job. Because hotel work involves large amounts of exposure to customers for low entry-level wages, in many cases resident managers must have the ability to select qualified employees and keep them motivated.

Increasingly, resident managers will need computer skills to manage their activities efficiently.

On a personal level, resident managers must exhibit stress management skills to deal with the pressures of being "on call" 24 hours a day.

Unions and Associations

As hotel executives, resident managers generally do not belong to a national union. Their primary national trade organization is the American Hotel and Motel Association (AHMA), located in Washington, D.C. AHMA offers seminars, conventions, trade shows, publications, and training programs for front-line employees that resident managers can use at their properties.

Tips for Entry

1. Strengthen your skills in business management, accounting, and human resources management through courses or direct work experience.

2. Begin your exposure to the hotel industry by working part time as a desk clerk, bellman, concierge, night auditor, or a similar position. Most hotels prefer to promote from within; in fact, several hotel company CEOs trace their careers back to a part-time position.

3. Broaden your knowledge of current hospitality issues by reading AHMA publications such as *Lodging*, the AHMA membership magazine, and other trade magazines.

4. Consider whether your interpersonal skills—especially your ability to supervise and relate to entry-level employees—are strong enough for a people-intensive position in hotel management.

5. Write hotel companies for information about internships and on-the-job management training programs. Many large hotel chains and management companies offer such tracks for liberal arts college graduates, so that these new trainees can learn the hospitality business from their employers.

DIRECTOR OF SALES AND MARKETING, HOTEL

CAREER PROFILE

Duties: Prepares marketing plans to solicit individual guests and groups; coordinates advertising, public relations, direct-mail, and other marketing campaigns; schedules presentations and makes sales calls on travel companies and other large-volume buyers

Alternate Title(s): Sales manager

Salary Range: $15,000 to $140,000

Employment Prospects: Very good

Best Geographic Location: Most regions of the country offer job possibilities.

Prerequisites:

Education and Training—High school diploma required, with courses in business management helpful; additional training in direct sales; college degree helpful, with courses in business management, sales, and hospitality management

Experience—Direct sales; customer relations; work experience in a tour company, travel agency, or a travel supplier (e.g., theme park, airline)

Special Skills and Personality Traits—Sales ability; business management skills; strong oral and written communication skills; interpersonal skills; group presentation skills

CAREER LADDER

General Manager, Hotel

Director of Sales and Marketing, Hotel

Account Executive, Hotel

Clerk, Hotel

Position Description

Before individual travelers, tour groups, business travelers, and other guests can enjoy the amenities and services of a hotel, they must be informed about the hotel and persuaded to reserve rooms. That responsibility rests with the hotel's director of sales and marketing. Using all available avenues, directors plan, coordinate, and execute the sales and marketing activities for the hotel.

Ideally, directors will first establish the strategic marketing plan for the hotel. This process begins with an examination of the hotel's capacity and resources, as directors work closely with the general manager and

other staffers to decide which aspects of the hotel (e.g., the types of rooms, the rates, the hotel's proximity to corporate headquarters or vacation attractions) will draw the most attention from potential guests.

Based on the hotel's best attributes, directors identify the most promising market segments. Today many hotels rely on a number of different market segments to fill rooms: individual travelers, families, international inbound travelers, corporate travelers, meetings and conventions, tour groups, and other niches.

As the product types and market segments are being determined, directors also must decide on the hotel's positioning in the marketplace compared to other companies. For example, should the hotel focus on serving the needs of business travelers or leisure travelers? Will most guests come from the United States or from other countries? Positioning will be critical in deciding what types of promotions and what future services will make the hotel a success.

Once these basic decisions have been made, directors will begin identifying prospective customers and soliciting their business. For large-volume customers such as preformed groups, tour operators, and companies, directors will likely follow up direct-mail letters and catalogs and telemarketing calls with personal presentations to the group or selected decision makers. Therefore, directors need to be adept at speaking in front of groups and planning creative presentations to sell the hotel.

For the most part, however, directors will rely on standard marketing techniques such as advertising, public relations, and direct-mail brochures. Directors must design and plan the advertisements for the hotel, choose the media involved, and make the final placement decisions. Directors usually will coordinate press releases and serve as spokespeople for the company to journalists. Using in-house staffers or an outside firm, directors will design and supervise the production of the hotel's brochures and other printed materials; once these pieces are printed, directors will decide strategies for sending them to prospective guests.

To gauge the effectiveness of these marketing efforts, directors must research the targeted market segments and track the number of customers who stayed in the hotel and their satisfaction with the stay. In many companies, this market research includes focus groups and evaluation forms completed by guests before they check out.

Salaries

Salaries of hotel directors of sales and marketing range widely, depending on the size of the hotel, its position in the marketplace, and other factors. Among smaller hotels, the director of sales and marketing may be the only sales employee (in fact, the owner or general manager will assume these duties in the smallest firms), with salaries beginning at $15,000. Larger companies with strong niche markets or national reputations will pay $50,000 and more for a qualified director. Vice presidents of marketing with the largest hotel chains may earn $140,000 or more, including bonuses.

Employment Prospects

Any region in the United States should offer the full range of hotel properties, from all-inclusive, deluxe inns to budget motels. Therefore, qualified directors of sales

and marketing with proven track records in generating business should find openings around the country.

They can improve their chances if they have a graduate degree, a certificate from a recognized continuing education program, or additional skills such as foreign language fluency.

Advancement Prospects

The primary track for promotions in this field is moving to similar positions at larger hotels, within the same company or within another hotel management firm or chain. With additional management training, some directors decide to become general managers. Other directors can advance in terms of salary by switching to another segment of the travel industry or by opening or purchasing their own properties.

Education and Training

Directors of sales and marketing can complete the Certified Hotel Sales Executive (CHSE) designation offered by the Hotel Sales and Marketing Association International in Washington, D.C.

Within the hospitality industry, another route for continuing education is the Certified Hotel Administrator (CHA) program offered by the American Hotel & Motel Association in Washington, D.C.

In certain cases, directors whose properties depend greatly on tour operator business will complete the Certified Tour Professional (CTP) program of the National Tour Association in Lexington, Kentucky.

Additional courses in foreign languages and sales management will be helpful.

Experience, Skills, and Personality Traits

Directors of sales and marketing must demonstrate direct sales abilities and group presentation skills to discover prospective clients and persuade them to book hotel space. If they manage account executives, they should have the interpersonal skills, oral and written communication skills, and supervisory skills to keep them motivated.

Increasingly, directors will need computer skills to manage their activities efficiently.

Unions and Associations

As hotel executives, directors of sales and marketing generally do not belong to a national union. Their primary national trade organization is the Hotel Sales and Marketing Association International (HSMAI), located in Washington, D.C. HSMAI offers publications, training manuals, and other assistance to directors of sales and marketing.

Tips for Entry

1.   Strengthen your skills in business management and sales, through courses or direct work experience.

2.   Begin your exposure to the hotel industry by working part time as a desk clerk, bellman, concierge, night auditor, or a similar position. Most hotels prefer to promote from within; in fact, many directors can trace their careers to a part-time position.

3.   Broaden your knowledge of current hospitality issues by reading AHMA publications such as *Lodging*, the AHMA membership magazine, and other trade magazines.

4.   Consider whether your interpersonal skills—especially supervising sales assistants and other office support staffers as well as relaying client arrangements and requests to desk clerks and other employees—are strong enough to survive in the people-intensive environment of a hotel.

5.   Write hotel companies for information about internships and on-the-job management training programs. Many large hotel chains and management companies offer such tracks for liberal arts college graduates, so that these new trainees can learn the hospitality business from their employers.

6.   Do not be discouraged by the relatively low entry-level salaries in this field, compared to figures in other areas of sales. Directors who prove their ability to attract business generally can double their initial salaries within three to five years, counting bonuses, according to HSMAI.

ACCOUNT EXECUTIVE, HOTEL

CAREER PROFILE

Duties: Prepares marketing plans to solicit individual guests and groups; designs advertisements, letters, and proposals for specific clients; schedules presentations and makes sales calls on travel companies and other large-volume buyers

Alternate Title(s): Salesperson

Salary Range: $15,000 to $35,000

Employment Prospects: Very good

Best Geographic Location: Most regions of the country offer job possibilities.

Prerequisites:

Education and Training—High school diploma required, with courses in business management helpful; additional training in direct sales; college degree helpful, with courses in business management, sales, and hospitality management

Experience—Direct sales; customer relations; work experience in a tour company, travel agency, or a travel supplier (e.g., theme park, airline)

Special Skills and Personality Traits—Sales ability; business management skills; strong oral and written communication skills; interpersonal skills; group presentation skills

CAREER LADDER

```
┌─────────────────────────────────┐
│                                 │
│     General Manager, Hotel      │
│                                 │
└─────────────────────────────────┘

┌─────────────────────────────────┐
│                                 │
│  Director of Sales and Marketing,│
│             Hotel               │
│                                 │
└─────────────────────────────────┘

┌─────────────────────────────────┐
│                                 │
│    Account Executive, Hotel     │
│                                 │
└─────────────────────────────────┘

┌─────────────────────────────────┐
│                                 │
│         Clerk, Hotel            │
│                                 │
└─────────────────────────────────┘
```

Position Description

Account executives in a hotel perform the bread-and-butter work of contacting prospective clients and persuading them to book hotel space, while the director of sales and marketing writes the sales letters, makes the telephone calls, and prepares the proposals and presentations for specific clients.

Working from the hotel's strategic marketing plan, account executives must learn the hotel's capacity and resources. They must have a firsthand knowledge of the types of room, the various room rates and discounts, amenities for corporate travelers and tour groups, and any other background information that future guests may request.

Under the supervision of the director of sales and marketing, account executives will be given specific market segments for which they must be responsible: individual travelers, families, international inbound travelers, corporate travelers, meetings and conventions, tour groups, and other niches. In the largest hotels, account executives may be given a list of individual accounts rather than an entire segment.

Account executives must become very familiar with the dynamics and needs of their accounts. They should know the booking patterns, rates, itineraries, special needs, and other characteristics that distinguish these guests from others. Successful account executives round out their knowledge of their accounts by studying the hotel's files on these guests, reading their trade publications, establishing a personal rapport with the decision makers at these accounts, and networking with other travel suppliers in the city or state. Also, they will investigate the office or city "politics" of dealing with specific clients.

Armed with this information, account executives will begin identifying prospective customers and soliciting their business. For large-volume customers such as pre-formed groups, tour operators, and companies, account executives will follow up direct-mail letters, brochures, and telemarketing calls with personal presentations to the group or selected decision makers. Account executives must be able to support the director of sales in planning creative presentations for clients.

Working together with other account executives, they will respond to leads generated by standard marketing techniques such as advertising, public relations, and direct-mail campaigns. Account executives may help to design and plan advertisements for the hotel, choose the media involved, and make the final placement decisions. They also may assist in public relations work such as greeting visiting clients and arranging familiarization tours.

When they have clients staying in the hotel, account executives monitor complaints and questions that may arise. If the clients have arranged special billing procedures, the account executive may oversee the preparation of those bills.

To gauge the effectiveness of these marketing efforts, account executives must research the targeted market segments and conduct research that tracks the number of their customers who stayed in the hotel and their satisfaction with the stay. For the most part, this research includes focus groups and evaluation forms completed by guests before they check out.

Salaries

Salaries of hotel account executives range widely, depending on the size of the hotel, its position in the marketplace, and other factors. Among smaller hotels, sales will be handled by only one person (in fact, the owner or general manager will assume these duties in the smallest firms), with salaries beginning at $15,000. Hotels in metropolitan areas may pay $30,000 or more.

Employment Prospects

Any region in the United States should offer the full range of hotel properties, from all-inclusive, deluxe inns to budget motels. Therefore, qualified account executives with proven track records in generating business should find openings around the country.

Though additional degrees or supplementary abilities such as foreign language fluency may help to some degree, the basic qualification for account executives—especially neophytes in the lodging industry—will be work experience as a sales representative.

Advancement Prospects

The primary track for promotions in this field is moving to similar positions at larger hotels, within the same company or within another hotel management firm or chain. With additional management training and a track record of sales success, account executives may seek promotions as directors of sales and marketing. Sometimes account executives can advance in terms of salary by switching to another segment of the travel industry or by opening or purchasing their own properties.

Education and Training

Account executives can complete the Certified Hotel Sales Executive (CHSE) designation offered by the Hotel Sales and Marketing Association International in Washington, D.C.

Within the hospitality industry, another route for continuing education is the Certified Hotel Administrator (CHA) program offered by the American Hotel & Motel Association in Washington, D.C.

In certain cases, account executives whose accounts are primarily tour operators will complete the Certified Tour Professional (CTP) program of the National Tour Association in Lexington, Ky.

Additional courses in foreign languages and sales management will be helpful.

Experience, Skills, and Personality Traits

Account executives must demonstrate the direct sales abilities and group presentation skills to discover prospective clients and persuade them to book hotel space. Oral and written communication skills will prove critical as they prepare sales presentations and proposals.

Increasingly, account executives will need computer skills to manage their activities efficiently.

Unions and Associations

As hotel executives, account executives generally do not belong to a national union. Their primary national trade organization is the Hotel Sales and Marketing Association International (HSMAI), located in Washington, D.C. HSMAI offers publications, training manuals, and other assistance to account executives.

Tips for Entry

1. Strengthen your skills in business management and sales, through courses or direct work experience.

2. Begin your exposure to the hotel industry by working part time as a desk clerk, bellman, concierge, night auditor, or a similar position. Most hotels prefer to promote from within.

3.   Broaden your knowledge of current hospitality issues by reading AHMA publications such as *Lodging,* the AHMA membership magazine, and other trade magazines.

4.   Consider whether your interpersonal skills—especially your ability to supervise and relate to different types of clients—are strong enough for a people-intensive position in hotel management.

5.   Write hotel companies for information about internships and on-the-job management training programs. Many large hotel chains and management companies offer such tracks for liberal arts college graduates, so that these new trainees can learn the hospitality business from their employers.

6.   Do not be discouraged by the relatively low entry-level salaries in this field, compared to figures in other areas of sales. Salespersons who prove their ability to attract business can generally double their initial salaries within three to five years, counting bonuses, according to HSMAI.

FOOD AND BEVERAGE MANAGER, HOTEL

CAREER PROFILE

Duties: Supervises the food, banquet, and beverage services in the hotel; coordinates the staffing and equipment needs in these areas for the hotel; supervises food and beverage preparation and meal service for clients; insures the quality of the food and the service; serves as liaison between clients and food and beverage employees

Alternate Title(s): Director of catering services

Salary Range: $22,000 to $62,800

Employment Prospects: Good

Best Geographic Location: Most regions of the United States offer job possibilities.

Prerequisites:

Education and Training—High school diploma required, with courses in business management and home economics helpful; additional training in culinary arts, including a certificate or diploma from a recognized cooking school or academy; college degree helpful, with courses in business management and hospitality management

Experience—Hospitality and restaurant management; work experience as a chef, cook, or caterer; customer relations; work experience in a hotel or restaurant

Special Skills and Personality Traits—Supervisory skills; business management skills; strong oral and written communication skills; interpersonal skills; negotiating skills; creativity

CAREER LADDER

General Manager, Hotel

Assistant Manager, Hotel

Food and Beverage Manager, Hotel

Chef or Head Waiter, Hotel

Position Description

From a supper ordered from room service to the continental breakfast prepared for an early-morning business meeting, guests depend on the hotel's coffee shops, restaurants, room service, and catering service for snacks and meals during their stay. Coordinating these services is the food and beverage manager, who supervises staffers and manages the resources and facilities to accommodate these needs.

For banquets and catered meals, food and beverage managers begin the process by meeting with the clients to select the menu, decorations, schedule, and other aspects of each meal. These preferences will be recorded on function sheets that will guide the cooks and wait staffers who will be on duty during the meal. In a small

hotel, the food and beverage manager also may be asked to reserve the necessary rooms and equipment (e.g., tables and chairs, dance floors, audiovisual equipment) for the event.

Working with the chefs or caterers, managers will order the proper food items for the menus requested by clients and supervise the preparation of dishes for each meal. If additional services will be needed, such as security or press accommodations, managers may work with other hotel executives to meet these needs.

Although some hotels employ independent managers for their restaurants and room service units, food and beverage managers usually exert some supervisory authority over these areas of the hotel. Managers may hire and oversee the activities of restaurant staffers, establish service policies and menus for each unit, and determine the budgets and prices for menu items.

While food and beverage managers depend on a knowledge of catering practices and culinary arts, they also need supervisory skills to manage large numbers of entry-level employees—waiters, servers, and kitchen assistants—who work long hours for low wages.

Salaries

Smaller hotels may combine the job of head chef or cook with the food and beverage manager position; even with the added responsibilities, starting salaries may barely exceed $20,000. With several years of experience in the field, salaries can range beyond $60,000, depending on the size of the hotel and its number of restaurants and food service units.

Employment Prospects

Any region in the United States should offer the full range of hotel properties, from all-inclusive, deluxe inns to budget motels. Therefore, qualified food and beverage managers with a track record of managing restaurant units should find openings around the country.

Though additional culinary training may help to some degree, the basic qualification for food and beverage managers will be work experience as a restaurant manager or catering director.

Advancement Prospects

The primary track for promotions in this field is moving to similar positions at larger hotels, within the same company or within another hotel management firm or chain. With additional management training and several years of running food and beverage services, these managers may seek promotions as resident managers or general managers. Sometimes food and beverage managers can advance in terms of salary by switching to another segment of the travel industry or by opening or purchasing their own restaurants or hotels.

Education and Training

Within the hospitality industry, the primary route for continuing education is the Certified Hotel Administrator (CHA) program offered by the American Hotel & Motel Association in Washington, D.C.

Additional courses in culinary arts or business management will be helpful.

Experience, Skills, and Personality Traits

Food and beverage managers must demonstrate the interpersonal skills, oral and written communication skills, and supervisory skills to manage large numbers of employees and keep them motivated to do a good job. (The supervisory role can be difficult because many food service employees will be hired for minimal wages to perform tasks with high exposure to guests.)

Increasingly, food and beverage managers will need computer skills to manage their activities efficiently.

Unions and Associations

Food and beverage managers who have risen through the ranks may belong to the Hotel Employees and Restaurant Employees International Union in Washington, D.C.

The primary trade association is the American Hotel and Motel Association (AHMA) in Washington, D.C. AHMA offers seminars, trade shows, publications, and training materials to help food and beverage managers handle their assignments.

Managers who supervise restaurant units also may become involved in the National Restaurant Association in Washington, D.C.

Tips for Entry

1. Strengthen your skills in business management and food preparation, through courses or direct work experience.

2. Begin your exposure to the hotel industry by working part time as a waiter, server, bartender, or cook. Most hotels prefer to promote from within; in fact, many food and beverage managers can trace their careers to a part-time position.

3. Broaden your knowledge of current hospitality issues by reading AHMA publications such as *Lodging*, the AHMA membership magazine, and other trade magazines.

4. Consider whether your interpersonal skills—especially your ability to supervise and relate to demanding clients—are strong enough for a people-intensive position in hotel management.

5. Write hotel companies for information about internships and on-the-job management training programs. Many large hotel chains and management companies offer such tracks for liberal arts college graduates, so that these new trainees can learn the hospitality business from their employers.

FRONT OFFICE MANAGER, HOTEL

CAREER PROFILE

Duties: Coordinates front office activities of the hotel, including check-in, billing, and checkout procedures for guests; resolves complaints from guests and enforces hotel policies; supervises shifts of workers at front desk

Alternate Title(s): Front desk manager

Salary Range: $18,000 to $42,000

Employment Prospects: Very good

Best Geographic Location: Most regions in the United States offer job possibilities.

Prerequisites:

Education and Training—High school diploma required, with courses in accounting and business management helpful; additional training in computer systems; college degree with a major in hospitality management, travel and tourism, or business management helpful for advancement

Experience—Bookkeeping or accounting; customer relations; work experience in another segment of the travel industry

Special Skills and Personality Traits—Courtesy and tact; interpersonal skills; problem-solving ability; ability to make quick decisions; supervisory skills

CAREER LADDER

```
┌─────────────────────────────────┐
│                                 │
│     Resident Manager, Hotel     │
│                                 │
└─────────────────────────────────┘

┌─────────────────────────────────┐
│                                 │
│    Front Office Manager, Hotel  │
│                                 │
└─────────────────────────────────┘

┌─────────────────────────────────┐
│                                 │
│       Desk Clerk, Hotel         │
│                                 │
└─────────────────────────────────┘
```

Position Description

Because the guests in a hotel have more personal contact with the employees at the front desk than with any other workers in the hotel, this department must impress guests with efficient, friendly service. As head of the department, the front office manager must train and supervise the staffers and establish service guidelines to meet that goal.

Guests will be involved with the front office area of the hotel from the moment they arrive until they check out at the end of their stay. Front office managers set policies and supervise desk clerks in the following check-in functions: greeting guests and requesting proper identification, assigning rooms, securing credit card information or an advance deposit, registering guests, issuing keys, and instructing bellhops.

During the average shift at the front desk, managers will schedule one or more clerks to answer telephones and route incoming messages and mail deliveries, answer questions from guests, and handle other assignments that may arise.

When guests check out, front office managers again supervise workers in collecting keys, reviewing room charges with guests, and securing final payments.

Through the desk clerks on duty or a separate department, front office managers direct the receipt and confirmation of reservations for rooms. Depending on the responsibilities given to other departments, front office managers also may be responsible for posting charges to individual guest bills, storing valuables in a safe at the request of guests, and assorted duties related to the safety and security of guests.

Besides desk clerks, front office managers usually supervise the door attendants, parking valets, bellhops and other workers charged with greeting guests, and helping them during check-in or checkout.

Salaries

While many smaller hotels will combine the position of front office manager with the job of general manager, resident manager, or desk clerk, entry-level front office managers in the average hotel can expect beginning salaries starting at $18,000. With several years of experience in the field, salaries can range beyond $40,000, depending on the size of the hotel and the number of front office employees.

Employment Prospects

Any region in the United States should offer the full range of hotel properties, from all-inclusive, deluxe inns to budget motels. Therefore, qualified front office managers—particularly those with accounting or business management backgrounds—should find openings around the country.

Although additional hospitality training may help to some degree, the basic qualification for front office managers will be work experience and supervisory skills in a hotel front office. In fact, many front office managers begin their careers as desk clerks.

Advancement Prospects

The primary track for promotions in this field is moving to similar positions at larger hotels, within the same company or within another hotel management firm or chain. With additional management training and several years of running the hotel front office, these managers may seek promotions as resident managers or general managers. Sometimes they can advance in terms of salary by switching to another segment of the travel industry or by opening or purchasing their own hotels or inns.

Education and Training

Within the hospitality industry, the primary route for continuing education is the Certified Hotel Administrator (CHA) program offered by the American Hotel & Motel Association in Washington, D.C.

Additional courses in accounting or customer relations will be helpful.

Experience, Skills, and Personality Traits

Front office managers must demonstrate the interpersonal skills, oral and written communication skills, and supervisory skills to manage large numbers of employees and keep them motivated to do a good job. Because hotel work involves large amounts of exposure to customers for low entry-level wages, in many cases, front office managers must have the ability to select qualified employees and keep them motivated.

Increasingly, front office managers will need computer skills to manage their activities efficiently.

Unions and Associations

Front office managers who have risen through the ranks of bellhops, desk clerks, and other entry-level positions may belong to the Hotel Employees and Restaurant Employees International Union in Washington, D.C.

The primary trade association is the American Hotel and Motel Association (AHMA) in Washington, D.C. AHMA offers seminars, trade shows, publications, and training materials to help front office managers handle their assignments and train their workers.

Tips for Entry

1. Strengthen your skills in business management and accounting, through courses or direct work experience.

2. Begin your exposure to the hotel industry by working part time as a desk clerk, bellhop, or door attendant. Most hotels prefer to promote from within; in fact, many front office managers can trace their careers to a part-time position. Also, front office management is considered the primary route to becoming a general manager.

3. Broaden your knowledge of current hospitality issues by reading AHMA publications such as *Lodging*, the AHMA membership magazine, and other trade magazines.

4. Consider whether your interpersonal skills—especially your ability to supervise and relate to different types of clients—are strong enough for a people-intensive position in hotel management.

5. Write hotel companies for information about internships and on-the-job management training programs. Many large hotel chains and management companies offer such tracks for liberal arts college graduates, so that these new trainees can learn the hospitality business from their employers.

EXECUTIVE HOUSEKEEPER, HOTEL

CAREER PROFILE

Duties: Oversees the overall cleanliness and physical condition of the hotel; establishes standards for and supervises work of housekeeping staffers; inspects condition of rooms and recommends renovations; inventories supplies and trains housekeeping staffers

Alternate Title(s): Administrative housekeeper; head housekeeper

Salary Range: $15,000 to $35,000

Employment Prospects: Very good

Best Geographic Location: Most regions in the United States offer job possibilities.

Prerequisites:

Education and Training—High school diploma required, with courses in business management and home economics helpful; college degree, with a major in hospitality management or business management, helpful for advancement

Experience—Work experience in the custodial field; business management

Special Skills and Personality Traits—Supervisory skills; organization; strong oral and written communication skills; interpersonal skills

CAREER LADDER

```
┌─────────────────────────────────────┐
│                                      │
│      Resident Manager, Hotel         │
│                                      │
└─────────────────────────────────────┘

┌─────────────────────────────────────┐
│                                      │
│    Executive Housekeeper, Hotel      │
│                                      │
└─────────────────────────────────────┘

┌─────────────────────────────────────┐
│                                      │
│       Housekeeper, Hotel             │
│                                      │
└─────────────────────────────────────┘
```

Position Description

Because hotels depend on using the same guest rooms, meeting spaces, and food service units again and again, executive housekeepers must direct an institutional custodial program to maintain the cleanliness and appealing appearance of the hotel for guests and clients.

To provide guidelines for the hotel's housekeepers, executive housekeepers will establish standards and policies that housekeepers will follow during their shifts, as they clean and service different areas of the hotel. For example, how many times per day will the carpet in the hotel lobby be vacuumed? How many towels should be left in the bathroom of a guest room? What types of guest amenities (e.g., soaps, shampoos) will the hotel provide in each guest room? Relying on budget figures, bids from suppliers, and accepted housekeeping practices in other hotels, executive housekeepers must balance the goal of efficient cleaning operations with the hotel's available staffing and financial resources.

With these standards in place, executive housekeepers will organize work schedules for the various shifts of custodians and housekeepers on duty in the hotel. Enough workers must be on duty at all times, even in the late evening and early morning, to handle standard cleaning duties and emergencies.

Executive housekeepers will inspect and evaluate the physical condition of the hotel, from individual guest rooms and meeting halls to common areas such as the lobby and the restaurant. If these areas need renovations or safety improvements, executive housekeepers will research those needs, solicit bids, and recommend actions to the general manager of the hotel.

Because the hotel must carry an adequate supply of cleaning products and equipment, executive housekeepers must conduct periodic inventories of these stores.

Executive housekeepers organize and direct training programs for staffers, from refresher training in using common cleaning equipment to advanced topics such as adapting and maintaining rooms for disabled guests. As the primary department manager, executive housekeepers will resolve personnel conflicts and enforce the hotel's personnel policies.

Salaries

Executive housekeepers at smaller properties will earn starting salaries in the range of $18,000. With several years of experience in the field, salaries can range beyond $35,000, depending on the size of the hotel and the number of housekeeping employees.

Employment Prospects

Any region in the United States should offer the full range of hotel properties, from all-inclusive, deluxe inns to budget motels. Therefore, qualified executive housekeepers should find openings around the country.

Although additional hospitality training may help to some degree, the basic qualification for executive housekeepers will be work experience and supervisory skills in custodial management or hospitality management. Many hotels will expect some background as a front-line housekeeper.

Advancement Prospects

The primary track for promotions in this field is moving to similar positions at larger hotels, within the same company or within another hotel management firm or chain. With additional management training and several years of running the housekeeping department, executive housekeepers may seek promotions as resident managers or general managers. Sometimes they can advance in terms of salary by switching to another segment of the travel industry or by opening or purchasing their own hotels or inns.

Education and Training

Within the hospitality industry, the primary route for continuing education is the Certified Hotel Administrator (CHA) program offered by the American Hotel & Motel Association in Washington, D.C.

Additional courses in custodial management or hospitality management will be helpful.

Experience, Skills, and Personality Traits

Executive housekeepers must demonstrate the interpersonal skills, oral and written communication skills, and supervisory skills to manage large numbers of employees and keep them motivated to do a good job. (Supervising housekeeping employees can be challenging, because most of them have been hired for minimal wages to complete tasks that may mean frequent exposure to guests.)

Unions and Associations

Executive housekeepers who have been promoted from housekeeping positions may belong to the Hotel Employees and Restaurant Employees International Union in Washington, D.C.

The primary trade association is the American Hotel and Motel Association (AHMA) in Washington, D.C. AHMA offers seminars, trade shows, publications, and training materials to help executive housekeepers handle their assignments and train their workers.

Tips for Entry

1. Strengthen your skills in custodial techniques and hospitality management, through courses or direct work experience.

2. Begin your exposure to the hotel industry by working part time as a housekeeper or other entry-level job. Most hotels prefer to promote from within; in fact, many executive housekeepers can trace their careers to a part-time position.

3. Broaden your knowledge of current hospitality issues by reading AHMA publications such as *Lodging*, the AHMA membership magazine, and other trade magazines.

4. Consider whether your interpersonal skills—especially your ability to supervise and relate to different types of clients—are strong enough for a people-intensive position in hotel management.

5. Write hotel companies for information about internships and on-the-job management training programs. Many large hotel chains and management companies offer such tracks for liberal arts college graduates, so that these new trainees can learn the hospitality business from their employers.

CONCIERGE, HOTEL

CAREER PROFILE

Duties: Provides personal services for hotel guests, including directions, restaurant reservations, entertainment recommendations, and other types of assistance

Alternate Title(s): None

Salary Range: $17,000 to $25,000

Employment Prospects: Fair

Best Geographic Location: Most opportunities for employment as a concierge will be found in metropolitan areas and resorts, primarily at hotels that cater to business travelers and deluxe leisure travelers.

Prerequisites:

Education and Training—High school diploma required, with business management courses helpful

Experience—Customer relations; work experience in a hotel or another segment of the travel industry

Special Skills and Personality Traits—Problem-solving ability; strong oral and written communication skills; interpersonal skills

CAREER LADDER

```
┌─────────────────────────────────┐
│                                 │
│    Front Office Manager, Hotel  │
│                                 │
└─────────────────────────────────┘

┌─────────────────────────────────┐
│                                 │
│        Concierge, Hotel         │
│                                 │
└─────────────────────────────────┘

┌─────────────────────────────────┐
│                                 │
│        Desk Clerk, Hotel        │
│                                 │
└─────────────────────────────────┘
```

Position Description

During the course of a guest's stay in the hotel, numerous questions and difficulties may arise. Where can movie or show tickets be bought? Can cellular telephones, computers, or automobiles be rented? Which area restaurants offer the best service?

Answering these questions falls on the shoulders of concierges, members of the hotel's front office department who usually staff a table or podium in the hotel lobby. From this location, concierges respond to guest requests in many different arenas: restaurant recommendations and reservations, walking and driving directions, admissions prices and operating hours for local attractions and events, entertainment recommendations and reservations, rentals of business equipment, and other needs.

Concierges maintain an extensive file of contact persons and background information on these topics, so that answers can be found quickly and efficiently. In fact, guests value the help of concierges in these matters over their ability to flip through telephone directories or call other sources for help.

Salaries

Even though concierges are normally veteran employees with several years of experience in front office operations, entry-level salaries in the position remain relatively low: $17,000 for the first year, with raises progressing to $25,000 after several years of experience.

Employment Prospects

Concierges will be found primarily in hotels located in major metropolitan areas and resorts, where many hotels cater to business travelers and deluxe leisure travelers (since these guests will be most likely to request the restaurants, shows, and other services offered by a concierge). In other parts of the country, opportunities for concierges will be quite limited.

Advancement Prospects

Concierges with several years of experience can progress to become front office manager, especially if they also have a background as a desk clerk. Another avenue is applying for concierge positions at larger properties, in the same hotel chain or with a different chain or hotel management company.

Education and Training

Within the hospitality industry, the primary route for continuing education is the Certified Hotel Administrator (CHA) program offered by the American Hotel & Motel Association in Washington, D.C.

Additional courses in custodial management or hospitality management will be helpful.

Experience, Skills, and Personality Traits

Successful concierges must have a thorough knowledge of the city or region surrounding the hotel, so that they can advise guests properly. Because they have such close personal contact with guests, they should have strong interpersonal skills and problem-solving abilities to handle the wide variety of challenges which may arise.

Unions and Associations

Concierges who have been promoted from front desk positions may belong to the Hotel Employees and Restaurant Employees International Union in Washington, D.C.

The primary trade association is the American Hotel and Motel Association (AHMA) in Washington, D.C. AHMA offers seminars, trade shows, publications, and training materials to help concierges handle their assignments.

Tips for Entry

1. Strengthen your skills in business management and hospitality management, through courses or direct work experience.

2. Begin your exposure to the hotel industry by working part time as a front desk clerk, bellhop, or door attendant. Most hotels prefer to promote from within.

3. Broaden your knowledge of current hospitality issues by reading AHMA publications such as *Lodging*, the AHMA membership magazine, and other trade magazines.

4. Consider whether your interpersonal skills—especially your ability to supervise and relate to different types of clients—are strong enough for a people-intensive position in hotel management.

5. Write hotel companies for information about internships and on-the-job management training programs. Many large hotel chains and management companies offer such tracks for liberal arts college graduates, so that these new trainees can learn the hospitality business from their employers.

6. Before you go into an interview at a hotel, research the surrounding area thoroughly. If you can name neighboring restaurants or mention the local theatrical productions currently running, you will stand out as being eager and qualified for this type of work.

DESK CLERK, HOTEL

CAREER PROFILE

Duties: Conducts front office activities of the hotel, including check-in, billing, and checkout procedures for guests; resolves complaints from guests and enforces hotel policies

Alternate Title(s): None

Salary Range: $15,000 to $25,000

Employment Prospects: Very good

Best Geographic Location: Most regions in the United States offer job possibilities.

Prerequisites:

Education and Training—High school diploma required, with courses in accounting and business management helpful; additional training in computer systems; college degree, with a major in hospitality management, travel and tourism, or business management, helpful for advancement

Experience—Bookkeeping or accounting; customer relations; work experience in another segment of the travel industry

Special Skills and Personality Traits—Courtesy and tact; interpersonal skills; problem-solving ability; ability to make quick decisions

CAREER LADDER

```
┌─────────────────────────────────┐
│                                 │
│     Resident Manager, Hotel     │
│                                 │
└─────────────────────────────────┘

┌─────────────────────────────────┐
│                                 │
│    Front Office Manager, Hotel  │
│                                 │
└─────────────────────────────────┘

┌─────────────────────────────────┐
│                                 │
│        Desk Clerk, Hotel        │
│                                 │
└─────────────────────────────────┘
```

Position Description

Regardless of the size, location, or budget category of any hotel, guests form the bulk of their impressions about a particular hotel by their close, personal contact with the desk clerks at the front desk.

Guests will be involved with hotel desk clerks from the moment they arrive until they check out at the end of their stay. Desk clerks greet guests and request proper identification as they check into the hotel. The clerks assign rooms, secure credit card information or an advance deposit, register guests, issue keys, and instruct bellhops.

During the average shift at the front desk, desk clerks will answer telephones, route incoming messages and mail deliveries, answer questions from guests, and handle other assignments that may arise.

When guests check out, desk clerks collect keys, review room charges with guests, and secure final payments.

Unless the hotel has established a separate department for reservations, desk clerks will receive and confirm reservations for rooms. Depending on the responsibilities given to other departments, desk clerks also may post charges to individual guest bills, store valuables in a safe at the request of guests, and complete assorted duties related to the safety and security of guests.

Beyond greeting customers and answering questions, therefore, many tasks performed by desk clerks will require highly developed clerical skills, such as operating cash registers, entering data in credit card readers, and typing information into computer reservations terminals.

Desk clerks work closely with the door attendants, parking valets, bellhops, and other employees charged with greeting guests and helping them during check-in or checkout.

Salaries

The position of desk clerk is considered one of the primary entry-level jobs in hotels. Most beginning desk clerks will earn starting salaries approaching $15,000. After several years of experience, desk clerks may advance to salaries of $25,000 or more.

Employment Prospects

Any region in the United States should offer the full range of hotel properties, from all-inclusive, deluxe inns to budget motels. Therefore, beginning or experienced desk clerks—especially those with backgrounds in hospitality management or accounting—should find openings around the country.

Though additional hospitality training may help to some degree, the basic qualifications for desk clerks will be an aptitude for working with the public and the ability to handle clerical work. The job of desk clerk is traditionally seen as the training ground for future hotel general managers.

Advancement Prospects

The primary track for promotions in this field is moving up to front office manager, within the same hotel or within another hotel management firm or chain. With additional management training and several years of running the hotel front office, these managers may seek promotions as resident managers or general managers. Sometimes they can advance in terms of salary by switching to another segment of the travel industry.

Education and Training

Within the hospitality industry, the primary route for continuing education is the Certified Hotel Administrator (CHA) program offered by the American Hotel & Motel Association in Washington, D.C.

Additional courses in accounting or customer relations will be helpful.

Experience, Skills, and Personality Traits

Desk clerks must demonstrate the interpersonal skills and oral and written communication skills to organize and conduct the business of the hotel's front desk. Stress management skills and the ability to make quick decisions will prove crucial, because the front desk is considered the hub of the hotel and draws much activity during the average day.

Increasingly, desk clerks will need computer skills to manage their activities efficiently.

Unions and Associations

Desk clerks may belong to the Hotel Employees and Restaurant Employees International Union in Washington, D.C.

The primary trade association is the American Hotel and Motel Association (AHMA) in Washington, D.C. AHMA offers seminars, trade shows, publications, and training materials to help desk clerks handle their assignments.

Tips for Entry

1.   Strengthen your skills in business management and accounting, through courses or direct work experience.

2.   Begin your exposure to the hotel industry by working part time, as a desk clerk, bellhop, or door attendant. Most hotels prefer to promote from within; in fact, many hotel managers can trace their careers to a part-time position. Also, front office management is considered the primary route to becoming a general manager.

3.   Broaden your knowledge of current hospitality issues by reading AHMA publications such as *Lodging*, the AHMA membership magazine, and other trade magazines.

4.   Consider whether your interpersonal skills—especially your ability to supervise and relate to different types of clients—are strong enough for a people-intensive position in hotel management.

5.   Write hotel companies for information about internships and on-the-job management training programs. Many large hotel chains and management companies offer such tracks for liberal arts college graduates, so that these new trainees can learn the hospitality business from their employers.

GUEST SERVICES MANAGER, RESORT/SPA

CAREER PROFILE

Duties: Coordinates guest services activities of the resort or spa, including check-in, billing, and checkout procedures for guests; resolves complaints from guests and enforces resort or spa policies; maintains recreational facilities; plans special events and handles other requests from guests

Alternate Title(s): Assistant manager

Salary Range: $18,000 to $42,000

Employment Prospects: Good

Best Geographic Location: Most resorts and spas that hire guest services managers will be found in traditional resort areas, particularly the Southwest and the West Coast.

Prerequisites:

Education and Training—High school diploma required, with courses in accounting and business management helpful; college degree helpful, with a major in hospitality management, travel and tourism, recreation management or business management

Experience—Bookkeeping or accounting; customer relations; work experience in another segment of the travel industry, especially managing a recreational facility

Special Skills and Personality Traits—Courtesy and tact; interpersonal skills; problem-solving ability; ability to make quick decisions; supervisory skills

CAREER LADDER

```
┌─────────────────────────────────┐
│                                 │
│   Resident Manager or General   │
│      Manager, Resort/Spa        │
│                                 │
└─────────────────────────────────┘

┌─────────────────────────────────┐
│                                 │
│  Guest Services Manager, Resort/Spa │
│                                 │
└─────────────────────────────────┘

┌─────────────────────────────────┐
│                                 │
│  Desk Clerk or Concierge, Resort/Spa │
│                                 │
└─────────────────────────────────┘
```

Position Description

Guests who stay at resorts or spas generally expect a higher level of service and attention than those frequenting the average hotel or inn. Guest services managers must train and supervise the staffers and establish service guidelines to meet those expectations.

Guest services managers set policies and supervise desk clerks in greeting guests and requesting proper identification, assigning rooms, securing credit card information or an advance deposit, registering guests, issuing keys, and instructing bellhops. They will schedule one or more clerks to answer telephones and route incoming messages and mail deliveries, answer questions from guests, and handle other assignments that may arise.

Working with grounds crews and other department managers, guest services managers will oversee the maintenance and improvement of the spa's recreational and training facilities and grounds. They will develop and oversee budgets for the department. As guests use the spa's facilities, guest services managers and their staffers will reserve times, schedule lessons or consultations with trainers and specialists on staff, and rent or sell equipment.

If guests need special arrangements during their stay, guest services managers will go to great lengths to satisfy those requests. They will plan special events and activities for guests as well.

When guests check out, guest services managers supervise workers in collecting keys, reviewing room charges with guests, and securing final payments.

Through the desk clerks on duty or a separate department, guest services managers direct the receipt and confirmation of reservations. Depending on the responsibilities given to other departments, guest services managers also may be responsible for posting charges to individual guest bills, storing valuables in a safe at the request of guests, and assorted duties related to the safety and security of guests.

Guest services managers may also supervise the door attendants, parking valets, bellhops, and other employees such as nutritionists and sports instructors whose work is critical to guests' satisfaction.

Salaries

Though many resorts and spas charge higher rates than the average hotel, salaries of guest services managers remain in line with those found at other lodging facilities. Beginning guest services managers will earn $18,000 or more. After several years of experience in the position, they may progress to salaries exceeding $40,000.

Employment Prospects

Most resorts and spas that hire guest services managers will be found in the traditional resort areas, such as the West Coast and the Southwest.

Though additional hospitality training may help to some degree, the basic qualification for guest service managers will be work experience and supervisory skills in hotels, especially in assignments with extensive amounts of guest contact, such as front office managers or desk clerks.

Advancement Prospects

The primary track for promotions in this field is moving to similar positions at larger resorts and spas, within the same company or within another hotel management firm or chain. With additional management training and several years of running the guest services department, these managers may seek promotions as resident managers or general managers. Sometimes they can advance in terms of salary by switching to another segment of the travel industry or by opening or purchasing their own spas.

Education and Training

Within the hospitality industry, the primary route for continuing education is the Certified Hotel Administrator (CHA) program offered by the American Hotel & Motel Association in Washington, D.C.

Additional courses in accounting or customer relations will be helpful.

Experience, Skills, and Personality Traits

Guest services managers must demonstrate the interpersonal skills, oral and written communication skills, and supervisory skills to manage large numbers of employees and keep them motivated to do a good job (given the higher service expectations of guests in these facilities).

Increasingly, guest services managers will need computer skills to manage their activities efficiently.

Unions and Associations

As resort or spa executives, guest services managers generally do not belong to a national union.

The primary trade association is the American Hotel and Motel Association (AHMA) in Washington, D.C. AHMA offers seminars, trade shows, publications, and training materials to help guest services managers handle their assignments and train their workers.

Tips for Entry

1. Strengthen your skills in business management and accounting, through courses or direct work experience.

2. Begin your exposure to resorts and spas by working part time as a desk clerk, sports instructor, or bellhop. Most hotels prefer to promote from within; in fact, many guest services managers can trace their careers to a part time position. Also, guest services management is considered the primary route to becoming a general manager at a resort or spa.

3. Broaden your knowledge of current hospitality issues by reading AHMA publications such as *Lodging*, the AHMA membership magazine, and other trade magazines.

4. Consider whether your interpersonal skills—especially your ability to supervise and relate to different types of clients—are strong enough for a people-intensive position in hotel management.

5. Write resorts and spas for information about internships and on-the-job management training programs. Many large resorts, spas, and hotel management firms offer such tracks for liberal arts college graduates, so that these new trainees can learn the hospitality business from their employers.

SPORTS INSTRUCTOR, RESORT/SPA

CAREER PROFILE

Duties: Provides practice lessons and training in various sports; recommends playing gear and training regimens; plays practice games with guests; manages playing areas and stocks supplies; plans tournaments

Alternate Title(s): Sports pro(fessional)

Salary Range: $15,000 to $65,000

Employment Prospects: Good

Best Geographic Location: Most resorts and spas that hire sports instructors will be found in traditional resort areas such as the Southwest and the West Coast.

Prerequisites:

Education and Training—High school diploma required, with courses in business management helpful; advanced training with recognized sports instructors; completion of sports training programs at recognized camps and schools; college degree, with a major in hospitality management, travel and tourism, recreation management, or business management, helpful for advancement

Experience—Advanced proficiency or professional-level playing ability in a given sport; customer relations; work experience in another segment of the travel industry, especially managing a recreational facility

Special Skills and Personality Traits—Courtesy and tact; interpersonal skills; teaching skills

CAREER LADDER

```
Resident Manager or General
Manager, Resort/Spa
```

```
Guest Services Manager, Resort/Spa
```

```
Sports Instructor, Resort/Spa
```

Position Description

Many guests choose to stay at resorts and spas for the chance to improve their ability to play golf or tennis or to ski. Sports instructors work with guests to develop playing and practice habits that will increase their proficiency in the chosen sport.

They achieve this objective primarily by providing hands-on lessons in the game, on an individual basis or in a group of students. They review the basic rules of the sport, introduce and demonstrate training drills to help guests work on basic skills, and assess guest weaknesses that should be worked on the most.

With this information in hand, they develop and recommend training regimens for guests to follow during their stay and at home. They will schedule practice games among guests and in many cases play games themselves with guests.

To maintain the ski runs, tennis courts, golf courses, pools, or other playing areas, sports instructors will supervise grounds crews and other employees in their cleaning assignments. They will keep stores of supplies and handle budgets for their areas. They may recommend and sell sports equipment and gear to guests.

Sports instructors will plan, promote, and operate tournaments and other competitions to exercise the skills of guests and to generate attention for the resort or spa. The instructors may use direct-mail brochures, advertisements, or other means to encourage guests to come to the resort or spa and use the instructional services available.

Salaries

Salaries of sports instructors vary greatly, depending on the ability and reputation of the instructor and the size and reputation of the resort or spa. Beginning sports instructors with intermediate skills will earn $15,000 or more. Instructors with national reputations may earn $65,000 or more.

Employment Prospects

Most resorts and spas that hire sports instructors will be found in the traditional resort areas, such as the West Coast and the Southwest for golf and tennis or the Rocky Mountains for skiiing.

Though hospitality management training may help to some degree, the basic qualification for sports instructors will be the individual's ability to play the sport involved.

Advancement Prospects

The primary track for promotions in this field is moving to similar positions at larger resorts and spas, within the same company or within another hotel management firm or chain. With additional hospitality management training and experience, sports instructors may seek promotions as resident managers or general managers. Other avenues for advancement include increasing their proficiency in the sport (thereby earning raises from the resort or spa) or developing ancillary income from sports products and training aids.

Education and Training

Within the hospitality industry, the primary route for continuing education is the Certified Hotel Administrator (CHA) program offered by the American Hotel & Motel Association in Washington, D.C. This route will apply mainly to sports instructors who want to become resort or spa managers.

Additional courses in business management or customer relations will be helpful. Also, many resorts will value certification in first-aid techniques and CPR training.

Experience, Skills, and Personality Traits

Sports instructors must demonstrate the interpersonal skills and teaching skills to work with guests at varying levels of playing ability. Patience and creativity will help them as well.

If they manage budgets or employees, they will need supervisory skills and financial management abilities to run the department efficiently.

Unions and Associations

Sports instructors generally do not belong to a national union. However, they may participate in professional sports organizations that sponsor and manage tournaments.

The primary trade association for tennis instructors is the American Tennis Professionals Association. Golf pros may belong to the U.S. Professional Golfers Association.

Tips for Entry

1. Strengthen your playing skills in the sport, through achieving professional recognition, playing in major tournaments, or qualifying for a professional league. Also, consider completing a course in a camp or school that is recognized for its top-flight graduates.

2. If you want to advance to become a guest services manager or general manager, consider courses or a degree or certification in hospitality management.

3. Propose becoming an intern or assistant instructor for a sports instructor working in your field. At the least, begin establishing a network of contacts by writing sports instructors for career advice.

4. Consider whether your interpersonal skills—especially your ability to supervise and relate to different types of clients—are strong enough for a people-intensive position working in a resort or spa.

5. Become familiar with the latest training techniques, regimens, and equipment available in your sport.

NUTRITIONIST, RESORT/SPA

CAREER PROFILE

Duties: Plans nutrition programs and supervises the preparation and serving of meals; promotes healthful eating habits among guests; evaluates guests' diets and recommends changes

Alternate Title(s): Dietitian

Salary Range: $23,300 to $34,800

Employment Prospects: Good

Best Geographic Location: Most resorts and spas that hire nutritionists will be found in traditional resort areas such as the West Coast.

Prerequisites:

Education and Training—High school diploma required, with courses in sciences and home economics helpful; bachelor's degree required, with a major in dietetics, nutrition, or food service management; graduate degree in dietetics, nutrition, or food service management helpful for advancement

Experience—Nutritional planning; meal service and preparation; customer relations; business management

Special Skills and Personality Traits—Interpersonal skills; strong teaching skills; oral and written communication skills

CAREER LADDER

```
┌─────────────────────────────────────┐
│  Resident Manager or General         │
│  Manager, Resort/Spa                 │
└─────────────────────────────────────┘

┌─────────────────────────────────────┐
│  Nutritionist, Resort/Spa            │
└─────────────────────────────────────┘

┌─────────────────────────────────────┐
│  Chef or Cook, Resort/Spa            │
└─────────────────────────────────────┘
```

Position Description

Nutritionists work with guests at resorts and spas to develop healthful eating habits and to improve their physical condition. In the controlled environment of the resort or spa, they will prescribe food, supplements, and even fitness regimens to address the health needs of guests.

When guests arrive at the resort or spa, they may be interviewed or examined by the nutritionists for an assessment of their dietetic needs. Depending on the specialties of the spa, nutritionists may confer with doctors or other health care professionals on staff to review each guest profile.

With this information in hand, they will develop nutritional programs for guests and recommend modifications in their diets. For example, guests who suffer from hypertension may be offered low-sodium meals.

Nutritionists will plan and supervise the preparation and serving of meals that are consistent with these nutritional programs. In this capacity, they may work in the kitchens and supervise the efforts of chefs and other employees; also, they may plan budgets and manage the purchasing of foodstuffs and kitchen equipment.

After guests begin their nutritional regimens, nutritionists will evaluate their progress during their stay. Changes may be made in the program to keep guests on track toward improvements.

Nutritionists may promote healthful eating habits by conducting seminars and classes for guests or by scheduling individual counseling sessions. When guests leave, nutritionists will prescribe additional steps and menus that will help them to continue improving their physical condition.

Salaries

Beginning nutritionists may earn salaries ranging from $23,000, while nutritionists with advanced training or at larger properties may progress to $35,000 and beyond.

Employment Prospects

The number of nutritionists employed at resorts and spas will be minimal, due to the limited number of spas in the United States that offer nutritional counseling and dietary programs. Nutritionists who possess a hospitality management background or who have experience in dealing with resort guests will have the greatest chance of being employed.

Advancement Prospects

If they want to remain in the travel industry, nutritionists can progress to become guest service managers, resident managers, or general managers if they gain additional training in hospitality management. Otherwise, nutritionists can apply for similar posts in larger resorts or spas, or they can become independent nutritional consultants or representatives for equipment or food manufacturers.

Education and Training

The primary avenue for continuing professional education is the Registered Dietitian certification offered by the Commission on Dietetic Registration of the American Dietetic Association, given to nutritionists who pass a certification exam.

Many colleges that train nutritionists combine internships or supervised work experiences with the coursework needed to earn a major in nutrition or dietetics.

Experience, Skills, and Personality Traits

Nutritionists who work in a resort or spa must possess the interpersonal skills and teaching skills to counsel and recommend lifestyle changes to guests who may be struggling with health problems.

Unions and Associations

As health professionals, nutritionists generally do not belong to a national union.

Their primary trade association is the American Dietetic Association (ADA) in Chicago, Illinois. ADA offers seminars, publications, and other assistance for practicing nutritionists.

Tips for Entry

1.   Strengthen your skills in business management and hospitality management, through courses or direct work experience, so that you can supervise food service employees in your department properly.

2.   Begin your exposure to the hotel industry by working part time as a front desk clerk, bellhop, or door attendant. You can earn extra money for school while deciding if you want to work in this setting.

3.   If your college requires an internship or supervised work experience as part of your degree program, request a position with a hotel, resort, or spa.

4.   Broaden your knowledge of current hospitality issues by reading AHMA publications such as *Lodging*, the AHMA membership magazine, and other trade magazines.

5.   Consider whether your interpersonal skills—especially your ability to supervise and relate to different types of clients—are strong enough for a people-intensive position in dietetics.

FLOOR MANAGER, CASINO

CAREER PROFILE

Duties: Coordinates gaming, food service, and entertainment activities in a section of the casino; supervises employees at different work stations; enforces casino policies and insures the security of the gaming stations; greets guests and resolves complaints; oversees deposits and money exchanges on the floor

Alternate Title(s): Crew boss

Salary Range: $18,000 to $45,000

Employment Prospects: Good

Best Geographic Location: Most job opportunities will be concentrated in traditional gambling centers such as Las Vegas and Atlantic City and in new casinos and riverboats approved in various parts of the country, especially the Midwest and Southeast.

Prerequisites:

Education and Training—High school diploma required, with courses in business management and accounting helpful; completion of courses in gaming and casino operations from a recognized academy; college degree, with a major in business management or accounting, helpful for advancement

Experience—Accounting and financial management; customer relations; work experience in a hotel or another segment of the travel industry

Special Skills and Personality Traits—Financial management skills; interpersonal skills; supervisory skills; customer relations skills

CAREER LADDER

General Manager, Casino

Floor Manager, Casino

Croupier or Cashier, Casino

Position Description

As more cities and states around the country approve gambling operations within their borders, many people will visit casinos and riverboats to place wagers and to play games of chance, to sample the food served in these establishments, and to enjoy the different types of entertainment offered. In each section of the casino, floor managers supervise and control these activities and insure that guests have a positive experience during their visit.

Floor managers assign duties and schedule shifts of workers to staff the various stations in each section of the casino, from croupiers and dealers at the different gaming tables and singers and musicians in performing areas to waiters and cooks in the restaurants. During a shift, floor managers will walk through their areas and monitor the performance of workers at various stations.

Because the croupiers and cashiers process large amounts of currency, change, and gaming chips during each shift, floor managers must supervise the accounting and cash management activities of these workers. Managers will check the balances in the drawers of each croupier and cashier, prepare and schedule deposits, and resolve any discrepancies at the end of the shift.

Floor managers will be the primary supervisors available to enforce casino policies during the shift. They will consider options and decide actions to take regarding gambling and credit limits for individual patrons, the acceptance of personal checks, and similar matters that might arise. In these duties, they will work closely with security officers to prevent cheating and to maintain order.

To build goodwill and to encourage repeat visits, floor managers will greet customers and answer questions as they walk through their areas. If the casino has invited VIP guests during a shift, floor managers will welcome them, escort them through the casino, and arrange accommodations and other details of their stay. Floor managers will resolve complaints that guests may make during the shift.

Salaries

Beginning floor managers with little experience in the gaming industry may expect to earn salaries starting at $18,000. Floor managers who have progressed through the ranks and possess several years of gaming industry experience may progress to $45,000 or more. While salaries in established gaming centers such as Las Vegas and Atlantic City may be static, new casinos in other parts of the country have been forced to pay premiums in order to hire qualified floor managers.

Employment Prospects

Currently the number of floor manager positions remains relatively limited to casinos in Nevada and Atlantic City and riverboats in the Midwest. However, many Native American reservations around the country have opened new gaming resorts in recent years, and there has been an explosion in the number of cities and states considering the legalization of gambling. Therefore, the number of positions in this field should expand rapidly in coming years.

Advancement Prospects

Most floor managers will advance into higher management positions within their current casinos or in larger gaming resorts around the United States. They may move laterally to become resident or general managers in other lodging facilities.

Education and Training

Floor managers should earn a college degree in business management or a similar field in order to qualify for advanced management positions. In gaming centers such as Nevada and Atlantic City, gaming academies offer specific training for floor managers in casino management and the rules of games of chance. However,

most casinos will value on-the-job experience as a croupier, cashier, or assistant floor manager most highly.

Experience, Skills, and Personality Traits

Because they motivate large numbers of entry-level employees, floor managers must possess the supervisory skills and organizational skills to assign the proper duties and to handle employee needs and problems. Also, they should have high levels of courtesy and tact since they deal closely with the public. Accounting or financial management training will help floor managers as they track the large amounts of money processed during a shift.

Unions and Associations

Floor managers generally do not belong to a national union. If the casino offers lodging, floor managers may belong to the Hotel Employees and Restaurant Employees International Union in Washington, D.C.

No national association has been established for the gaming industry. However, casinos and riverboats may belong to the American Hotel and Motel Association in Washington, D.C., or the National Tour Association in Lexington, Kentucky. Both groups offer seminars, publications, training materials, and other aids for floor managers.

Tips for Entry

1. Strengthen your skills in business management and hospitality management, through courses or direct work experience, so that you will be prepared for advanced management positions.

2. Begin your exposure to the gaming industry by working part time as a cashier, croupier, or hotel clerk. You can earn extra money for school while deciding if you want to work in this setting. Try to target both the established properties and the brand-new casinos.

3. If your college requires an internship or supervised work experience as part of your degree program, request a position with a casino or riverboat.

4. Broaden your knowledge of current hospitality issues by reading AHMA publications such as *Lodging*, the AHMA membership magazine, and other trade magazines.

5. Consider whether your interpersonal skills—especially your ability to supervise and relate to different types of clients—are strong enough for a people-intensive position as a floor manager.

CROUPIER, CASINO

CAREER PROFILE

Duties: Coordinates the activities at a gaming table, including dealing cards, posting bets, collecting chips, and operating other gaming equipment; enforces casino policies and insures the security of the gaming stations; greets guests and resolves complaints; prepares deposits and money exchanges for the floor manager

Alternate Title(s): Dealer

Salary Range: $12,000 to $25,000

Employment Prospects: Good

Best Geographic Location: Most job opportunities will be concentrated in traditional gambling centers such as Las Vegas and Atlantic City and in new casinos and riverboats approved in various parts of the country, especially the Midwest and Southeast.

Prerequisites:

Education and Training—High school diploma required, with courses in business management and accounting helpful; completion of courses in gaming and casino operations from a recognized academy; college degree, with a major in business management or accounting, helpful for advancement

Experience—Customer relations; work experience in a hotel or another segment of the travel industry; bookkeeping or financial management

Special Skills and Personality Traits—Customer relations skills; interpersonal skills; physical dexterity

CAREER LADDER

```
┌─────────────────────────────────┐
│                                 │
│     Floor Manager, Casino       │
│                                 │
└─────────────────────────────────┘

┌─────────────────────────────────┐
│                                 │
│  Assistant Floor Manager, Casino│
│                                 │
└─────────────────────────────────┘

┌─────────────────────────────────┐
│                                 │
│   Croupier or Cashier, Casino   │
│                                 │
└─────────────────────────────────┘
```

Position Description

Every gaming establishment—from the most ostentatious casinos in Las Vegas and Atlantic City to the newest gambling riverboats in Iowa and Mississippi—depends on the work of croupiers and dealers in its operations. Croupiers carry out the specific tasks required at each gaming station.

Their primary responsibility is operating the mechanics of the games of chance. For example, croupiers at a blackjack table must explain the basic rules of the game to players, supervise the placing of bets, shuffle and deal the cards, and pay winning players. They must possess a certain degree of physical dexterity to handle the cards and gaming chips in a quick, efficient manner.

Most gaming establishments rely on the use of plastic chips, rather than currency and change, at gaming stations. Croupiers must track the chips used at each station, group them in trays for easy handling, and exchange different denominations of chips for guests. (Guests will need to exchange their cash for chips at cashier stations.) Croupiers will complete reports at the beginning and end of their shifts regarding the number of chips collected at their station.

Working with the floor manager and security officers, croupiers will enforce casino policies and applicable federal, state, and local laws at their stations. Examples include limits on the credit of specific patrons or alcohol consumption. They will report suspected cases of cheating to the floor manager.

Because they have direct contact with members of the public, croupiers must be ready to answer questions about different games of chance, the casino's facilities, and other matters that may arise. If they cannot resolve the guests' complaints, they will refer the guests to a floor manager.

Salaries

Beginning croupiers with little experience in the gaming industry may expect to earn salaries starting at $12,000. In fact, they may be paid on an hourly basis. Croupiers who have learned to operate different games of chance and possess several years of gaming industry experience may progress to $25,000 or more. While salaries in established gaming centers such as Las Vegas and Atlantic City may be static, new casinos in other parts of the country have been forced to pay premiums in order to hire qualified croupiers.

Employment Prospects

Currently the number of croupier positions remains relatively limited to casinos in Nevada and Atlantic City and riverboats in the Midwest. However, many Native American reservations around the country have opened new gaming resorts in recent years, and there has been an explosion in the number of cities and states considering the legalization of gambling. Therefore, the number of positions in this field should expand rapidly in coming years.

Advancement Prospects

Most croupiers will advance into floor manager jobs or higher management positions within their current casinos or in larger gaming resorts around the United States. They may move laterally to positions in other attractions or lodging facilities.

Education and Training

Croupiers should possess at least a high school diploma. They will need a college degree in business management or a similar field in order to qualify for advanced management positions. In gaming centers such as Nevada and Atlantic City, gaming academies offer specific training for croupiers in casino management and the rules of games of chance. However, most casinos will conduct their own orientation sessions and on-the-job training programs.

Experience, Skills, and Personality Traits

Because they must operate the mechanics of a game of chance (e.g., the dice at the craps table, the wheel and ball at the roulette table), they should possess some degree of manual dexterity in order to operate the games quickly and efficiently. Also, they should have high levels of courtesy and tact since they deal closely with the public. Basic math skills will help croupiers as they track the large amounts of money processed during a shift.

Unions and Associations

Croupiers belong to the Hotel Employees and Restaurant Employees International Union in Washington, D.C.

No national association has been established for the gaming industry. However, casinos and riverboats may belong to the American Hotel and Motel Association in Washington, D.C., or the National Tour Association in Lexington, Kentucky. Both groups offer seminars, publications, training materials, and other activities to help casinos and riverboats attract gamblers and manage operations.

Tips for Entry

1. Increase your knowledge of the rules and operations of different games of chance. You can read books on the subject or complete a training program offered by a gaming academy.

2. Begin your exposure to the gaming industry by working part time as a cashier, clerk, or a similar entry-level position. You can earn extra money for school while deciding if you want to work in this setting. Try to target both the established properties and the brand-new casinos.

3. If your college requires an internship or supervised work experience as part of your degree program, request a position with a casino or riverboat.

4. Broaden your knowledge of current hospitality issues by reading AHMA publications such as *Lodging*, the AHMA membership magazine, and other trade magazines.

5. Consider whether your interpersonal skills—especially your ability to supervise and relate to different types of clients—are strong enough for a people-intensive position as a croupier.

OWNER/MANAGER, BED-AND-BREAKFAST INN

CAREER PROFILE

Duties: Manages the overall operations of a bed-and-breakfast inn; supervises staffers in various departments of the inn; sets rates and guest policies; markets the inn to prospective guests

Alternate Title(s): Innkeeper

Salary Range: $21,000 to $45,000

Employment Prospects: Fair

Best Geographic Location: Most regions of the United States offer job possibilities, particularly in rural scenic areas and in traditional resort locations.

Prerequisites:

Education and Training—High school diploma required, with courses in business management and home economics helpful; college degree helpful, with a major in business management, hospitality management, or travel and tourism; completion of an innkeeping training course offered by a recognized expert

Experience—Work experience in a hotel; work experience in another segment of the travel industry; business management

Special Skills and Personality Traits—Supervisory skills; strong oral and written communication skills; interpersonal skills; financial management skills

CAREER LADDER

```
┌─────────────────────────────┐
│                             │
│      Owner/Manager,         │
│    Bed-and-Breakfast Inn    │
│                             │
└─────────────────────────────┘

┌─────────────────────────────┐
│                             │
│      Assistant Manager,     │
│    Bed-and-Breakfast Inn    │
│                             │
└─────────────────────────────┘

┌─────────────────────────────┐
│                             │
│    Chef or Reservationist,  │
│    Bed-and-Breakfast Inn    │
│                             │
└─────────────────────────────┘
```

Position Description

Seeking a change of pace from run-of-the-mill hotels, many travelers today choose to stay in bed-and-breakfasts—private homes and small hotels that have been renovated into distinctive inns. These inns are run by general managers, who supervise inn employees and allocate resources so that guests will be satisfied and the inn will realize a profit on its operations. (In many cases, the managers are also the owners.)

These managers exert authority over every facet of the inn's operations. This process begins at the front desk, where they approve the different rates charge to guests (such as the standard rate and the discounted rate for repeat visitors), the check-in procedures by which guests register and receive their keys, and the billing procedures by which guest charges are recorded and payments collected.

Working with interior designers and housekeepers, innkeepers plan the overall look and design of the inn grounds and interior, from the types of shrubs planted along walkways to the color schemes used in hotel guest rooms. Many inns feature historic antique furnishings or unique themes that appeal to their market niches. The innkeepers approve the custodial schedules and practices that the housekeeping staff follows in maintaining the inn's appearance.

To attract guests to the inn, managers design and schedule advertisements for magazines and newspapers. Also, they write and send press releases to generate mentions in the media. They work with travel agents, tour operators, and other travel professionals to solicit business. If the inn is historic, the innkeepers will cooperate with local historic preservation boards to promote the inn's place in local history.

When guests finalize their plans for staying at the inn, the managers oversee the handling of reservation requests and confirmations. Because computers play an increasingly important role in this process, managers should understand basic principles of automated reservation systems and computer systems.

Because most bed-and-breakfasts are small-scale lodging facilities, owners and managers develop a close rapport with their guests. In fact, many inns take on the air of a private home, with the innkeepers acting as gracious family hosts. They must respond to questions about the inn's furnishings and grounds, assist guests who want to purchase similar furniture or accessories for their own homes, and recommend activities for visitors in the area surrounding the inn.

Many inns also offer meals, from continental breakfast to sumptuous dinner buffets. The manager will supervise the preparation of menus and dishes; in some cases, the manager also may serve as the chef.

Many owners and managers opt for this career during retirement or as a second income, because the salaries and profit levels are normally lower than those found in other segments of the lodging industry.

Salaries

Given the small scale of bed-and-breakfast inns, salaries for owners and managers tend to range lower than comparable figures for managers in other segments of the travel industry. Beginning salaries for managers of smaller inns may start at $21,000, proceeding to $45,000 or more for experienced managers who run inns in the most popular resort areas of the United States. Salaries function largely in relation to the size of the inn, its rates, and the popularity of its location. If the manager also owns the inn, the low salary may be balanced by the increasing value of the owner's equity.

Employment Prospects

Most areas of the United States now have a fair share of bed-and-breakfast inns, though the concept remains most popular in areas such as the Northeast and Northwest. While this fact offers some mobility for qualified owners and managers, many managers will find that they have to invest in an inn or purchase it outright in order to create an opening (since many owners manage their inns themselves).

Advancement Prospects

The primary avenue for managers to advance in this field is buying their own inn. If they have sufficient experience, they may transfer laterally to become managers in other lodging facilities.

Education and Training

Within the innkeeping industry, the primary route for continuing education is courses and seminars offered by groups such as the Professional Association of Innkeepers International in Santa Barbara, California.

Additional courses in financial management, marketing, and hospitality management will be helpful.

Experience, Skills, and Personality Traits

Innkeepers must demonstrate the interpersonal skills, oral and written communication skills, and supervisory skills to manage their numbers of employees and keep them motivated to do a good job. These same skills will help innkeepers relate to their guests, who generally require closer contact from innkeepers than from employees in traditional hotels.

Increasingly, these managers will need computer skills to manage their activities efficiently.

Unions and Associations

As owners and managers, innkeepers generally do not belong to a national union. Their primary national trade organization is the Professional Association of Innkeepers International (PAII) in Santa Barbara, California. PAII offers seminars, publications, and training programs that innkeepers can use to improve their operations.

Tips for Entry

1. Read book and magazines (many offered by PAII) about what it takes to run a bed-and-breakfast inn.

2. Attend classes offered by PAII and inn consultants in various cities around the country. Hear successful inn owners describe their jobs and investments. Also, consider talking to an inn broker who sells bed-and-breakfasts.

3. Visit an inn when you travel. Ask the innkeepers if you can follow them during a typical day, to discover whether this line of work appeals to you.

4. If you have picked an area of the country where you want to open an inn, review the types of inns already operating there. Also, consider the popularity of that location for travelers.

5. Write PAII for information about serving as an intern or apprentice at an inn.

OWNER/MANAGER, RESTAURANT

CAREER PROFILE

Duties: Manages the overall operations of a restaurant; selects menu items and sets prices; orders foodstuffs and supplies; recruits and trains workers; oversees food preparation and service

Alternate Title(s): None

Salary Range: $15,000 to $56,000

Employment Prospects: Very good

Best Geographic Location: Most regions of the United States offer job possibilities.

Prerequisites:

Education and Training—High school diploma required, with courses in business management and home economics helpful; college degree helpful, with a major in business management or restaurant administration

Experience—Work experience in a restaurant; customer relations; work experience in another segment of the travel industry; business management

Special Skills and Personality Traits—Supervisory skills; strong oral and written communication skills; interpersonal skills; financial management skills

CAREER LADDER

```
+-----------------------------------+
|                                   |
|   Owner/Manager, Restaurant       |
|                                   |
+-----------------------------------+


+-----------------------------------+
|                                   |
|   Assistant Manager, Restaurant   |
|                                   |
+-----------------------------------+


+-----------------------------------+
|                                   |
|   Chef or Head Waiter, Restaurant |
|                                   |
+-----------------------------------+
```

Position Description

Millions of Americans eat meals out of the home each day, from continental breakfast at a fast-food restaurant to elaborate multicourse dinners at four-star restaurants. Coordinating the meals and service are restaurant owners and managers, who oversee the planning, preparation, and service of meals to patrons.

Restaurant managers exert authority over every facet of the restaurant's operations. This process begins with the menu, as managers select the various dishes that the restaurant will offer. The managers analyze the recipes for these menu items to break out the cost of ingredients and labor; then, they price the items. In today's health-censcious environment, managers will pay considerable attention to the nutritional content of these dishes.

They order supplies for the restaurant, from the ingredients for various dishes and uniforms to pots and pans, cutlery and cleaning products. Managers track the amount of supplies inventoried, so that the restaurant does not run out. They deal with vendors and suppliers, placing orders and checking invoices. When the supplies arrive, they check the deliveries for quality. They oversee the maintenance and repair of restaurant equipment and furnishings.

To staff the restaurant fully, owners and managers recruit and train workers. They provide orientation sessions and teach new employees the routines and work practices of the restaurant. They schedule shifts of workers so that the restaurant has enough employees available during the busiest times.

During each shift, managers supervise the operations of the kitchen and dining areas. They oversee food preparation and service, insuring that portions are adequate and that the wait staff delivers the dishes with the proper presentation. Managers handle questions and complaints from patrons. They also direct the cleaning of the restaurant.

Managers also may devote time to bookkeeping and record-keeping responsibilities. For example, they will record the number of hours worked in various shifts by different employees, the amounts of supplies used during a shift, and the cash and credit card payments taken from customers. The managers will make bank deposits at the end of each shift or day.

To attract patrons to the restaurant, managers plan advertisements in magazines and newspapers, public relations campaigns to draw media attention, and other marketing techniques.

Salaries

In smaller restaurants, owners and managers will handle many aspect of restaurant operations personally, without the help of assistant managers. Entry-level salaries will begin at $15,000. By progressing to larger restaurants or to management positions in restaurant companies, a manager can boost salary levels to $56,000 and beyond. In the case of owners, salaries will be supplemented by the increasing value of the owner's equity.

Employment Prospects

Any region in the United States will offer openings in this field. In fact, the number of restaurant jobs should continue to increase faster than opportunities in other sectors of the travel industry. Therefore, qualified managers with demonstrable experience in restaurant administration should find openings around the country.

Advancement Prospects

The primary track for promotions in this field is moving to the manager's position at larger restaurants or within a restaurant management firm or chain. Many managers can advance in terms of salary by switching to another segment of the travel industry. For some, the biggest dream is opening their own restaurant; however, such a step will require extensive planning and, in many cases, access to significant amounts of capital (from loans or investors).

Education and Training

Within the restaurant industry, there is no continuing education program at present that leads to a professional certification.

In certain cases, owners and managers whose properties depend greatly on tour operator business will complete the Certified Tour Professional (CTP) program of the National Tour Association in Lexington, Kentucky.

Additional courses in financial management and human resources management will be helpful.

Experience, Skills, and Personality Traits

Restaurant managers must demonstrate the interpersonal skills, oral and written communication skills, and supervisory skills to manage large numbers of employees and keep them motivated to do a good job. (Supervising restaurant employees can be difficult, because many of them have been hired for minimal wages to perform tasks that are menial in nature or that require direct exposure to paying customers.)

Surprisingly, many managers note that culinary skills are not a critical matter for them—not nearly as important to the success of the restaurant as business management skills.

Unions and Associations

Restaurant owners and managers generally do not belong to a national union.

Their primary national trade organization is the National Restaurant Association (NRA), located in Washington, D.C. NRA offers seminars, conventions, trade shows, publications, and training programs for frontline employees that restaurant managers can use at their properties.

Tips for Entry

1. Strengthen your skills in business management, accounting, and human resources management, through courses or direct work experience.

2. Begin your exposure to restaurant operations by working part time as a busboy, waiter or waitress, cook, or a similar position. Most restaurants prefer to promote from within; in fact, many owners and managers trace their careers to a part-time position.

3. Broaden your knowledge of current restaurant issues by reading publications such as *Restaurants USA*, the NRA magazine, and other trade magazines.

4. Consider whether your interpersonal skills—especially your ability to supervise and relate to entry-level employees—are strong enough for a people-intensive position in restaurant management.

5. Write restaurants for information about internships and on-the-job management training programs. Many large chains and management companies offer such tracks for liberal arts college graduates, so that these new trainees can learn the restaurant business from their employers.

CHEF, RESTAURANT

CAREER PROFILE

Duties: Supervises operations of the kitchen in a restaurant or similar establishment; oversees preparation of various dishes; purchases foodstuffs and other supplies; selects and develops recipes; trains kitchen staffers

Alternate Title(s): Executive chef; cook

Salary Range: $12,000 to $55,000

Employment Prospects: Very good

Best Geographic Location: Most regions of the United States offer job possibilities, although the most prestigious restaurants will be located in major cities.

Prerequisites:

Education and Training—High school diploma required, with courses in business management and home economics helpful; completion of an apprenticeship program offered by an accredited cooking school or academy; college degree helpful, with a major in culinary arts or food preparation

Experience—Work experience in a kitchen or restaurant; customer relations; work experience in another segment of the travel industry; business management

Special Skills and Personality Traits—Culinary skills; strong oral and written communication skills; interpersonal skills; supervisory skills

CAREER LADDER

```
┌─────────────────────────────────────┐
│                                      │
│      Owner/Manager, Restaurant       │
│                                      │
└─────────────────────────────────────┘

┌─────────────────────────────────────┐
│                                      │
│     Assistant Manager, Restaurant    │
│                                      │
└─────────────────────────────────────┘

┌─────────────────────────────────────┐
│                                      │
│          Chef, Restaurant            │
│                                      │
└─────────────────────────────────────┘
```

Position Description

Chefs are the primary supervisors and artists who set the menu and the tone for most restaurants. They oversee the planning, preparation, and service of meals to patrons.

Working with the owner or manager, chefs select the specific dishes that will appear on the menu. They develop and analyze recipes, test them for flavor and appearance, and decide on the ingredients that will be used to prepare each dish. In today's health-conscious environment, chefs will pay considerable attention to the nutritional content of these dishes.

They estimate the amount of each item that will be ordered by patrons on a regular basis, and they purchase the ingredients needed to satisfy that demand. When foodstuffs are delivered, chefs inspect the deliveries for quality and color. They also may order cooking utensils, china, cutlery, and kitchen equipment, under the supervision of the owner or manager.

Chefs usually will be involved (under the manager's supervision) in recruiting and training workers for the kitchen. They teach new employees the routines and work practices of the restaurant. They schedule shifts of workers so that the kitchen has enough employees available during the busiest times. (In small restaurants, they may be directly responsible for all personnel matters, from hiring new workers to keeping time sheets and processing paychecks.)

During each shift, chefs supervise the operations of the kitchen and participate in the preparation and cooking of various dishes. For example, they may cut or carve meats, mix sauces and dressings, and bake desserts. They insure that portions are adequate and that the wait staff delivers the dishes with the proper presentation. If needed, they will handle questions and complaints from patrons. They also direct the cleaning of the kitchen, including all work areas and utensils.

Chefs may be asked to keep kitchen records such as inventories of foodstuffs and supplies, employee time sheets, and other paperwork.

To attract patrons to the restaurant, chefs may participate in promotional activities such as fund-raisers and advertisements, as directed by the owner or manager.

Salaries

In smaller restaurants, chefs will run many aspects of the kitchen personally, without the help of assistant chefs or cooks. Entry-level salaries will begin as low at $12,000. By progressing to larger restaurants or to management positions in restaurant companies, a chef can boost salary levels to $55,000 and beyond. If the chef owns part or all of the restaurant, the salary will be supplemented by the increasing value of the owner's equity.

Employment Prospects

Any region in the United States will offer openings in this field. In fact, the number of restaurant jobs should continue to increase faster than opportunities in other sectors of the travel industry. Therefore, qualified chefs with demonstrable experience in culinary skills should find openings around the country.

Advancement Prospects

The primary track for promotions in this field is moving to positions at larger restaurants or within a restaurant management firm or chain. Many chefs launch their own restaurants, shouldering more management responsibility in return for higher earnings.

Education and Training

The American Culinary Federation offers a tiered certification program that tests culinary abilities and awards the following designations: cook, working chef, executive chef, and master chef.

Experience, Skills, and Personality Traits

Chefs must demonstrate the interpersonal skills, oral and written communication skills, and supervisory skills to manage their employees and keep them motivated to do a good job. (Supervising restaurant workers can be difficult, due to the low wages normally paid in relation to the high degree of customer service expected.)

More important, chefs must exhibit advanced culinary skills—gained from work experience, an apprenticeship, or a cooking school—to function effectively in a restaurant kitchen.

Unions and Associations

Chefs generally do not belong to a national union.

The primary national trade organization for chefs is the American Culinary Federation (ACF), located in St. Augustine, Florida. ACF offers a certification program, publications, seminars, and other support materials for chefs and their employees.

The primary national trade organization for restaurants is the National Restaurant Association (NRA), located in Washington, D.C. NRA offers seminars, conventions, trade shows, publications, and training programs for restaurant owners and managers.

Tips for Entry

1.   Strengthen your cooking skills, through working in a restaurant, signing on as an apprentice to a master chef, or completing a culinary arts degree program at a recognized cooking school or academy.

2.   Begin your exposure to restaurant operations by working part time as a busboy, waiter or waitress, cook, or a similar position. Most restaurants prefer to promote from within; in fact, many owners and managers trace their careers to a part-time position. If possible try to switch assignments in the kitchen (e.g., sauces to pastries to main courses) so that you get a wide range of experience.

3.   Broaden your knowledge of current restaurant issues by reading publications such as *Restaurants USA*, the NRA magazine, and other trade magazines.

4.   Consider whether your interpersonal skills—especially your ability to supervise and relate to entry-level employees—are strong enough for a people-intensive position as a chef and kitchen manager.

5.   Write restaurants for information about internships and on-the-job management training programs. Many large chains and management companies offer such tracks for liberal arts college graduates, so that these new trainees can learn the restaurant business from their employers.

DISTRICT SALES MANAGER, AIRLINE

CAREER PROFILE

Duties: Prepares marketing plans to solicit leisure and business travelers; coordinates advertising, public relations, direct-mail, and other marketing campaigns; schedules presentations and makes sales calls on travel agents, corporate travel managers, and other large-volume buyers

Alternate Title(s): None

Salary Range: $25,000 to $85,000

Employment Prospects: Fair

Best Geographic Location: Most job openings will be found in large cities that the major airlines use as "hubs" for their routes.

Prerequisites:

Education and Training—High school diploma required, with courses in business management helpful; college degree required, with courses in business management, sales, and hospitality management helpful; additional training in direct sales

Experience—Direct sales; customer relations; work experience in a tour company, travel agency, or travel supplier (e.g., theme park, hotel)

Special Skills and Personality Traits—Sales ability; business management skills; strong oral and written communication skills; interpersonal skills; group presentation skills

CAREER LADDER

```
┌─────────────────────────────────┐
│   Vice President of Sales and    │
│        Marketing, Airline        │
└─────────────────────────────────┘

┌─────────────────────────────────┐
│   District Sales Manager, Airline│
└─────────────────────────────────┘

┌─────────────────────────────────┐
│    Sales Representative, Airline  │
└─────────────────────────────────┘

┌─────────────────────────────────┐
│      Reservationist, Airline      │
└─────────────────────────────────┘
```

Position Description

Although many Americans who travel via airplanes understand the procedures for booking a ticket by calling a travel agent or the corporate travel manager, they may not understand the dynamics by which the airlines promote their services to these buyers. In various sales districts around the country (and around the world), district sales managers use all available avenues to plan, coordinate, and execute the sales and marketing activities of the airline.

Ideally, the district sales managers first will adapt the airline's overall strategic marketing plan to fit their districts. This process begins with an examination of the airline's capacity and resources, as the district sales managers work closely with the vice president of sales and marketing and other staffers to decide which features of the airline (e.g., the types of flights, the fares, the district's proximity to corporate headquarters or vacation attractions) will draw the most attention from potential customers.

Based on the airline's best attributes, district sales managers then identify the most promising market segments. Today many airlines rely on a number of different market segments to fill seats: individual travelers, families, international inbound travelers, corporate travelers, meetings and convention delegates, tour groups, and other niches.

As the product types and market segments are being determined, district sales managers also must take into account the carrier's positioning in the marketplace, compared to other airlines. For example, should the airline focus on serving the needs of business travelers or leisure travelers? Will most passengers come from the United States or from other countries abroad? Positioning will be critical in deciding what types of promotions and what future services will make the airline a success in each district.

Once these basic decisions have been made, district sales managers will begin identifying prospective customers and soliciting their business. For large-volume customers such as travel agencies and major companies, the managers and their sales representatives will likely follow up direct-mail letters and telemarketing calls with personal presentations to the groups or selected decision makers. Therefore, managers need to be adept at speaking in front of groups and planning creative presentations to sell the airline.

For the most part, however, district sales managers will rely on standard marketing techniques such as advertising, public relations, and direct-mail brochures. District sales managers must design and plan local advertisements for the airline (building on materials used in the airline's national advertising campaigns), choose the media involved, and make the final placement decisions. Managers usually will coordinate press releases and serve as spokespeople for the company to journalists. Using in-house staffers or an outside firm, district sales managers will design and supervise the production of the airline's schedules, brochures, and other printed materials; once these pieces are printed, managers will decide strategies for sending them to prospective passengers.

To gauge the effectiveness of these marketing efforts, district sales managers must research the targeted market segments and track the number of passengers who traveled on the airline as a result.

Salaries

Salaries of district sales managers reflect their years of sales experience and their responsibility for an entire district. Managers in the smallest districts may earn $25,000 or more, while managers who control the most lucrative districts or who work overseas may earn $120,000 or more (plus bonuses).

Employment Prospects

Opportunities in this field will remain very limited, as America's nine major "national" carriers cut back their staffs. However, a surge in the number of start-up airlines means that more positions will become available in the future. They will be found primarily in larger cities that serve as "hubs" for airline routes or that contain significant numbers of corporate headquarters or other large-volume buyers.

Advancement Prospects

The primary track for promotions in this field is moving to similar positions at other airlines or progressing to higher management positions within the same airline. Other district sales managers can advance in terms of salary by switching to another segment of the travel industry.

Education and Training

Currently there is no continuing education program for professional certification of district sales managers.

In certain cases, managers who target certain niches may seek specialized designations such as the Certified Tour Professional (CTP) program of the National Tour Association in Lexington, Kentucky, or the Certified Travel Counselor (CTC) program of the Institute of Certified Travel Agents in Wellesley, Massachusetts.

Additional courses in foreign languages and sales management may be helpful.

Experience, Skills, and Personality Traits

District sales managers must demonstrate the direct sales abilities and group presentation skills to discover prospective clients and persuade them to book seats. If they manage sales representatives, they should have the interpersonal skills, oral and written communication skills, and supervisory skills to keep them motivated.

Increasingly, these managers will need computer skills to manage their activities efficiently.

Unions and Associations

As airline executives, district sales managers generally do not belong to a national union, nor do they have a professional association.

The primary national trade organization for airlines is the Air Transport Association (ATA) in Washington, D.C. ATA offers publications, training manuals, government representation, and other assistance to U.S. airlines.

Tips for Entry

1. Strengthen your skills in business management and sales, through courses or direct work experience.

2. Begin your exposure to the airline industry by working part time as a sales representative, reservationist, flight attendant, or a similar position. Most airlines prefer to promote from within.

3.   Broaden your knowledge of current airline issues by reading trade magazines such as *Airline Executive* and *Air Transport World*.

4.   Write the major airlines for information about internships and on-the-job management training programs. Many airlines offer such tracks for college graduates, so that these new trainees can learn the airline business from their employers.

SALES REPRESENTATIVE, AIRLINE

CAREER PROFILE

Duties: Prepares marketing plans to solicit individual clients; designs advertisements, letters, and proposals for these clients; schedules presentations and makes sales calls on travel companies and other large-volume buyers

Alternate Title(s): Account executive

Salary Range: $15,000 to $85,000

Employment Prospects: Fair

Best Geographic Location: Most job openings will be found in large cities that the major airlines use as "hubs" for their routes.

Prerequisites:

Education and Training—High school diploma required, with courses in business management helpful; college degree required, with courses in business management, sales, and hospitality management helpful; additional training in direct sales

Experience—Direct sales; customer relations; work experience in a tour company, travel agency, or travel supplier (e.g., theme park, hotel)

Special Skills and Personality Traits—Sales ability; business management skills; strong oral and written communication skills; interpersonal skills; group presentation skills

CAREER LADDER

```
┌─────────────────────────────┐
│  Vice President of Sales and │
│       Marketing, Airline     │
└─────────────────────────────┘

┌─────────────────────────────┐
│  District Sales Manager, Airline │
└─────────────────────────────┘

┌─────────────────────────────┐
│  Sales Representative, Airline │
└─────────────────────────────┘

┌─────────────────────────────┐
│   Reservationist, Airline    │
└─────────────────────────────┘
```

Position Description

Airline sales representatives perform the bread-and-butter work of contacting prospective clients and persuading them to book seats on the airline. These representatives will write the sales letters, make the telephone calls, and prepare the proposals and presentations for specific clients.

Working from the airline's strategic marketing plan, account executives must learn the airline's capacity and resources. They must have a firsthand knowledge of the types of flights, the various fares and discounts, amenities for corporate travelers and tour groups, and any other background information that future passengers may request.

Under the supervision of the district sales manager, sales representatives will be given specific market segments for which they must be responsible: individual travelers, families, international inbound travelers, corporate travelers, meetings and conventions, tour groups, and other niches. In many districts, sales representatives may be given a list of individual accounts rather than an entire segment.

Sales representatives must become very familiar with the dynamics and needs of their accounts. They should know the booking patterns, fares, itineraries, special needs, and other characteristics that distinguish these clients from others. Successful sales representatives round out their knowledge of their accounts by studying the airline's files on these travelers, reading their trade publications, establishing a personal rapport with the decision makers at these accounts, and networking with other travel suppliers in the city or state.

Armed with this information, sales representatives will begin identifying prospective customers and soliciting their business. For large-volume customers such as travel agencies and major corporations, sales representatives will follow up direct-mail letters, brochures, and telemarketing calls with personal presentations to the groups or selected decision makers. Sales representatives must be able to speak in front of groups and plan creative presentations to sell the airline.

Working together with other sales representatives, they will respond to leads generated by standard marketing techniques such as advertising, public relations, trade shows, and direct-mail campaigns. Sales representatives may help to design and plan advertisements for the airline, choose the media involved, and make the final placement decisions. They also may assist in public relations work such as greeting visiting clients and arranging familiarization tours. In some cases, they will staff booths at trade shows.

Sales representatives monitor complaints and questions that may arise. If the clients have arranged special billing procedures, the sales representative may oversee the preparation of those bills.

To gauge the effectiveness of these marketing efforts, sales representatives must research the targeted market segments and track the number of their clients who have booked space on the airline.

Salaries

Salaries of airline sales representatives depend on the size of the airline, its position in the marketplace, and other factors. Salaries for new representatives may begin at $15,000, but experienced sales representatives with proven track records of generating business may earn $85,000 or more (including bonuses).

Employment Prospects

Opportunities in this field will remain very limited, as America's nine major "national" carriers cut back their staffs. However, a surge in the number of start-up airlines means that more positions will become available in the future. They will be found primarily in larger cities that serve as "hubs" for airline routes or that contain significant numbers of corporate headquarters or other large-volume buyers.

Advancement Prospects

The primary track for promotions in this field is moving to similar positions at other airlines or progress-

ing to become a district sales manager within the same airline. Other sales representatives can advance in terms of salary by switching to another segment of the travel industry.

Education and Training

Currently there is no continuing education program for professional certification of airline sales representatives.

In certain cases, sales representatives who target certain niches may seek specialized designations such as the Certified Tour Professional (CTP) program of the National Tour Association in Lexington, Kentucky, or the Certified Travel Counselor (CTC) program of the Institute of Certified Travel Agents in Wellesley, Massachusetts.

Additional courses in foreign languages and sales management may be helpful.

Experience, Skills, and Personality Traits

Airline sales representatives must demonstrate the direct sales abilities and group presentation skills to discover prospective clients and persuade them to book seats. They must have organizational skills and attention to detail to handle service requests from clients.

Increasingly, sales representatives will need computer skills to manage their activities efficiently.

Unions and Associations

As airline executives, sales representatives generally do not belong to a national union, nor do they have a professional association.

The primary national trade organization for airlines is the Air Transport Association (ATA) in Washington, D.C. ATA offers publications, training manuals, government representation, and other assistance to U.S. airlines.

Tips for Entry

1. Strengthen your skills in business management and sales, through courses or direct work experience.

2. Begin your exposure to the airline industry by working part time as a baggage handler, reservationist, flight attendant, or a similar position. Most airlines prefer to promote from within; in fact, many sales representatives can trace their careers to a part-time position.

3. Broaden your knowledge of current airline issues by reading trade magazines such as *Airline Executive* and *Air Transport World*.

4. Consider whether your interpersonal skills are strong enough for a people-intensive position in airline sales.

5. Write the major airlines for information about internships and on-the-job management training programs. Many airlines offer such tracks for college graduates, so that these new trainees can learn the airline business from their employers.

6. When you apply for airline sales positions, highlight any experience you have had in customer relations and direct sales, from part-time jobs to volunteer assignments.

ADVERTISING ASSISTANT, AIRLINE

CAREER PROFILE

Duties: Conducts marketing and media research for advertising campaigns; prepares advertising materials; acts as liaison to advertising agencies; designs and prepares collateral materials

Alternate Title(s): None

Salary Range: $15,000 to $25,000

Employment Prospects: Fair

Best Geographic Location: Most job openings will be found at the airlines' corporate headquarters or in large cities that the major airlines use as "hubs" for their routes.

Prerequisites:

Education and Training—High school diploma required, with courses in business management helpful; college degree required, with courses in advertising and business management helpful

Experience—Work experience in an advertising firm or the advertising sales department of a media company; work experience in a tour company, travel agency, or travel supplier (e.g., theme park, hotel)

Special Skills and Personality Traits—Creativity; organizational skills; attention to detail; strong oral and written communication skills; interpersonal skills

CAREER LADDER

```
┌─────────────────────────────┐
│                             │
│   Vice President of Sales and│
│     Marketing, Airline       │
│                             │
└─────────────────────────────┘

┌─────────────────────────────┐
│                             │
│  Director of Advertising, Airline│
│                             │
└─────────────────────────────┘

┌─────────────────────────────┐
│                             │
│  Advertising Assistant, Airline│
│                             │
└─────────────────────────────┘
```

Position Description

Advertising assistants for airlines perform research tasks, prepare materials, and work in teams with advertising professionals to promote the airline to potential travelers.

Working from the airline's strategic marketing plan, advertising assistants conduct research programs to determine which market segments the airline should target in its campaigns. They use computerized databases, passenger focus groups, comments from district sales offices, and other sources of information to carry out their research plans.

Also, they examine potential media—magazines, newspapers, radio and TV stations, and other forms—to decide where the airline's advertisements should appear. They will review media rate cards, audiences, editorial slants, and other factors in making these decisions.

Then they will prepare advertising materials for the airline. If the airline works with an outside advertising agency, advertising assistants will work in a support and advisory role to the agency staffers working on the airline account. In other cases, advertising assistants will work with the vice president of sales and marketing to develop a theme, prepare "slicks" and videos containing the ads, and request space in the targeted media for these ads.

Beyond support services, advertising assistants will serve as liaisons between the outside advertising agency and other airline departments.

For marketing campaigns in individual districts or other targeted efforts, advertising assistants may design and produce brochures, newspaper inserts, and other collateral materials for specific district sales managers and sales representatives to use for their clients.

As media placements and other expenses arise, advertising assistants track invoices from these vendors, check their accuracy, and forward them to the accounting department for payment.

Salaries

Salaries of advertising assistants depend on the size of the airline, its position in the marketplace, and other factors. Salaries for new assistants may begin at $15,000 and progress to $25,000.

Employment Prospects

Opportunities in this field will remain very limited, as America's nine major "national" carriers cut back their staffs. However, a surge in the number of start-up airlines means that more positions will become available in the future. They will be found primarily at the airline's corporate headquarters or in larger cities that serve as "hubs" for airline routes.

Advancement Prospects

The primary track for promotions in this field is moving to similar positions at other airlines or progressing to become director of advertising. Other advertising assistants can advance in terms of salary by switching to another segment of the travel industry or to an advertising agency that specializes in travel accounts.

Education and Training

Currently there is no continuing education program for professional certification of advertising assistants.

Additional courses in advertising, graphic arts, and marketing may be helpful.

Experience, Skills, and Personality Traits

Advertising assistants must have the creativity to develop advertisements and collateral materials that will promote the airline effectively. They must have organizational skills and attention to detail to handle service requests from media and from outside agencies.

Increasingly, advertising assistants will need computer skills to manage their activities efficiently.

Unions and Associations

Advertising assistants generally do not belong to a national union.

The primary national trade organization for airlines is the Air Transport Association (ATA) in Washington, D.C. ATA offers publications, training manuals, government representation, and other assistance to U.S. airlines.

Tips for Entry

1. Strengthen your skills in advertising and marketing, through courses or direct work experience.

2. Begin your exposure to the airline industry by working part time as a baggage handler, reservationist, flight attendant, or a similar position. Most airlines prefer to promote from within; in fact, many airline executives can trace their careers to a part-time position.

3. Broaden your knowledge of current airline issues by reading trade magazines such as *Airline Executive* and *Air Transport World.*

4. Consider whether you would prefer working inside the airline, as opposed to an independent advertising agency. Some advertising professionals like the variety of working for more than one type of client.

5. Write the major airlines for information about internships and on-the-job management training programs. Many airlines offer such tracks for college graduates, so that these new trainees can learn the airline business from their employers.

PUBLIC RELATIONS ASSISTANT, AIRLINE

CAREER PROFILE

Duties: Prepares press releases and other public relations materials; handles media calls and interview requests; serves as liaison to outside public relations firms; handles industry affairs duties

Alternate Title(s): None

Salary Range: $15,000 to $25,000

Employment Prospects: Fair

Best Geographic Location: Most job openings will be found at the airlines' corporate headquarters or in large cities that the major airlines use as "hubs" for their routes.

Prerequisites:

Education and Training—High school diploma required, with courses in journalism and writing helpful; college degree required, with courses in English, journalism, and public relations helpful

Experience—Work experience in a public relations firm or in the field of journalism; work experience in a tour company, travel agency, or travel supplier (e.g., theme park, hotel)

Special Skills and Personality Traits—Writing ability; creativity; organizational skills; attention to detail; very strong oral and written communication skills; interpersonal skills

CAREER LADDER

```
┌─────────────────────────────────────┐
│     Vice President of Sales and      │
│          Marketing, Airline          │
└─────────────────────────────────────┘

┌─────────────────────────────────────┐
│   Director of Public Relations, Airline   │
└─────────────────────────────────────┘

┌─────────────────────────────────────┐
│   Public Relations Assistant, Airline   │
└─────────────────────────────────────┘
```

Position Description

Public relations assistants for airlines create written materials, work with journalists, and conduct industry affairs programs to promote the airline.

Working from the airline's strategic marketing plan, public relations assistants write press releases, media alerts, briefing papers, and other materials to promote the airline to journalists. Working with other departments, they also may prepare lobbying position papers and other materials for government relations as well as annual reports and other brochures for investor relations. They write comments and speeches for the airline's leading executives.

Public relations assistants field calls from journalists who want information or background on a story involving the airline. They will refer some calls and interview requests to other airline executives, briefing them on the situation before comments are made. In many cases,

public relations assistants will act as the airline's spokespeople.

To encourage travel writers and other journalists to mention the airline in their stories, public relations assistants will work with national and state tourism officers and with local convention and visitors bureau directors to plan familiarization tours and to provide transportation as journalists cover some stories.

If the airline retains an outside public relations firm, public relations assistants will act as liaisons linking the firm with other airline departments. They may review invoices from the firm and forward them to the accounting department for processing.

Public relations assistants will handle industry affairs assignments for the airline to strengthen relations with other segments of the travel industry. For example, the airline may provide free tickets as contest prizes during National Tourism Week in May, or public relations assistants may serve on an industry task force to develop a public service campaign promoting the benefits of traveling. In these cases, public relations assistants will represent the airline.

If the airline produces an inflight magazine for passengers to read, public relations assistants may help to develop story ideas. They also will insure that each issue contains updated information about airline services and flights, and they may draft a column or welcome statement from the airline's chief executives.

Salaries

Salaries of public relations assistants depend on the size of the airline, its position in the marketplace, and other factors. Salaries for new assistants may begin at $15,000 and progress to $25,000.

Employment Prospects

Opportunities in this field will remain very limited, as America's nine major "national" carriers cut back their staffs. However, a surge in the number of start-up airlines means that more positions will become available in the future. They will be found primarily at the airline's corporate headquarters or in larger cities that serve as "hubs" for airline routes.

Advancement Prospects

The primary track for promotions in this field is moving to similar positions at other airlines or progressing to become director of public relations. Other public relations assistants can advance in terms of salary by switching to another segment of the travel industry or to a public relations firm that specializes in travel accounts.

Education and Training

Currently there is no continuing education program for professional certification of public relations assistants. However, once they have accrued five years of work experience, they can qualify to take an exam to become accredited (with the "APR" designation) by the Public Relations Society of America.

Additional courses in public relations, journalism, and writing may be helpful.

Experience, Skills, and Personality Traits

Public relations assistants must have strong writing skills to prepare press releases and other written materials that will promote the airline effectively. They must have organizational skills and attention to detail to handle service requests from media and from outside agencies.

Increasingly, public relations assistants will need computer skills to manage their activities efficiently.

Unions and Associations

Public relations assistants generally do not belong to a national union.

Their primary national association is the Public Relations Society of America (PRSA) in New York City. PRSA offers seminars, publications, training materials and videos, and other services to support public relations practitioners.

The primary national trade organization for airlines is the Air Transport Association (ATA) in Washington, D.C. ATA offers publications, training manuals, government representation, and other assistance to U.S. airlines.

Tips for Entry

1. Strengthen your skills in journalism and public relations, through courses or direct work experience.

2. Broaden your knowledge of current airline issues by reading trade magazines such as *Airline Executive* and *Air Transport World*.

3. Consider whether you would prefer working inside the airline, as opposed to an independent public relations firm. Some public relations practitioners like the variety of working for more than one type of client.

4. Write the major airlines for information about internships and on-the-job management training programs. Many airlines offer such tracks for college graduates, so that these new trainees can learn the airline business from their employers.

RESERVATIONIST, AIRLINE

CAREER PROFILE

Duties: Reserves flights and prepares tickets for passengers; confirms, changes, and cancels reservations; tags luggage and issues boarding passes at the airport; issues boarding announcements and collects tickets before the flight

Alternate Title(s): Ticket agent; gate agent

Salary Range: $16,000 to $45,000

Employment Prospects: Good

Best Geographic Location: Most job openings will be found in large cities that the major airlines use as "hubs" for their routes as well in as any city with an airport.

Prerequisites:

Education and Training—High school diploma required, with courses in business management helpful; college degree preferred, with courses in business management, sales, and travel and tourism helpful; additional training in customer relations

Experience—Customer relations; computer operations; work experience in a tour company, travel agency, or travel supplier (e.g., theme park, hotel)

Special Skills and Personality Traits—Courtesy and tact; computer operating skills; strong oral and written communication skills; interpersonal skills; problem-solving ability

CAREER LADDER

District Sales Manager, Airline

Sales Representative, Airline

Reservationist, Airline

Position Description

Airline reservationists field questions from consumers, book them on flights, issue tickets, and check them on the flights before departure.

This process begins when the reservations are made. Working in airline reservation centers, city ticket offices, and airport ticket counters, reservationists answer calls from consumers who want information about booking a ticket. They field questions about different fares, routes, departure and arrival times, and airline policies. They access this information with the help of computer terminals that tap into the airline's computerized reservations system (CRS). Therefore, reservationists must be able to type rapidly in order to process calls from consumers quickly.

Using the CRS terminals, reservationists can reserve space on any flight for a caller. If the caller offers a credit card number or an approved billing arrangement, reser-

vationists can issue tickets and send them via mail or arrange for another pickup. The tickets that they "write" include the passenger's name, flight times, fare, and other information about the flights involved.

Reservationists also may help callers who want to change their flight arrangements or cancel their seats altogether. If the passenger presents his or her frequent flyer number, reservationists can insure credit for future free flights or upgrades in service.

Reservationists become ticket agents when they work behind the counter at an airport. As passengers arrive to check in for their flights, ticket agents review their flight arrangements, check in and tag luggage, and issue boarding passes.

When passengers arrive at the designated gate to board the airplane, reservationists working as gate agents make boarding announcements, check and collect tickets, offer additional boarding help for children or passengers who have special needs, and answer final questions from consumers before the flight leaves.

Because they have primary contact with passengers, reservationists must be able to remain calm under pressure and pay attention to the complex details of ticketing.

Salaries

Salaries of airline reservationists depend on the size of the airline, its position in the marketplace, and other factors. Salaries for new reservationists may begin at $16,000, but experienced employees may progress with seniority to $45,000 or more.

Employment Prospects

Opportunities in this field will remain competitive, as America's nine major "national" carriers cut back their staffs. However, a surge in the number of start-up airlines means that more positions will become available in the future. They will be found primarily in larger cities that serve as "hubs" for airline routes or in any city with an airport served by that airline.

Advancement Prospects

The primary track for promotions in this field is moving to similar positions at other airlines or progressing to become a sales representative within the same airline. Sometimes reservationists can advance in terms of salary by switching to another segment of the travel industry.

Education and Training

Currently there is no continuing education program for professional certification of airline reservationists.

Most reservationists will complete an on-the-job training program to learn how to operate the airline's CRS terminals.

Experience, Skills, and Personality Traits

Airline reservationists must have computer skills to operate the airline CRS terminals quickly and effi-

ciently. Also, they need courtesy and tact to deal with the numerous questions and complaints from traveling consumers.

Unions and Associations

Airline reservationists generally belong to a national union such as the International Brotherhood of Airline and Railway Clerks.

The primary national trade organization for airlines is the Air Transport Association (ATA) in Washington, D.C. ATA offers publications, training manuals, government representation, and other assistance to U.S. airlines.

Tips for Entry

1. Strengthen your computer operating skills, through courses or direct work experience.

2. Begin your exposure to the airline industry by working part time as a baggage handler, flight attendant, or a similar position. Most airlines prefer to promote from within; in fact, many airline executives can trace their careers to a part-time position.

3. Broaden your knowledge of current airline issues by reading trade magazines such as *Airline Executive* and *Air Transport World*.

4. Consider whether your interpersonal skills—especially your ability to relate to passengers who may be disgruntled at times—are strong enough for a people-intensive position in airline reservations.

5. Write the major airlines for information about internships and on-the-job management training programs. Many airlines offer such tracks for college graduates, so that these new trainees can learn the airline business from their employers.

6. When you apply for airline reservations positions, highlight any experiences you have had in customer relations and computer operations, from part-time jobs to volunteer assignments.

CAPTAIN, AIRLINE

CAREER PROFILE

Duties: Flies commercial aircraft with passengers, crew, and cargo between destinations; plots courses and conducts safety checks; supervises other crew members; enforces federal laws and airline policies; completes flight reports and other paperwork

Alternate Title(s):   Pilot

Salary Range: $25,000 to $145,000

Employment Prospects: Good

Best Geographic Location: Most job openings will be found in large cities that the major airlines use as "hubs" for their routes.

Prerequisites:

   Education and Training—High school diploma required; at least two years of college required, with college degree preferred; commercial pilot's license (with instrument rating), flight engineer's license, and airline transport pilot's license (all from the Federal Aviation Administration) required; physical exam and FAA exam required; 1,500 hours of flying time required

   Experience—At least 1,500 hours of flying time required, including night and instrument flying

   Special Skills and Personality Traits—Ability to make quick decisions under pressure; attention to detail; interpersonal skills

CAREER LADDER

```
┌─────────────────────────────┐
│                             │
│     Captain, Airline        │
│                             │
└─────────────────────────────┘

┌─────────────────────────────┐
│                             │
│   First Officer, Airline    │
│                             │
└─────────────────────────────┘

┌─────────────────────────────┐
│                             │
│  Flight Engineer, Airline   │
│                             │
└─────────────────────────────┘
```

Position Description

Captains manage the flight crews aboard a commercial airplane and operate the instruments and controls that direct the airplane between destinations. They assume full responsibility for the safety and comfort of the passengers, crew, and cargo.

Along with the flight attendants, captains normally fly with a first officer or copilot who helps monitor instruments and communicate with air traffic controllers. While many flights today still carry a third pilot, the flight engineer, who helps navigate the aircraft, the newest airplanes contain sophisticated computer equipment that no longer necessitates taking the flight engineer along.

Before the flight departs, captains confer with air traffic controllers and weather forecasters prior to finalizing the flight's route, altitude, and speed. Captains will file a flight plan with air traffic controllers specifying these details, especially in cases when pilots will rely heavily on their instruments (if the weather is poor).

Captains and first officers run through an extensive check of all onboard instruments and systems as well as the engines and wing controls. They confirm that the luggage and cargo have been safely loaded, and they brief flight attendants on the conditions for the flight.

Once the passengers have been secured in their seats, captains back the airplane from the gate for takeoff. Takeoff and landing present special challenges for captains. As captains accelerate the aircraft down the runway, first officers help calculate the proper takeoff speed; once that speed is reached, captains ease the controls back to guide the airplane into the air.

Once the airplane has reached its cruising altitude, captains pilot it along the predetermined route. Along the way, they check with air traffic controllers and monitor conditions on the instruments. If the weather changes or other conditions worsen, captains will decide to alter the route, altitude, speed, or other factors to compensate.

If visibility is poor, captains must rely heavily on their instruments. Advances in computer technology help captains to pinpoint their location, avoid obstacles, and land the airplane safely even if their vision is obscured.

Once the airplane lands and the passengers have deplaned, captains file reports on the flight for the airline and the FAA.

Although the glamour of shuttling around the world draws many potential airline pilots, the pressures of a constant travel schedule can wear heavily upon a captain's family and friends.

Salaries

Salaries of captains reflect the many years of experience and training that they must have to qualify to fly commercial aircraft. While captains may begin their careers as flight engineers earning $25,000, they progress quickly according to established rules of seniority. Top salaries at major airlines can exceed $145,000.

Employment Prospects

Opportunities in this field will remain very limited, as America's nine major "national" carriers cut back their staffs. However, a surge in the number of start-up airlines means that more positions will become available in the future. They will be found primarily in larger cities that serve as "hubs" for airline routes.

Advancement Prospects

Once pilots have reached the level of captain, prospects for advancement will be limited to applying for higher salaries at competing airlines. The major airlines have mandatory retirement ages at 50 years and older; after retirement, captains can serve as instructors or in other ancillary occupations.

Education and Training

Pilots who want to become captains must pass a comprehensive physical exam (including a stringent visual acuity test) and a written exam covering FAA regulations. Also, they need to log at least 1,500 hours of flying time, including night and instrument flying. Many captains rack up these hours by flying for the military or by serving as instructors.

Most commercial airlines require their captains to hold three FAA licenses: commercial pilot (with instrument rating), flight engineer, and airline transport pilot.

Experience, Skills, and Personality Traits

Airline captains must possess the ability to make quick decisions under pressure, as flight conditions change and safety concerns arise during a flight. They must have the interpersonal skills to supervise other crew members on the flight.

Additional training, such as foreign languages, may be important if captains seek international routes.

Unions and Associations

Most airline captains belong to the major U.S. union for pilots: the Air Line Pilots Association. Some captains opt to join the Allied Pilots Association union.

The primary national trade organization for airlines is the Air Transport Association (ATA) in Washington, D.C. ATA offers publications, training manuals, government representation, and other assistance to U.S. airlines.

Tips for Entry

1. Earn the necessary number of hours of flying time, by joining the military for pilot training or by serving as an instructor for private students.

2. Begin your exposure to the airline industry by working part time as a baggage handler, reservationist, flight attendant, or a similar position. You can earn extra money for school or flying lessons while deciding if you enjoy working for the airline.

3. Broaden your knowledge of current airline issues by reading trade magazines such as *Airline Executive* and *Air Transport World*.

4. As you choose a college, try to select a school that offers a major in aviation or a related field. Many programs include flight training as part of the curriculum.

FLIGHT ATTENDANT, AIRLINE

CAREER PROFILE

Duties: Greets passengers as they board the airplane; conducts safety briefings and demonstrates the use of safety equipment; serves meals and beverages; answers passenger questions

Alternate Title(s): "Steward" and "stewardess" are no longer used.

Salary Range: $12,000 to $45,000

Employment Prospects: Good

Best Geographic Location: Most job openings will be found in large cities that the major airlines use as "hubs" for their routes.

Prerequisites:

Education and Training—High school diploma required; college degree helpful; completion of an approved flight attendant training program

Experience—Customer relations; work experience in a tour company, travel agency, or travel supplier (e.g., theme park, hotel)

Special Skills and Personality Traits—Interpersonal skills; strong oral communication skills; interpersonal skills; first-aid training

CAREER LADDER

```
+------------------------------------------+
|                                          |
|   Customer Service Director, Airline     |
|                                          |
+------------------------------------------+

+------------------------------------------+
|                                          |
|          Lead Attendant, Airline         |
|                                          |
+------------------------------------------+

+------------------------------------------+
|                                          |
|         Flight Attendant, Airline        |
|                                          |
+------------------------------------------+
```

Position Description

Once on board the aircraft, airline flight attendants are the primary contacts the passengers have with the airline. They assume responsibility for the comfort and safety of passengers during each flight.

Flight attendants prepare for each departure by checking stores of meals, beverages, safety equipment, reading materials, blankets and pillows, and other supplies. Also, they undergo a flight briefing with the captain.

As passengers board the airplane, flight attendants greet them, check their seating assignments, and help them to store carry-on luggage.

After insuring that passengers have fastened their safety belts, flight attendants brief them on safety procedures, including evacuation routes, flotation cushions, and oxygen masks.

Once the airplane reaches its cruising altitude, flight attendants heat prepackaged meals and serve them with beverages. They hand out reading materials, headphones, blankets, and pillows as requested. They answer passengers' questions about the flight or connections at the arrival airport.

Once the airplane lands, the flight attendants assist passengers in leaving the aircraft. Then the lead attendant will file reports on medications given to passengers, specific complaints filed, and other matters that arose during the flight.

In the rare event of an emergency, flight attendants supervise preparations for a crash landing and/or the evacuation of the aircraft. They assist passengers in securing flotation cushions, deploy evacuation slides, attach oxygen masks, and provide other help as needed until the situation is stable.

While the idea of flying around the world may seem glamorous at first, potential flight attendants should consider the pressures of spending many days on the road, away from family and friends.

Salaries

After they complete their training period, new flight attendants will earn beginning salaries from $12,000. As they rise in seniority, their salaries will progress to $25,000 and more.

Employment Prospects

Opportunities in this field will remain competitive, as America's nine major "national" carriers cut back their staffs. However, a surge in the number of start-up airlines means that more positions will become available in the future. They will be found primarily in larger cities that serve as "hubs" for airline routes.

Advancement Prospects

The primary track for promotions in this field is earning the seniority to qualify as a lead attendant, in charge of other attendants on the flight. Some attendants will move to similar positions at other airlines or progress to become a customer service director within the same airline. Sometimes they will switch to another segment of the travel industry.

Education and Training

Currently there is no continuing education program for professional certification of flight attendants.

However, most commercial airlines require flight attendants to complete a training course in an airline-approved school. (Most approved schools are run by the major airlines.) The course will include training in emergency procedures, flight regulations and duties, and customer service principles.

Additional courses in foreign languages may be helpful.

Experience, Skills, and Personality Traits

Flight attendants must have courtesy and tact as they deal with the demands of passengers. Strong oral communication skills will help as they explain safety regulations and other policies to passengers.

Unions and Associations

Most flight attendants belong to a major national union such as the Association of Flight Attendants or the Transport Workers Union of America.

The primary national trade organization for airlines is the Air Transport Association (ATA) in Washington, D.C. ATA offers publications, training manuals, government representation, and other assistance to U.S. airlines.

Tips for Entry

1. Strengthen your skills in customer relations, through courses or direct work experience.

2. Begin your exposure to the airline industry by working part time as a baggage handler, reservationist, or a similar position. Most airlines prefer to promote from within.

3. Broaden your knowledge of current airline issues by reading trade magazines such as *Airline Executive* and *Air Transport World*.

4. Consider whether your interpersonal skills—especially your ability to respond to the demands and needs of passengers—are strong enough for a people-intensive position as a flight attendant.

5. Write the major airlines for information about internships and on-the-job management training programs. Many airlines offer such tracks for college graduates, so that these new trainees can learn the airline business from their employers.

6. When you apply for flight attendant positions, highlight any experience you have had in customer relations, from part-time jobs to volunteer assignments.

GUIDE, ADVENTURE TOUR COMPANY

CAREER PROFILE

Duties: Serves as the primary contact person for passengers during an adventure tour; arranges and oversees all aspects of the tour during the actual trip; provides commentary on the different sites visited; helps passengers with sightseeing excursions, currency exchanges, meal preparations, and other needs

Alternate Title(s): Tour manager; escort

Salary Range: $12,000 to $35,000

Employment Prospects: Good

Best Geographic Location: Most regions of the United States offer job possibilities, especially among smaller operators who specialize in adventure tours or "ecotours."

Prerequisites:

Education and Training—High school diploma required, with courses in public speaking, travel and tourism, foreign languages, and geography helpful; completion of a tour management program in a recognized travel academy; college degree helpful, with courses in public speaking, foreign languages, and geography

Experience—Travel planning and operations; customer relations; work experience in a tour company, travel agency, or travel supplier (e.g., hotel, airline); volunteer experience as a museum or city guide; public speaking

Special Skills and Personality Traits—Strong oral and written communication skills; interpersonal skills; public speaking skills; foreign language fluency; first-aid training

CAREER LADDER

President, Adventure Tour Company

Director of Operations or Director of Sales and Marketing, Adventure Tour Company

Tour Planner or Salesperson, Adventure Tour Company

Guide, Adventure Tour Company

Position Description

Adventure tours are packaged vacations to destinations that are more rugged or primitive than the standard escorted tours. These tours require participants to be more active and involved, from hiking trails and climbing mountains to paddling down rivers and pitching tents for the evening. During adventure tours, the guide is the primary person upon whom the tour group will rely.

Once the operations department has planned the itinerary for a tour, the company assigns a guide to each departure. (In many tour companies, the same itinerary will be repeated throughout the year by different groups of passengers departing at different times.) Guides will review the company's materials—topographical and geographical survey maps, videos, reports from the operations department, even evaluations from previous tour groups—to learn as much as possible about the trip.

When passengers assemble for the trip, guides greet each person and checks him or her onto the tour. Final payments may be collected, and release forms and other travel documents distributed before the group leaves. Through activities on the first day or at a welcome dinner or reception, guides arrange introductions among the different passengers and review safety procedures.

Each day of the tour, guides are responsible for keeping the group on time and following the itinerary as closely as possible. Guides handle payments for meals included in the tour package, coordinate the cooking of other meals, distribute room keys at each lodge or supervise the pitching of tents, and arrange admissions at attractions or sightseeing tours that are part of the tour package. The guide's basic goal is handling the administrative and logistical details of the trip, so that the passengers can concentrate on enjoying the experience.

During the tour, guides will provide commentary on famous sights and scenes along the way, the history of the region, and other topics of interest to the group. While the company and state or local tourism offices will provide the bulk of this information, guides may have to read on their own to round out their knowledge of an area. In fact, some guides prefer to specialize in accompanying tours to a particular region year after year.

Because the passengers view a guide as the tour operator's primary representative during the trip, they may call upon him or her for personal assistance, ranging from mailing postcards to exchanging currency. In rare instances, guides may be required to enforce tour company rules or local laws (e.g., artifacts may not be removed from archaeological sites) or to arrange emergency medical care. Therefore, guides must possess the presence of mind to handle unexpected situations that may arise on any tour.

At the end of the trip, guides distribute evaluation forms for the passengers to complete and arrange or confirm return transportation once the tour ends.

Along with the pressures of insuring the safety of tour participants, guides also must contend with the inconveniences of being away from home for days and weeks at a time.

Salaries

Salaries in tour companies range widely, depending on the size of the company, its position in the marketplace, and other factors. However, tour guides typically rank as the lowest paid employees in the company, primarily due to the part-time nature of the work involved and the status of guides as entry-level employees. Also, most guides serve as independent contractors, not full-fledged employees, limiting their benefits.

Guides in smaller companies may earn $300 to $500 plus gratuities on each trip, which can last from one day to a week or longer. Guides who work with adventure tour companies that sell nationwide or that specialize in extremely hazardous itineraries can earn substantially more money.

Employment Prospects

Almost every region in the United States boasts several strong tour operators. However, the entire industry is limited in terms of employment prospects. Of the estimated 3,000 tour operators in business in the United States, only about 100 have established themselves as adventure tour companies.

Employment prospects will depend heavily on a guide's ability to network with adventure tour operators in search of job leads. Guides who can accept a very flexible work schedule or who offer additional skills (e.g., foreign languages) will stand the best chances of being hired.

Advancement Prospects

Because guiding is traditionally seen as the "ground-floor opportunity" for tour operators, guides who succeed at working with groups and who seem willing to accept additional responsibilities have excellent chances of moving into tour planning or sales and marketing. Successful guides set up as independent contractors may opt to work for more than one tour company (provided that the companies do not compete directly) or to launch their own adventure tour companies.

Education and Training

A number of travel academies and colleges around the country offer tour management and tour guiding curricula (which last one month to one year) that grant certificates and diplomas to graduates. Before enrolling in a program, check its reputation among adventure tour companies and ask about placement assistance upon graduation.

Within the tour industry, the primary avenue for advanced training is the Certified Tour Professional program offered by the National Tour Association.

Additional training in foreign languages, geography, and emergency medical procedures (such as first-aid training or CPR) will be helpful.

Experience, Skills, and Personality Traits

Guides must have strong oral communication skills and public speaking experience to adopt a confident pose and assume direction of a large group of passengers. Also, they need organizational skills to keep track of their specific tasks at each stop along the tour.

Interpersonal skills will be critical, as guides deal with the many different personalities found in the average adventure tour group.

Unions and Associations

There are no unions for tour guides. The most active associations in the tour industry are two national organizations that accept tour companies as members: the National Tour Association in Lexington, Kentucky, and the U.S. Tour Operators Association in New York City.

These groups sponsor educational seminars and publications that tour operators use to train new guides.

Tips for Entry

1. Develop your public speaking and organizational skills, through courses or direct working experience. Tour operators value these abilities highly.

2. Learn about the tour business by taking an adventure tour offered by a local operator—or by tour companies that you plan to target in your job search. Your cover letter and resume will carry more weight if you can include details and procedures that you observed as a passenger.

3. Build a network of contacts in tour companies by writing adventure tour operators for career advice, by working part time in a tour company, or by serving as an intern in an adventure tour company.

4. Gain a broad knowledge of the travel industry by reading trade publications for hotels, restaurants, travel agencies, and other travel businesses. Tour companies deal with many different segments of travel, so you will need to be familiar with them in order to understand the demands of a tour company.

5. If you can demonstrate your expertise in a hobby or special interest that would serve you well on an adventure tour, that information may help you in getting your foot in the door at some tour companies. For example, if you minored in college in anthropology and studied the islands in the South Pacific, mention that fact in your letters to operators who offer itineraries in that region.

6. If you want to specialize in a particular region, take courses or read books dealing with that area's history and culture. Become fluent in the language, if English is not the primary language.

DIRECTOR OF SALES AND MARKETING, CAR RENTAL COMPANY

CAREER PROFILE

Duties: Prepares marketing plans to solicit individual and group business; coordinates advertising, public relations, direct-mail, and other marketing campaigns; schedules presentations and makes sales calls on travel agencies, corporate travel managers, and other large-volume buyers

Alternate Title(s): Sales manager

Salary Range: $25,000 to $120,000

Employment Prospects: Fair

Best Geographic Location: Most job openings will be found only in cities that have a car rental company headquarters.

Prerequisites:

Education and Training—High school diploma required, with courses in business management helpful; additional training in direct sales; college degree required, with courses in business management, sales, and travel and tourism helpful

Experience—Direct sales; customer relations; work experience in a tour company, travel agency, or travel supplier (e.g., theme park, airline)

Special Skills and Personality Traits—Sales ability; business management skills; strong oral and written communication skills; interpersonal skills; group presentation skills

CAREER LADDER

```
┌─────────────────────────────────┐
│  Vice President of Sales and     │
│  Marketing, Car Rental Company   │
└─────────────────────────────────┘

┌─────────────────────────────────┐
│  Director of Sales and Marketing, Car │
│  Rental Company                  │
└─────────────────────────────────┘

┌─────────────────────────────────┐
│  Account Executive, Car Rental   │
│  Company                         │
└─────────────────────────────────┘

┌─────────────────────────────────┐
│  Sales Clerk, Car Rental Company │
└─────────────────────────────────┘
```

Position Description

Many Americans traveling on business or pleasure rent cars to drive to their destinations. Car rental companies employ many methods to promote their services and to persuade more travelers to rent from them. Using all available avenues, directors of sales and marketing for a car rental company plan, coordinate, and execute these promotions.

Directors will first establish the strategic marketing plan for the company. This process begins with an examination of the company's capacity and resources, as directors work closely with the vice president of sales and marketing and other staffers to decide which features of the company (e.g., the types of cars, the rates, the proximity of the company's locations to various corporate headquarters or vacation attractions) will draw the most attention from potential renters.

Based on the company's best attributes, directors will identify the most promising market segments. Today many car rental firms rely on a number of different market segments to rent vehicles: individual travelers, families, international inbound travelers, corporate travelers, meetings and convention delegates, and other niches.

Once these basic decisions have been made, directors will begin identifying prospective customers and soliciting their business. For large-volume customers such as travel agency chains and major corporations, directors will likely follow up direct-mail letters and telemarketing calls with personal presentations to the groups or selected decision makers. Therefore, directors need to be adept at speaking in front of groups and planning creative presentations to sell the company's services.

For the most part, however, directors will rely on standard marketing techniques such as advertising, public relations, and direct-mail brochures. Directors must design and plan the advertisements for the company, choose the media involved, and make the final placement decisions. Directors usually will coordinate press releases and serve as spokespeople for the company to journalists. Using in-house staffers or an outside firm, directors will design and supervise the production of the firm's brochures and other printed materials; once these pieces are printed, directors will decide strategies for sending them to prospective renters.

To gauge the effectiveness of these marketing efforts, directors must research the targeted market segments and conduct research that tracks the number of customers who rented cars and their satisfaction with the rental. In many companies, this market research includes focus groups and evaluation forms completed by renters when they return the cars.

Salaries

Salaries of directors of sales and marketing for car rental companies range widely, depending on the size of the company, its position in the marketplace, and other factors. Directors at the smallest regional firms may earn $25,000 per year, while directors at companies with locations around the world may earn $120,000 or more (including bonuses).

Employment Prospects

Most opportunities in this field will be confined to the headquarters of car rental companies.

Directors can improve their chances if they have a strong track record of sales success, a graduate degree, a certificate from a recognized continuing education program, or additional skills such as foreign language fluency.

Advancement Prospects

The primary track for promotions in this field is moving to similar positions at other companies or becoming vice president of sales and marketing. With additional management training, some directors become general managers or presidents of their companies. Other directors can advance in terms of salary by switching to another segment of the travel industry or by opening or purchasing franchise locations from their company.

Education and Training

Directors of sales and marketing currently do not have a professional certification program.

Additional courses in foreign languages and sales management will be helpful.

Experience, Skills, and Personality Traits

Directors of sales and marketing must demonstrate the direct sales abilities and group presentation skills to discover prospective clients and persuade them to rent cars. If they manage account executives, they should have the interpersonal skills, oral and written communication skills, and supervisory skills to keep them motivated.

Increasingly, directors will need computer skills to manage their activities efficiently.

Unions and Associations

As company executives, directors of sales and marketing generally do not belong to a national union.

The primary national trade association for car rental firms is the American Car Rental Association (ACRA) in Washington, D.C. ACRA offers publications, training manuals, and other assistance to car rental company members.

Tips for Entry

1. Strengthen your skills in business management and sales, through courses or direct work experience.

2. Begin your exposure to the car rental industry by working part time as a counter clerk, attendant, or a similar position. Most car rental companies promote from within; in fact, many directors can trace their careers to a part-time position. As you earn money for school, you can decide if you enjoy working in a car rental firm.

3. Write these companies for information about internships and on-the-job management training programs. Many large car rental companies offer such tracks for liberal arts college graduates, so that these new trainees can learn the car rental business from their employers.

CITY MANAGER, CAR RENTAL COMPANY

<table>
<tr><td>

CAREER PROFILE

Duties: Oversees the operations of a car rental company outlet (company-owned or franchised); directs counter workers in renting and checking in cars; recruits and trains workers

Alternate Title(s): None

Salary Range: $18,000 to $35,000

Employment Prospects: Fair

Best Geographic Location: Most job openings will be found in cities with airports or large numbers of companies located nearby.

Prerequisites:

Education and Training—High school diploma required, with courses in business management helpful; additional training in direct sales; college degree preferred, with courses in business management, sales, and travel and tourism helpful

Experience—Direct sales; customer relations; work experience in a tour company, travel agency, or travel supplier (e.g., theme park, airline)

Special Skills and Personality Traits—Sales ability; business management skills; strong oral and written communication skills; interpersonal skills; supervisory skills

</td><td>

CAREER LADDER

```
┌─────────────────────────────────┐
│                                 │
│  President, Car Rental Company  │
│                                 │
└─────────────────────────────────┘

┌─────────────────────────────────┐
│                                 │
│      Regional Manager,          │
│      Car Rental Company         │
│                                 │
└─────────────────────────────────┘

┌─────────────────────────────────┐
│                                 │
│ City Manager, Car Rental Company│
│                                 │
└─────────────────────────────────┘

┌─────────────────────────────────┐
│                                 │
│ Counter Clerk, Car Rental Company│
│                                 │
└─────────────────────────────────┘
```

</td></tr>
</table>

Position Description

City managers of car rental companies oversee all activities in local company outlets. Whether these outlets are owned directly by the company or operated by franchise holders, city managers supervise workers in renting cars to customers and insuring that they have a satisfactory experience with their cars.

When customers approach a counter in the airport or another location, the city manager supervises counter clerks who process the rental. Identification cards and driver's licenses must be checked, credit card slips or a deposit collected, contracts signed, and keys issued. Unless the customer has adequate insurance, the clerks should recommend the purchase of additional coverage for the duration of the rental.

If customers need to make additional reservations for future trips, the city manager will direct clerks in taking this information or contacting the company's central reservation service. Based on reports from clerks and the company's files, the manager will forecast the number of cars needed in the near future.

When cars are returned, the manager checks the work of clerks who collect payments. The manager resolves disputes if a car is returned damaged; in many cases, the manager will collect insurance information and file a damage report.

City managers recruit and train workers as counter clerks, parking lot attendants, mechanics, and other crucial positions.

City managers file sales reports for the owners or company managers as well as employee time records and other forms. They make daily deposits of customers' payments. Therefore, city managers must have strong clerical skills, including data entry and basic accounting procedures.

To encourage more business from local travel agencies, corporations, and other sources, the city manager will conduct sales calls and contact potential customers via telemarketing calls and letters.

Salaries

Salaries for beginning city managers may start at $18,000, progressing to $35,000 or more with several years of experience and additional training.

Employment Prospects

Most opportunities in this field will be confined to cities with airports, large concentrations of corporate offices, or major vacation attractions.

Advancement Prospects

The primary track for promotions in this field is moving to similar positions at other companies or becoming a regional manager in charge of several locations. With additional management training, some city managers may become general managers or presidents of their companies. Other city managers can advance in terms of salary by switching to another segment of the travel industry or by opening or purchasing franchise locations from their company.

Education and Training

City managers of car rental firms do not have a professional certification program currently.

Additional courses in foreign languages and sales management will be helpful.

Experience, Skills, and Personality Traits

City managers must demonstrate the interpersonal skills and supervisory skills to recruit entry-level employees and keep them motivated.

Increasingly, managers will need computer skills to manage their activities efficiently.

Unions and Associations

As company executives, city managers generally do not belong to a national union.

The primary national trade association for car rental firms is the American Car Rental Association (ACRA) in Washington, D.C. ACRA offers publications, training manuals, and other assistance to car rental company members.

Tips for Entry

1. Strengthen your skills in business management and sales, through courses or direct work experience.

2. Begin your exposure to the car rental industry by working part time as a counter clerk, attendant, or a similar position. Most car rental companies promote from within; in fact, many managers can trace their careers to a part-time position. As you earn money for school, you can decide if you enjoy working in a car rental firm.

3. Consider whether your interpersonal skills—especially your ability to supervise and relate to entry-level employees—are strong enough for a people-intensive position in car rental management.

4. Write these companies for information about internships and on-the-job management training programs. Many large car rental companies offer such tracks for liberal arts college graduates, so that these new trainees can learn the car rental business from their employers.

DIRECTOR OF SALES AND MARKETING, MOTORCOACH COMPANY

CAREER PROFILE

Duties: Prepares marketing plans to satisfy current clients and secure new clients for the motorcoach company; schedules presentations and makes sales calls on individual customers and groups; confirms reservations and travel plans, as well as payment arrangements

Alternate Title(s):   Sales manager

Salary Range: $18,500 to $32,500

Employment Prospects: Fair

Best Geographic Location: Most regions of the country offer job possibilities, especially with smaller motorcoach companies.

Prerequisites:

Education and Training—High school diploma required, with courses in business management and geography helpful; additional training in direct sales; college degree helpful, with courses in business management and sales helpful

Experience—Direct sales; customer relations; work experience in a tour company, travel agency, or a travel supplier (e.g., hotel, airline)

Special Skills and Personality Traits—Sales ability; business management skills; strong oral and written communication skills; interpersonal skills; group presentation skills

CAREER LADDER

```
┌─────────────────────────────────────┐
│                                      │
│   President, Motorcoach Company      │
│                                      │
└─────────────────────────────────────┘

┌─────────────────────────────────────┐
│                                      │
│   Director of Sales and Marketing,   │
│        Motorcoach Company            │
│                                      │
└─────────────────────────────────────┘

┌─────────────────────────────────────┐
│                                      │
│   Salesperson, Motorcoach Company    │
│                                      │
└─────────────────────────────────────┘

┌─────────────────────────────────────┐
│                                      │
│   Clerk or Escort, Motorcoach        │
│            Company                   │
│                                      │
└─────────────────────────────────────┘
```

Position Description

Because motorcoach companies have huge investments in their equipment—motorcoaches, vans, and other mass-transit vehicles—owners and managers depend on their directors of sales and marketing to fill the motorcoaches with passengers. Directors plan, coordinate, and execute all sales and marketing activities for the motorcoach company.

Ideally, one primary responsibility of directors is establishing the strategic marketing plan for the company. This process begins when escorted tours are actually planned, as directors of sales and marketing work closely with the director of operations and other staffers to choose the destinations, routes, modes of transportation, sightseeing excursions, and other facets of each tour that will appeal to potential customers. In the case of charter rentals, directors review the equipment inventory of the company to gauge which types of customers—corporations, school groups, tour companies, airport-bound passengers—would be interested in the company's services.

Then directors identify potential markets for the company's services. Today many motorcoach companies rely on a number of different market segments to fill their vehicles. Acting as retailers, they may sell trips to individual travelers (these tours are called "independent tours" or "per-capita tours") or to civic clubs and other special-interest groups (known as "preformed groups"). Acting as wholesalers, they will market trips to travel agents, who in turn sell trips to consumers. They could provide airport shuttle service, rent their buses to school groups, charter vans for corporate trips, or provide charter service for any number of different groups.

As the product types and market segments are being determined, directors also must decide on the company's positioning in the marketplace, compared to its competitors. For example, will the company become known for its tours, or should it remain primarily a charter service? Will it become the low-cost provider, or should it strive to be the deluxe option?

Once these basic decisions have been made, directors will begin identifying prospective customers and soliciting their business. For large-volume customers such as preformed groups, schools, and companies, directors will likely follow up direct-mail letters and catalogs and telemarketing calls with personal presentations to the group or selected decision makers. Therefore, directors need to be adept at speaking in front of groups and planning creative presentations to sell the company's services.

For the most part, however, directors will rely on standard marketing techniques such as advertising, public relations, and direct-mail brochures. Directors must design and plan the advertisements for the company, choose the media involved, and make the final placement decisions. Directors usually will coordinate press releases and serve as spokespeople for the company to journalists. Using in-house staffers or an outside firm, directors will design and supervise the production of the company's catalogs and brochures; once these pieces are printed, directors will decide strategies for sending them to prospective customers.

To gauge the effectiveness of these marketing efforts, directors must research the targeted market segments and track the number of customers who purchased a tour or chartered a bus and their satisfaction with the service. In many companies, this market research includes focus groups and evaluation forms given to passengers at the end of the trip.

For certain types of customers such as government agencies, the marketing process will require paying attention to detailed regulations and bid procedures.

Salaries

Salaries in motorcoach companies range widely, depending on the size of the company, its position in the marketplace, and other factors. Among smaller bus companies, the director of sales and marketing may be the only sales employee (in fact, the owner will assume these duties in the smallest firms), with salaries beginning at $15,000. Larger companies with strong niche markets or national reputations will pay $50,000 and more for a qualified director.

Employment Prospects

Almost every region in the United States boasts several strong motorcoach companies. However, the entire industry is limited in terms of employment prospects; for example, the American Bus Association includes only 700 motorcoach company members. Nationwide, it is estimated that there are only about 5,000 motorcoach companies in business.

Employment prospects will depend heavily on a director's ability to network with bus companies in search of job leads. Directors who can prove a track record of successful sales efforts in the travel industry—even in other segments such as travel agencies, hotels, or airlines—will stand the best chances of being hired.

Advancement Prospects

Given the limited number of openings, directors of sales and marketing who wish to advance have few options. They might apply for positions at larger bus companies, but many decide to open their own bus companies or switch to another segment of the travel industry.

Education and Training

Within the tour industry, the primary avenue for advanced training is the Certified Tour Professional program offered by the National Tour Association.

Some directors with travel agency backgrounds also opt for the Certified Travel Counselor program or the Destination Specialist programs offered by the Institute of Certified Travel Agents.

Additional training in sales management, business administration, and marketing will be helpful.

Experience, Skills, and Personality Traits

Directors of sales and marketing for motorcoach companies must have direct sales training and sales management abilities to function effectively in this competitive environment. While high school and college courses will be helpful, most motorcoach companies will value on-the-job experience more highly.

Also, they must have strong communication skills and leadership abilities to motivate their staffers and other professionals involved in the sales and marketing activities.

Unions and Associations

There are no unions for directors of sales and marketing. Their primary trade associations are the Association of Travel Marketing Executives and the Association of Group Travel Executives, both located in New York City.

However, the most active associations for these directors are three national organizations that accept tour companies and motorcoach companies as members: the National Tour Association in Lexington, Kentucky, the American Bus Association in Washington, D.C., and the United Bus Owners of America in Washington, D.C. These groups sponsor annual conventions and trade shows at which directors of sales and marketing meet travel suppliers and learn about new destinations and attractions as well as new operating procedures.

Tips for Entry

1. Develop your sales and marketing skills, through courses or experience as a salesperson in another industry.

2. Learn about the bus business by working full or part time as an assistant, clerk, or guide in a motorcoach company. In fact, most motorcoach companies prefer to promote from within.

3. Build a network of contacts in bus companies by writing motorcoach operators for career advice, by working part time in a bus company, or by serving as an intern in a motorcoach company.

4. Gain a broad knowledge of the travel industry by reading trade publications for hotels, restaurants, travel agencies, and other travel businesses. Motorcoach companies deal with many different segments of travel, so you will need to be familiar with them in order to understand the demands of the job.

DIRECTOR OF OPERATIONS, MOTORCOACH COMPANY

CAREER PROFILE

Duties: Researches and plans itineraries for tours; selects travel suppliers and sets prices; sets policies for charter rentals; coordinates reservations and other arrangements for tours; prepares drivers and escorts for each trip; coordinates maintenance and repair of motorcoaches; files proper tax forms and legal permits

Alternate Title(s): None

Salary Range: $15,000 to $32,500

Employment Prospects: Fair

Best Geographic Location: Most regions of the United States offer job possibilities, especially among smaller motorcoach companies.

Prerequisites:

Education and Training—High school diploma required, with courses in business management, travel and tourism, and geography helpful; college degree helpful, with courses in business management and sales

Experience—Tour planning, escorting, and operations; motorcoach mechanics; customer relations; work experience in a bus company, travel agency, or travel supplier (e.g., hotel, airline)

Special Skills and Personality Traits—Strong organizational skills; business management skills; strong oral and written communication skills; interpersonal skills; negotiating skills

CAREER LADDER

President, Motorcoach Company

Director of Operations,
Motorcoach Company

Clerk or Driver,
Motorcoach Company

Position Description

Directors of operations for a motorcoach company shoulder the responsibility for researching, planning, routing, and scheduling each tour offered by the company throughout the year. Also, directors must oversee the maintenance of the fleet of motorcoaches and insure that the fleet meets government standards and regulations.

Working with the director of sales and marketing and other staffers, directors of operations begin the process by researching the anticipated demand for new tours and destinations. Relying on previous sales figures, announcements by travel suppliers of new services and locations, comments from customers, and personal site inspections by motorcoach company staffers, directors will decide the direction and focus of each tour for the coming year.

Once the foundation has been set, directors proceed in researching the attractions, hotels, restaurants, sightseeing operators, and other travel suppliers in that region. Directors also plot a tentative route for the tour—along interstates and highways for motorcoach tours, or among airports, terminals, and ports for trips involving buses combined with airlines, trains, and cruise ships.

With the tentative itinerary in hand, directors contact prospective suppliers to request availability and price quotes. Directors also may investigate the amenities and service record of these suppliers, so that the best ones will be selected. Using these data, directors will combine the quoted prices in a formula (adding the company's overhead and profit margins) to calculate the price of the tour. Depending on this price, directors may renegotiate prices with certain suppliers or choose different ones to reach an acceptable price level. Given the very competitive nature of the tour business, directors of operations must be savvy in negotiating techniques to confirm the best prices for the company's tours.

As the tours are marketed to customers, directors of operations oversee the recording of reservations for each tour. At a predetermined date before the tour departs, directors will make the necessary deposits or cancel reserved space with each supplier in the tour. Also, directors will forward tentative and final rooming lists and passenger numbers to suppliers, so that they can prepare for each group's arrival.

Directors of operations will interview, hire, and train the escorts who accompany the groups on each tour. Directors will prepare background manuals and other materials to support the escort who will accompany the group on the tour. Using evaluations from the escorts and passengers, directors of operations will consider changes in the tour for coming seasons.

Because federal and state regulators pay close attention to rules for motorcoach operations, directors must be very familiar with these regulations (e.g., fuel tax permits, Interstate Commerce Commission registrations, commercial driver licenses, and limits on driving time). Directors must complete the necessary forms, pay the fees, and instruct drivers and other employees in the proper ways to follow these rules.

Directors must inspect the physical and mechanical condition of the motorcoaches in the fleet at very regular intervals. Directors establish a maintenance schedule for the buses and authorize repairs as needed.

Salaries

Salaries in motorcoach companies range widely, depending on the size of the company, its position in the marketplace, and other factors. Among smaller bus companies, directors of operations may be the only tour planners and maintenance supervisors (in fact, the owner will assume these duties in the smallest firms), with salaries beginning at $15,000. Larger companies with strong niche markets or national reputations will pay $30,000 and more for a qualified director.

Employment Prospects

Almost every region in the United States boasts several strong motorcoach companies. However, the entire industry is limited in terms of employment prospects;

for example, the American Bus Association includes only 700 motorcoach company members. Nationwide, it is estimated that there are only about 5,000 motorcoach companies in business.

Employment prospects will depend heavily on a director's ability to network with bus companies in search of job leads. Directors who can prove a track record of successful management in the travel industry—even in other segments such as travel agencies, hotels, or airlines—will stand the best chances of being hired.

Advancement Prospects

Given the limited number of competitive openings, directors of operations who wish to advance have few options. They might apply for positions at larger bus companies, but many decide to open their own bus companies or switch to another segment of the travel industry.

Education and Training

Within the tour industry, the primary avenue for advanced training is the Certified Tour Professional program offered by the National Tour Association.

Additional training in mechanics, business administration, and government regulations will be helpful.

Experience, Skills, and Personality Traits

Directors of operations for motorcoach companies must have mechanical aptitude to manage effectively in this competitive environment. While high school and college courses will be helpful, most motorcoach companies will value on-the-job experience more highly.

Also, they must have strong communication skills and leadership abilities to motivate their employees.

Unions and Associations

There are no unions for directors of operations.

However, the most active associations for these directors are three national organizations that accept tour companies and motorcoach companies as members: the National Tour Association in Lexington, Kentucky, the American Bus Association in Washington, D.C., and the United Bus Owners of America in Washington, D.C.

Tips for Entry

1. Develop your management skills, through courses or experience as a supervisor in another industry.

2. Learn about the bus business by working full or part time as an assistant, driver, or guide in a motorcoach company. In fact, most motorcoach companies prefer to promote from within.

3. Build a network of contacts in bus companies by writing motorcoach operators for career advice, by working part time in a bus company, or by serving as an intern in a motorcoach company.

4. Gain a broad knowledge of the travel industry by reading trade publications for hotels, restaurants, travel agencies, and other travel businesses. Motorcoach companies deal with many different segments of travel, so you will need to be familiar with them in order to understand the demands of the company.

CAPTAIN, CRUISE LINE

CAREER PROFILE

Duties: Supervises the crew members and passengers aboard a cruise ship; sets course and speed of the ship; insures the safety and comfort of passengers; maintains proper logs and records

Alternate Title(s): None

Salary Range: $30,000 to $75,000

Employment Prospects: Poor

Best Geographic Location: Most captains of cruise ships will be based in or near major U.S. ports such as Miami and Los Angeles.

Prerequisites:

Education and Training—High school diploma required, with courses in geography helpful; degree from accredited merchant marine academy required; license required from the U.S. Coast Guard or the nation in which the ship is registered

Experience—Work experience aboard a cruise ship or merchant marine vessel; business management; work experience in another segment of the travel industry

Special Skills and Personality Traits—Nautical skills; supervisory skills; strong oral and written communication skills; ability to make quick decisions; self-confidence

CAREER LADDER

```
┌─────────────────────────────────────┐
│                                      │
│        Captain, Cruise Line          │
│                                      │
└─────────────────────────────────────┘

┌─────────────────────────────────────┐
│                                      │
│     Chief or First Mate, Cruise Line │
│                                      │
└─────────────────────────────────────┘

┌─────────────────────────────────────┐
│                                      │
│    Second Mate or Second Officer,    │
│              Cruise Line             │
│                                      │
└─────────────────────────────────────┘

┌─────────────────────────────────────┐
│                                      │
│     Third Mate or Third Officer,     │
│              Cruise Line             │
│                                      │
└─────────────────────────────────────┘
```

Position Description

Captains of cruise ships operate and maintain the ships during their scheduled voyages. They supervise all crew members on board to insure the safety, comfort, and enjoyment of the passengers who have purchased cruising vacations.

While passengers are boarding the cruise ship in port, captains will brief senior crew members about the conditions for the trip. Captains may take time to welcome passengers on board or to meet special VIP passengers or groups traveling on that cruise.

Once the ship has left port, captains spend most of the day on the bridge. They set the course and speed of the vessel, conferring with bridge officers about their decisions. Captains oversee the piloting of the ship, maneuvering to avoid hazards and weather problems where possible, and review the work of their officers in determining the ship's current position at sea.

Captains issue orders to crew members to operate and maintain the engines, signal to other vessels, steer into ports of call, and operate towing or dredging devices. They will inspect ship systems to insure that they are in working order, oversee the embarking and debarking of passengers in various ports of call, and conduct safety drills and review safety procedures with the crew and passengers.

Captains will maintain logs and other required records to preserve an accurate picture of the ship's movements and activities.

Along with the heavy responsibilities of running the ship, captains must contend with the pressures of being away from home for weeks and months at a time.

However, many captains consider their rooms on the ship to be their true home.

(Contrary to tradition, captains at sea no longer have the privilege of marrying passengers.)

Salaries

Qualifying to serve as captain of a cruise ship requires a degree from an accredited merchant marine academy and many years of seniority advancing through the ranks. Therefore, the salaries reflect that investment of time and effort. While the captains of the smallest vessels may earn $30,000 or more, those who command the most prestigious ships at sea will earn $75,000 or more per year.

Employment Prospects

Job openings in this field are extremely limited, due to the relatively small number of cruise ships in service today. In fact, most graduates of merchant marine academies fail to find employment as ship's officers (although they may find related jobs).

Advancement Prospects

Two avenues for advancement exist for cruise ship captains: moving to larger and more prestigious vessels, or becoming managers in the corporate headquarters of the cruise line.

Education and Training

Beyond the high school diploma, prospective cruise ship captains must qualify for a merchant marine license. That license requires a degree from an approved merchant marine academy (four-year programs) and a written exam. The degree and exam qualify the candidate as a third officer. Third officers with substantial experience and seniority can win promotion to become second officers and, later, captains.

Experience, Skills, and Personality Traits

Captains of cruise ships must display the maturity and self-confidence to command a large vessel with hundreds of crew members. They need strong supervisory skills to insure that the many duties necessary to the safe and efficient operation of the ship are carried out.

Unions and Associations

Cruise ship captains normally do not belong to a national union or professional association.

The primary national organization for cruise lines is the Cruise Lines International Association (CLIA) in New York City. CLIA sponsors marketing programs, seminars, publications, and other materials to support cruise lines.

Tips for Entry

1. To get an objective picture of life as a cruise ship captain, write major cruise lines for employment information. Try to correspond with captains on duty, to ask questions about their workloads and lifestyles.

2. If possible, shadow a captain for a day aboard a cruise ship. Visit the bridge and talk to other officers about the captain's duties.

3. Apply early for admission to an accredited merchant marine academy. Competition can be keen in the most prestigious academies.

4. Prepare for a very competitive struggle to be hired as a new third officer. There are many more applicants for each available opening than could possibly be hired.

CHIEF PURSER, CRUISE LINE

CAREER PROFILE

Duties: Serves as the ship's primary business officer; handles paperwork for the ship and passengers in different ports; provides banking services and related services for the crew and passengers

Alternate Title(s): Ship purser

Salary Range: $25,000 to $45,000

Employment Prospects: Poor

Best Geographic Location: Most chief pursers of cruise ships will be based in or near major U.S. ports such as Miami and Los Angeles.

Prerequisites:

Education and Training—High school diploma required, with courses in geography helpful; degree from accredited merchant marine academy required; license required from the U.S. Coast Guard or the nation in which the ship is registered

Experience—Work experience aboard a cruise ship or merchant marine vessel; business management or accounting work; work experience in another segment of the travel industry

Special Skills and Personality Traits—Accounting and bookkeeping skills; strong oral and written communication skills; organizational skills; interpersonal skills

CAREER LADDER

```
+--------------------------------------+
|                                      |
|    Chief or First Mate, Cruise Line  |
|                                      |
+--------------------------------------+

+--------------------------------------+
|                                      |
|    Chief Purser, Cruise Line         |
|                                      |
+--------------------------------------+

+--------------------------------------+
|                                      |
|    Assistant Purser, Cruise Line     |
|                                      |
+--------------------------------------+
```

Position Description

Chief pursers aboard a cruise ship act as the ship's primary business officers. Pursers coordinate the ship's paperwork in ports, control and disburse funds to crew members and passengers, and perform other business services for people aboard ship.

Working with an assistant purser and other crew members, pursers sign on members of the crew before the cruise begins. Pursers check qualifications of the crew members and prepare "shipping articles" (paperwork). During the voyage, pursers maintain accurate payroll records; at the end of the voyage, pursers pay crew members for their service.

Following government regulations, pursers check and maintain accurate records of passengers and crew members and submit these lists to the proper agencies.

When passengers leave the ship for port calls and at the end of the cruise, pursers and their crews review the forms they have filled out for customs and immigration authorities. If needed, they help to inspect agricultural items being brought home or immigration paperwork that needs additional scrutiny.

As the ship prepares to enter each port, pursers complete the necessary entrance and clearance procedure for local authorities. When cargo is unloaded, pursers file discharge forms. Pursers assume responsibility for the stowing, care, and removal of cargo and baggage stored in the ship's holds.

From pursers desks around the ship, pursers and their staffs work with passengers to schedule shore excursions and sightseeing tours during ports of call. They provide banking services ranging from exchanging currency to storing valuables in safety deposit boxes.

Working with cruise directors, pursers will supervise the writing, editing, and printing of the daily ship newspaper. Occasionally pursers may assist with other activities for passengers, arrange religious services, or administer first aid to passengers.

While pursers typically enjoy comfortable accommodations aboard the ship, the position requires extended periods of time away from family and friends.

Salaries

Qualifying to serve as purser of a cruise ship requires a degree from an accredited merchant marine academy and many years of seniority advancing through the ranks. New pursers may earn $25,000 or more, progressing with experience to $45,000 or more.

Employment Prospects

Job openings in this field are extremely limited, due to the relatively small number of cruise ships in service today. In fact, most graduates of merchant marine academies fail to find employment as ship's officers (although they may find related jobs).

Advancement Prospects

The avenues for advancement for cruise ship pursers include being promoted to chief or captain, moving to larger and more prestigious vessels, or becoming managers in the corporate headquarters of the cruise line.

Education and Training

Beyond a high school diploma, prospective cruise ship pursers must qualify for a merchant marine license. That license requires a degree from an approved merchant marine academy (four-year programs) and a written exam. The degree and exam qualify the candidate as a third officer. Third officers with substantial experience and seniority can win promotion to the second officer level, where most pursers are appointed.

Experience, Skills, and Personality Traits

Pursers of cruise ships must display the financial management and organizational skills to manage and track the many forms and reports that must be filed on behalf of the ship, crew members, and passengers.

Unions and Associations

Cruise ship pursers normally do not belong to a national union or professional association.

The primary national organization for cruise lines is the Cruise Lines International Association (CLIA) in New York City, N.Y. CLIA sponsors marketing programs, seminars, publications, and other materials to support cruise lines.

Tips for Entry

1. To get an objective picture of life as a cruise ship purser, write major cruise lines for employment information. Try to correspond with pursers on duty, to ask questions about their workloads and lifestyles.

2. If possible, follow a purser for a day aboard a cruise ship. Visit the purser's desk and talk to other officers about the purser's duties.

3. Apply early for admission to an accredited merchant marine academy. Competition can be keen in the most prestigious academies.

4. Prepare for a very competitive struggle to be hired as a new third officer. There are many more applicants for each available opening than could possibly be hired.

CRUISE DIRECTOR, CRUISE LINE

CAREER PROFILE

Duties: Serves as the chief social director for the cruise; organizes social activities that involve passengers; plans shore excursions and other events

Alternate Title(s): None

Salary Range: $18,000 to $35,000

Employment Prospects: Poor

Best Geographic Location: Most cruise directors will be based in or near major U.S. ports such as Miami and Los Angeles.

Prerequisites:

Education and Training—High school diploma required, with courses in geography helpful; college degree required for most cruise lines, with courses in business management and travel and tourism helpful

Experience—Work experience aboard a cruise ship; business management; work experience in another segment of the travel industry (e.g., travel agency, hotel)

Special Skills and Personality Traits—Courtesy and tact; very strong interpersonal skills; strong oral and written communication skills; organizational skills

CAREER LADDER

```
┌─────────────────────────────────────┐
│                                      │
│     Cruise Director, Cruise Line     │
│                                      │
└─────────────────────────────────────┘


┌─────────────────────────────────────┐
│                                      │
│   Passenger Services Representative, │
│             Cruise Line              │
│                                      │
└─────────────────────────────────────┘
```

Position Description

Cruise directors aboard a ship serve as the "masters of ceremonies" for the entire voyage. Cruise directors are responsible for organizing a wide range of social activities involving the passengers, guaranteeing them an enjoyable experience.

Cruise directors begin by examining the mix of passengers boarding the ship for the next cruise. Cruise directors will confer with group leaders and other sources to determine what types of activities will appeal most to this mix of passengers.

Cruise directors organize an extremely varied schedule of social activities and entertainment events during each day of the cruise. Physical activities using the ship's facilities will range from shuffleboard tournaments and swimming pool races to skeet shooting and basketball. More sedate events might include bingo and bridge tournaments or cooking classes in one of the ship's kitchens.

Cruise directors book entertainers for the ship's main showrooms, lounges, and dining areas. These entertainers will include dancers, singers, orchestras, and bands. In certain cases, cruise directors may schedule lectures or other special events to vary the pace.

Other events organized by cruise directors will include religious services, cocktail parties, themed dinners, and dances. When the ship enters a new port of call, cruise directors will work with the purser's desk to organize shore excursions and sightseeing tours.

Cruise directors supervise a social staff to coordinate these events, from an assistant director and social hosts to sports instructors and tour guides.

To inform passengers of their options, cruise directors work with pursers to prepare the ship's daily newspaper. Cruise directors will keep other essential records, such as employee time cards and passenger comment cards.

Although cruise directors normally will be assigned comfortable accommodations aboard the ship, the position requires extended periods of duty at sea, away from family and friends.

Salaries

Beginning cruise directors on the smallest ships will earn starting salaries of $18,000 or more, while experienced directors on the more prestigious vessels may earn $35,000 or more.

Employment Prospects

Job openings in this field are extremely limited, due to the relatively small number of cruise ships in service today and the large pool of candidates wanting to enter this "glamorous" field.

Advancement Prospects

The avenues for advancement for cruise directors are limited to moving to larger and more prestigious vessels or becoming managers in the corporate headquarters of the cruise line.

Education and Training

Beyond the high school diploma, cruise directors should earn a college degree in order to remain competitive. Courses in business management and travel and tourism will be most helpful.

Experience, Skills, and Personality Traits

Cruise directors must display the social skills and strong interpersonal skills to organize social events and encourage passengers to participate. Organizational skills and strong oral and written communication skills will be helpful in managing the events and preparing the ship's daily newspaper.

Unions and Associations

Cruise directors normally do not belong to a national union or professional association.

The primary national organization for cruise lines is the Cruise Lines International Association (CLIA) in New York City, N.Y. CLIA sponsors marketing programs, seminars, publications, and other materials to support cruise lines.

Tips for Entry

1. To get an objective picture of life as a cruise director, write major cruise lines for employment information. Try to correspond with directors on duty, to ask questions about their workloads and lifestyles.

2. If possible, shadow a director for a day aboard his or her cruise ship. Talk to other officers about the director's duties.

3. Earn a college degree to remain competitive in this very crowded field.

4. Prepare for a very competitive struggle to be hired as a new cruise director. There are many more applicants for each available opening than could possibly be hired.

PASSENGER SERVICES REPRESENTATIVE, CRUISE LINE

CAREER PROFILE

CAREER LADDER

Duties: Coordinates guest services activities of the cruise ship; resolves complaints from passengers and enforces cruise ship policies; confirms return airline flights and performs other services for passengers as requested

Alternate Title(s): Guest services representative

Salary Range: $15,000 to $25,000

Employment Prospects: Poor

Best Geographic Location: Most passenger services representatives will be based in or near major U.S. ports such as Miami and Los Angeles.

Prerequisites:

Education and Training—High school diploma required, with courses in geography helpful; completion of a travel agent training program at a recognized school; college degree helpful for most cruise lines, with courses in business management and travel and tourism

Experience—Work experience aboard a cruise ship; business management; work experience in another segment of the travel industry (e.g., travel agency, hotel)

Special Skills and Personality Traits—Courtesy and tact; very strong interpersonal skills; strong oral and written communication skills; organizational skills

```
┌─────────────────────────────────────┐
│                                      │
│     Cruise Director, Cruise Line     │
│                                      │
└─────────────────────────────────────┘


┌─────────────────────────────────────┐
│                                      │
│  Passenger Services Representative,  │
│            Cruise Line               │
│                                      │
└─────────────────────────────────────┘
```

Position Description

Passenger services representatives serve as ombudsmen for cruise ship passengers. They resolve problems and complaints that arise during the voyage.

As passengers board the ship, they may have questions or concerns about their initial bookings. Passenger services representatives will research their reservations, check the actual cabins, and insure that the passengers did indeed receive the correct accommodations. In some cases, representatives will authorize an upgrade to a higher class of cabin.

During the cruise, passengers may experience problems or have complaints about many different aspects of the trip, from their seating assignments at dinner or the availability of certain foods to the crowds at one of the swimming pools or advice in one port of call for purchasing souvenirs. Working with cruise directors, pursers and other ship officers, representatives will attempt to resolve these problems. Even when the problem cannot be resolved, representatives will explain the situation to the passengers and offer redress or compensation if needed.

In extreme cases such as medical emergencies, representatives will work with the ship's doctor and other officers to handle the needs of the passengers involved.

As the cruise nears its end, representatives will be available to reconfirm return airline flights and to make other arrangements for passengers as they prepare to leave.

Like other cruise ship officers, representatives will have to deal with the pressures of being away from family and friends for weeks or months at a time.

Salaries

Beginning passenger services representatives on the smallest ships will earn starting salaries of $15,000 or more, while experienced representatives on the more prestigious vessels may earn $25,000 or more.

Employment Prospects

Job openings in this field are extremely limited, due to the relatively small number of cruise ships in service today and the large pool of candidates wanting to enter this field.

Advancement Prospects

The avenues for advancement for passenger services representatives are limited to being promoted to cruise director, moving to larger and more prestigious vessels, or becoming managers in the corporate headquarters of the cruise line.

Education and Training

Beyond a high school diploma, representatives should earn a college degree in order to remain competitive. Courses in business management and travel and tourism will be most helpful as will training as a travel agent.

Experience, Skills, and Personality Traits

Passenger services representatives must display the courtesy and tact and strong interpersonal skills to listen to complaints and to resolve them amicably. Organizational skills and strong oral and written communication skills will be helpful in managing activities such as reconfirming flights for many different passengers.

Unions and Associations

Passenger services representatives normally do not belong to a national union or professional association.

The primary national organization for cruise lines is the Cruise Lines International Association (CLIA) in New York City. CLIA sponsors marketing programs, seminars, publications, and other materials to support cruise lines.

Tips for Entry

1. To get an objective picture of life as a passenger services representative, write major cruise lines for employment information. Try to correspond with representatives on duty, to ask questions about their workloads and lifestyles.

2. If possible, shadow a representative for a day aboard his or her cruise ship. Talk to other officers about the representative's duties.

3. Earn a college degree (or travel agency training) to remain competitive in this very crowded field.

4. Prepare for a very competitive struggle to be hired aboard a cruise ship today. There are many more applicants for each available opening than could possibly be hired.

DIRECTOR OF SALES AND MARKETING, CRUISE LINE

CAREER PROFILE

Duties: Prepares marketing plans to solicit leisure and business travelers; coordinates advertising, public relations, direct-mail, and other marketing campaigns; schedules presentations and makes sales calls on travel agents, tour operators, and other large-volume buyers

Alternate Title(s): None

Salary Range: $25,000 to $85,000

Employment Prospects: Fair

Best Geographic Location: Most job openings will be found in the primary port cities, such as Miami and Los Angeles, as well as other large U.S. cities with district sales offices.

Prerequisites:

Education and Training—High school diploma required, with courses in business management helpful; college degree required, with courses in business management, sales, and travel and tourism helpful; additional training in direct sales

Experience—Direct sales; customer relations; work experience in a tour company, travel agency, or travel supplier (e.g., theme park, hotel)

Special Skills and Personality Traits—Sales ability; business management skills; strong oral and written communication skills; interpersonal skills; group presentation skills

CAREER LADDER

```
┌─────────────────────────────────┐
│   Vice President of Sales and    │
│    Marketing, Cruise Line        │
└─────────────────────────────────┘

┌─────────────────────────────────┐
│  Director of Sales and Marketing,│
│          Cruise Line             │
└─────────────────────────────────┘

┌─────────────────────────────────┐
│  Sales Representative, Cruise Line│
└─────────────────────────────────┘

┌─────────────────────────────────┐
│    Reservationist, Cruise Line   │
└─────────────────────────────────┘
```

Position Description

Directors of sales and marketing for cruise lines use all available avenues to plan, coordinate, and execute the sales and marketing activities of the cruise line.

Directors will begin by developing a comprehensive strategic marketing plan for the cruise line. This process begins with an examination of the line's capacity and resources, as directors work closely with sales representatives and other staffers to decide which features of the line (e.g., the amenities of the line's different ships, their routes and ports of call) will draw the most attention from potential passengers.

Based on the cruise line's best attributes, directors then identify the most promising market segments. Today many cruise lines rely on a number of different market segments to fill cabins: individual travelers, families, international travelers, corporate executives on incentive trips, meetings and convention delegates, tour groups, and other niches.

As the product types and market segments are being determined, directors also must take into account the cruise line's positioning in the marketplace, compared to other lines and their ships. For example, should the cruise line focus on serving the mature market or young families? Will its ships operate on three- and four-day schedules or longer itineraries? Positioning will be critical in deciding what types of promotions and what future services will make the cruise line successful.

Once these basic decisions have been made, directors will begin identifying prospective customers and soliciting their business. For large-volume customers such as travel agencies and incentive travel specialists, directors and the line's sales representatives will likely follow up direct-mail letters and telemarketing calls with personal presentations to the groups or selected decision makers. Therefore, directors need to be adept at speaking in front of groups and planning creative presentations to sell the cruise line.

For the most part, however, directors will rely on standard marketing techniques such as advertising, public relations, and direct-mail brochures. Directors must design and plan local advertisements for the cruise line (working in some cases with an outside advertising agency), choose the media involved, and make the final placement decisions. Directors usually will coordinate press releases and serve as spokespeople for the company to journalists. Using in-house staffers or an outside firm, directors will design and supervise the production of the line's schedules, brochures, and other printed materials; once these pieces are printed, directors will decide strategies for sending them to prospective passengers.

To gauge the effectiveness of these marketing efforts, directors must research the targeted market segments and track the number of passengers who traveled on the line's ships as a result. For example, passengers may be asked to complete evaluation cards at the end of their voyage.

Salaries

Salaries of directors reflect their years of sales experience and their responsibility for the entire line. Directors with the smallest companies may earn $25,000 or more, while those working for more prestigious lines may earn $85,000 or more (plus bonuses).

Employment Prospects

Job openings in this field are extremely limited, due to the relatively small number of cruise lines and the large pool of candidates wanting to enter this "glamorous" field.

Advancement Prospects

The avenues for advancement for directors of sales and marketing include being promoted to vice president, moving to larger and more prestigious cruise lines, or switching to other areas of the travel industry.

Education and Training

Most cruise lines today will require a college degree for directors. Courses in business management, sales, and travel and tourism will be most helpful, as will additional training in direct sales.

Experience, Skills, and Personality Traits

Directors of sales and marketing for cruise lines must demonstrate the direct sales abilities and group presentation skills to discover prospective clients and persuade them to book cabins. They must have organizational skills and attention to detail to handle questions and requests from different clients.

Increasingly, directors will need computer skills to manage their activities efficiently.

Unions and Associations

As cruise line executives, directors of sales and marketing generally do not belong to a national union, nor do they have a professional association.

The primary national organization for cruise lines is the Cruise Lines International Association (CLIA) in New York City. CLIA sponsors marketing programs, seminars, publications, and other materials to support cruise lines.

Tips for Entry

1. Strengthen your skills in business management and sales, through courses or direct work experience.

2. Consider whether your interpersonal skills—especially your ability to supervise and relate to your sales representatives—are strong enough for a people-intensive position in cruise line sales.

3. When you apply for cruise line sales positions, highlight any experience you have had in customer relations and direct sales, from part-time jobs to volunteer assignments.

4. Prepare for a very competitive struggle to be hired by a cruise line today. There are many more applicants for each available opening than could possibly be hired.

SALES REPRESENTATIVE, CRUISE LINE

CAREER PROFILE

Duties: Prepares marketing plans to solicit individual clients; designs advertisements, letters, and proposals for these clients; schedules presentations and makes sales calls on travel companies and other large-volume buyers

Alternate Title(s): Account executive

Salary Range: $15,000 to $65,000

Employment Prospects: Fair

Best Geographic Location: Most job openings will be found in the primary port cities such as Miami and Los Angeles, as well as other large U.S. cities with district sales offices.

Prerequisites:

Education and Training—High school diploma required, with courses in business management helpful; college degree required, with courses in business management, sales, and travel and tourism helpful; additional training in direct sales

Experience—Direct sales; customer relations; work experience in a tour company, travel agency, or travel supplier (e.g., theme park, hotel)

Special Skills and Personality Traits—Sales ability; business management skills; strong oral and written communication skills; interpersonal skills; group presentation skills

CAREER LADDER

```
┌─────────────────────────────────┐
│   Vice President of Sales and    │
│     Marketing, Cruise Line       │
└─────────────────────────────────┘

┌─────────────────────────────────┐
│  Director of Sales and Marketing,│
│          Cruise Line             │
└─────────────────────────────────┘

┌─────────────────────────────────┐
│  Sales Representative, Cruise Line│
└─────────────────────────────────┘

┌─────────────────────────────────┐
│    Reservationist, Cruise Line   │
└─────────────────────────────────┘
```

Position Description

Cruise line sales representatives perform the bread-and-butter work of contacting prospective clients and persuading them to book cabins on the ships. These representatives will write the sales letters, make the telephone calls, and prepare the proposals and presentations for specific clients.

Working from the cruise line's strategic marketing plan, sales representatives must learn the line's capacity and resources. They must have a firsthand knowledge of the types of ships and cruises, the various fares and discounts, amenities for incentive travelers and tour groups, and any other background information that future passengers may request.

Under the supervision of the director of sales and marketing, sales representatives will be given specific market segments for which they must be responsible: individual travelers, families, international inbound travelers, incentive travelers, meetings and convention groups, tour groups, travel agencies, and other niches. In many districts, sales representatives may be given a list of individual accounts rather than an entire segment.

Sales representatives must become very familiar with the dynamics and needs of their accounts. They should know the booking patterns, fares, itineraries, special needs, and other characteristics that distinguish these clients from others. Successful sales representatives round out their knowledge of their accounts by studying the cruise line's files on these travelers, reading their trade publications, establishing a personal rapport with the decision makers at these accounts, and networking with other travel suppliers in the city or state.

Armed with this information, sales representatives will begin identifying prospective customers and soliciting their business. For large-volume customers such as travel agencies and tour operators, sales representatives will follow up direct-mail letters, brochures, and telemarketing calls with personal presentations to the groups or selected decision makers. Sales representatives must be able to speak in front of groups and plan creative presentations to sell the cruise line.

Working together with other sales representatives, they will respond to leads generated by standard marketing techniques such as advertising, public relations, trade shows, and direct-mail campaigns. Sales representatives may help to design and plan advertisements for the cruise line, choose the media involved, and make the final placement decisions. They also may assist in public relations work, such as greeting visiting clients and arranging familiarization tours. In some cases, they will staff booths at trade shows.

Sales representatives monitor complaints and questions that may arise. If the clients have arranged special billing procedures, sales representatives may oversee the preparation of those bills.

To gauge the effectiveness of these marketing efforts, sales representatives must research the targeted market segments and track the number of their clients who have booked cabins on the ships.

Salaries

Salaries of cruise line sales representatives depend on the size of the line, its position in the marketplace, and other factors. Salaries for new representatives may begin at $15,000, but experienced sales representatives with proven track records of generating business may earn $65,000 or more (including bonuses).

Employment Prospects

Job openings in this field are extremely limited, due to the relatively small number of cruise lines and the large pool of candidates wanting to enter this "glamorous" field.

Advancement Prospects

The avenues for advancement for sales representatives include being promoted to director of sales and marketing, moving to larger and more prestigious cruise lines, or switching to other areas of the travel industry.

Education and Training

Most cruise lines today will require a college degree for sales representatives. Courses in business management, sales, and travel and tourism will be most helpful as will additional training in direct sales.

Experience, Skills, and Personality Traits

Sales representatives for cruise lines must demonstrate the direct sales abilities and group presentation skills to discover prospective clients and persuade them to book cabins. They must have organizational skills and attention to detail to handle questions and requests from different clients.

Increasingly, sales representatives will need computer skills to manage their activities efficiently.

Unions and Associations

As cruise line executives, sales representatives generally do not belong to a national union, nor do they have a professional association.

The primary national organization for cruise lines is the Cruise Lines International Association (CLIA) in Washington, D.C. CLIA sponsors marketing programs, seminars, publications, and other materials to support cruise lines.

Tips for Entry

1. Strengthen your skills in business management and sales, through courses or direct work experience.

2. Consider whether your interpersonal skills are strong enough for a people-intensive position in cruise line sales.

3. When you apply for cruise line sales positions, highlight any experience you have had in customer relations and direct sales, from part-time jobs to volunteer assignments.

4. Prepare for a very competitive struggle to be hired by a cruise line today. There are many more applicants for each available opening than could possibly be hired.

RESERVATIONIST, CRUISE LINE

CAREER PROFILE

Duties: Reserves cabins and prepares boarding documents for passengers; confirms, changes, and cancels reservations; answers queries from travel agents and consumers

Alternate Title(s): None

Salary Range: $15,000 to $27,000

Employment Prospects: Fair

Best Geographic Location: Most job openings will be found in major port cities such as Miami and Los Angeles, where most cruise lines are headquartered.

Prerequisites:

Education and Training—High school diploma required, with courses in business management helpful; college degree preferred, with courses in business management, sales, and travel and tourism helpful; additional training in customer relations

Experience—Customer relations; computer operations; work experience in a tour company, travel agency, or travel supplier (e.g., theme park, hotel)

Special Skills and Personality Traits—Courtesy and tact; computer operating skills; strong oral and written communication skills; interpersonal skills; problem-solving ability

CAREER LADDER

```
┌──────────────────────────────────┐
│                                  │
│   Director of Sales and Marketing,│
│            Cruise Line            │
│                                  │
└──────────────────────────────────┘

┌──────────────────────────────────┐
│                                  │
│   Sales Representative, Cruise Line│
│                                  │
└──────────────────────────────────┘

┌──────────────────────────────────┐
│                                  │
│     Reservationist, Cruise Line   │
│                                  │
└──────────────────────────────────┘
```

Position Description

Cruise line reservationists field questions from consumers and travel agents, book cabins on upcoming ship departures, and issue boarding documents and invoices for the cruise.

This process begins when the reservations are made. Working in cruise line reservation centers, reservationists answer calls from consumers and travel agents who want information about booking a cruise. They field questions about different fares, routes, departure and arrival times, and cruise line policies. They access this information with the help of computer terminals that tap into the cruise line's computerized reservations system (CRS). Therefore, reservationists must be able to type rapidly in order to process calls quickly.

Using the CRS terminals, reservationists can reserve space on any cruise for a caller. If the caller offers a credit card number or an approved billing arrangement,

reservationists can issue booking documents and send them via mail or arrange for another pickup. The tickets that they "write" include the passenger's name, cruise dates, the fare, and other information about the voyages involved.

Reservationists also may help callers who want to change their cruise arrangements or cancel their cabins.

Because they have primary contact with passengers, reservationists must be able to remain calm under pressure and pay attention to the complex details of preparing booking documents.

Salaries

Salaries of cruise line reservationists depend on the size of the cruise line, its position in the marketplace, and other factors. Salaries for new reservationists may begin at $15,000, but experienced employees may progress with seniority to $27,000 or more.

Employment Prospects

Job openings in this field are extremely limited, due to the relatively small number of cruise lines and the large pool of candidates wanting to enter this "glamorous" field.

Advancement Prospects

The avenues for advancement for reservationists include being promoted to sales representative, moving to larger and more prestigious cruise lines, or switching to other areas of the travel industry.

Education and Training

Most cruise lines today prefer a college degree for reservationists. Courses in business management, sales, and travel and tourism will be most helpful as will additional training in direct sales.

Experience, Skills, and Personality Traits

Cruise line reservationists must have computer skills to operate the CRS terminals quickly and efficiently. Also, they need courtesy and tact to deal with the numerous questions and complaints from consumers and travel agents.

Unions and Associations

Cruise line reservationists generally do not belong to a national union or association.

The primary national organization for cruise lines is the Cruise Lines International Association (CLIA) in Washington, D.C. CLIA sponsors marketing programs, seminars, publications, and other materials to support cruise lines.

Tips for Entry

1. Consider whether your interpersonal skills—especially your ability to relate to the needs of consumers and travel agents—are strong enough for a people-intensive position in cruise line reservations.

2. When you apply for cruise line reservations, highlight any experience you have had in customer relations and direct sales, from part-time jobs to volunteer assignments.

3. Prepare for a very competitive struggle to be hired by a cruise line today. There are many more applicants for each available opening than could possibly be hired.

4. Strengthen your computer operating skills, through courses or direct work experience.

ADVERTISING ASSISTANT, CRUISE LINE

CAREER PROFILE

Duties: Conducts marketing and media research for advertising campaigns; prepares advertising materials; acts as liaison to advertising agencies; designs and prepares collateral materials

Alternate Title(s): None

Salary Range: $15,000 to $25,000

Employment Prospects: Fair

Best Geographic Location: Most job openings will be found at the cruise lines' corporate headquarters in major port cities such as Miami and Los Angeles.

Prerequisites:

    Education and Training—High school diploma required, with courses in business management helpful; college degree required, with courses in advertising and business management helpful

    Experience—Work experience in an advertising firm or the advertising sales department of a media company; work experience in a tour company, travel agency, or travel supplier (e.g., theme park, hotel)

    Special Skills and Personality Traits—Creativity; organizational skills; attention to detail; strong oral and written communication skills; interpersonal skills

CAREER LADDER

```
┌─────────────────────────────────┐
│    Vice President of Sales and   │
│      Marketing, Cruise Line      │
│                                  │
└─────────────────────────────────┘

┌─────────────────────────────────┐
│                                  │
│  Director of Advertising, Cruise Line │
│                                  │
└─────────────────────────────────┘

┌─────────────────────────────────┐
│                                  │
│  Advertising Assistant, Cruise Line │
│                                  │
└─────────────────────────────────┘
```

Position Description

Advertising assistants for cruise lines perform research tasks, prepare materials, and work in teams with advertising professionals to promote the line and its ships to potential passengers.

Working from the cruise line's strategic marketing plan, advertising assistants conduct research programs to determine which market segments the cruise line should target in its campaigns. They use computerized databases, passenger focus groups, comments from sales representatives, and other sources of information to carry out their research plans.

Also, they examine potential media—magazines, newspapers, radio and TV stations, and other forms—to decide where the cruise line's advertisements should appear. They will review media rate cards, audiences, editorial slants, and other factors in making these decisions.

Then, they will prepare advertising materials for the cruise line. If the cruise line works with an outside advertising agency, advertising assistants will work in a support and advisory role to the agency staffers working on the account. In other cases, advertising assistants will work with the vice president of sales and marketing to develop a theme, prepare "slicks" and videos containing the ads, and request space in the targeted media for these ads.

Beyond support services, advertising assistants will serve as liaisons between the outside advertising agency and other cruise line departments.

For marketing campaigns in individual districts or other targeted efforts, advertising assistants may design and produce brochures, newspaper inserts, and other collateral materials for specific sales representatives to use for their clients.

As media placements and other expenses arise, advertising assistants track invoices from these vendors, check their accuracy, and forward them to the accounting department for payment.

Salaries

Salaries of advertising assistants depend on the size of the cruise line, its position in the marketplace, and other factors. Salaries for new assistants may begin at $15,000 and progress to $25,000.

Employment Prospects

Job openings in this field are extremely limited, due to the relatively small number of cruise lines and the large pool of candidates wanting to enter this "glamorous" field.

Advancement Prospects

The primary track for promotions in this field is moving to similar positions at other cruise lines or progressing to become director of advertising. Other advertising assistants can advance in terms of salary by switching to another segment of the travel industry or to an advertising agency that specializes in travel accounts.

Education and Training

Currently there is no continuing education program for professional certification of advertising assistants.

Additional courses in advertising, graphic arts, and marketing may be helpful.

Experience, Skills, and Personality Traits

Advertising assistants must have the creativity to develop advertisements and collateral materials that will promote the cruise line effectively. They must have organizational skills and attention to detail to handle service requests from media and from outside agencies.

Increasingly, advertising assistants will need computer skills to manage their activities efficiently.

Unions and Associations

Advertising assistants generally do not belong to a national union.

The primary national organization for cruise lines is the Cruise Lines International Association (CLIA) in Washington, D.C. CLIA sponsors marketing programs, seminars, publications, and other materials to support cruise lines.

Tips for Entry

1. Strengthen your skills in advertising and marketing, through courses or direct work experience.

2. Consider whether you would prefer working inside the cruise line, as opposed to an independent advertising agency. Some advertising professionals like the variety of working for more than one type of client.

3. Write the major cruise lines for information about internships and on-the-job management training programs. Many cruise lines offer such tracks for college graduates, so that these new trainees can learn the business from their employers.

4. When you apply for cruise line positions, highlight any experience you have had in advertising, marketing, and direct sales, from part-time jobs to volunteer assignments.

5. Prepare for a very competitive struggle to be hired by a cruise line today. There are many more applicants for each available opening than could possibly be hired.

PUBLIC RELATIONS ASSISTANT, CRUISE LINE

CAREER PROFILE

Duties: Prepares press releases and other public relations materials; handles media calls and interview requests; serves as liaison to outside public relations firms; handles industry affairs duties

Alternate Title(s): None

Salary Range: $15,000 to $25,000

Employment Prospects: Fair

Best Geographic Location: Most job openings will be found at the cruise lines' corporate headquarters in major port cities such as Miami and Los Angeles.

Prerequisites:

Education and Training—High school diploma required, with courses in journalism and writing helpful; college degree required, with courses in English, journalism, and public relations helpful

Experience—Work experience in a public relations firm or in the field of journalism; work experience in a tour company, travel agency, or travel supplier (e.g., theme park, hotel)

Special Skills and Personality Traits—Writing ability; creativity; organizational skills; attention to detail; very strong oral and written communication skills; interpersonal skills

CAREER LADDER

```
┌─────────────────────────────────┐
│   Vice President of Sales and    │
│     Marketing, Cruise Line       │
└─────────────────────────────────┘


┌─────────────────────────────────┐
│   Director of Public Relations,  │
│          Cruise Line             │
└─────────────────────────────────┘


┌─────────────────────────────────┐
│   Public Relations Assistant,    │
│          Cruise Line             │
└─────────────────────────────────┘
```

Position Description

Public relations assistants for cruise lines create written materials, work with journalists, and conduct industry affairs programs to promote the cruise line.

Working from the cruise line's strategic marketing plan, public relations assistants write press releases, media alerts, briefing papers, and other materials to promote the cruise line to journalists. Working with other departments, they also may prepare lobbying position papers and other materials for government relations as well as annual reports and other brochures for investor relations. They will write comments and speeches for the cruise line's leading executives.

Public relations assistants field calls from journalists who want information or background on a story involving the cruise line. They will refer some calls and interview requests to other cruise line executives, briefing them on the situation before comments are made. In many cases, public relations assistants will act as the cruise line's spokesperson.

To encourage travel writers and other journalists to mention the cruise line in their stories, public relations assistants will work with national and state tourism officers and with local convention and visitors bureau directors to plan familiarization tours and to provide transportation as journalists cover some stories.

If the cruise line retains an outside public relations firm, public relations assistants will act as liaisons linking the firm with other cruise line departments. They may review invoices from the firm and forward them to the accounting department for processing.

Public relations assistants will handle industry affairs assignments for the cruise line to strengthen relations with other segments of the travel industry. For example, the cruise line may provide free tickets as contest prizes during National Tourism Week in May, or public relations assistants may serve on an industry task force to develop a public service campaign promoting the benefits of traveling. In these cases, public relations assistants will represent the cruise line.

If the cruise line produces an onboard magazine for passengers to read, public relations assistants may help to develop story ideas. They also will insure that each issue contains updated information about cruise line services and flights, and they may draft a column or welcome statement from the cruise line's chief executives.

Salaries

Salaries of public relations assistants depend on the size of the cruise line, its position in the marketplace, and other factors. Salaries for new assistants may begin at $15,000 and progress to $25,000.

Employment Prospects

Job openings in this field are extremely limited, due to the relatively small number of cruise lines and the large pool of candidates wanting to enter this "glamorous" field.

Advancement Prospects

The primary track for promotions in this field is moving to similar positions at other cruise lines or progressing to become director of public relations. Other public relations assistants can advance in terms of salary by switching to another segment of the travel industry or to a public relations firm that specializes in travel accounts.

Education and Training

Currently there is no continuing education program for professional certification of public relations assistants. However, once they have accrued five years of work experience, they can qualify to take an exam to become accredited (with the "APR" designation) by the Public Relations Society of America.

Additional courses in public relations, journalism, and writing may be helpful.

Experience, Skills, and Personality Traits

Public relations assistants must have strong writing skills to prepare press releases and other written materials that will promote the cruise line effectively. They must have organizational skills and attention to detail to handle service requests from media and from outside agencies.

Increasingly, public relations assistants will need computer skills to manage their activities efficiently.

Unions and Associations

Public relations assistants generally do not belong to a national union.

Their primary national association is the Public Relations Society of America (PRSA) in New York City. PRSA offers seminars, publications, training materials and videos, and other services to support public relations practitioners.

The primary national organization for cruise lines is the Cruise Lines International Association (CLIA) in Washington, D.C. CLIA sponsors marketing programs, seminars, publications, and other materials to support cruise lines.

Tips for Entry

1. When you apply for cruise line positions, highlight any experience you have had in public relations and journalism, from part-time jobs to volunteer assignments.

2. Strengthen your skills in journalism and public relations, through courses or direct work experience.

3. Consider whether you would prefer working inside the cruise line, as opposed to an independent public relations firm. Some public relations practitioners like the variety of working for more than one type of client.

4. Write the major cruise lines for information about internships and on-the-job management training programs. Many cruise lines offer such tracks for college graduates, so that these new trainees can learn the cruise line business from their employers.

5. Prepare for a very competitive struggle to be hired by a cruise line today. There are many more applicants for each available opening than could possibly be hired.

DIRECTOR OF SALES AND MARKETING, ATTRACTION/THEME PARK

CAREER PROFILE

Duties: Prepares marketing plans to solicit individual and group travelers; coordinates advertising, public relations, direct-mail, and other marketing campaigns; schedules presentations and makes sales calls on travel agents, tour operators, and other large-volume buyers

Alternate Title(s): None

Salary Range: $25,000 to $85,000

Employment Prospects: Fair

Best Geographic Location: Most regions of the United States will offer job possibilities.

Prerequisites:

Education and Training—High school diploma required, with courses in business management helpful; college degree required, with courses in business management, sales, and hospitality management helpful; additional training in direct sales

Experience—Direct sales; customer relations; work experience in a tour company, travel agency, or travel supplier (e.g., airline, hotel)

Special Skills and Personality Traits—Sales ability; business management skills; strong oral and written communication skills; interpersonal skills; group presentation skills

CAREER LADDER

```
┌─────────────────────────────────┐
│   Vice President of Sales and    │
│ Marketing, Attraction/Theme Park │
└─────────────────────────────────┘

┌─────────────────────────────────┐
│  Director of Sales and Marketing, │
│       Attraction/Theme Park       │
└─────────────────────────────────┘

┌─────────────────────────────────┐
│      Sales Representative,        │
│       Attraction/Theme Park       │
└─────────────────────────────────┘

┌─────────────────────────────────┐
│  Sales Clerk, Attraction/Theme Park │
└─────────────────────────────────┘
```

Position Description

Directors of sales and marketing for attractions or theme parks use all available avenues to plan, coordinate, and execute the sales and marketing activities of the attraction or theme park.

Directors will begin by developing a comprehensive strategic marketing plan for the attraction or theme park. This process begins with an examinations of the site's capacity and resources, as directors work closely with sales representatives and other staffers to decide which features of the attraction (e.g., the types of activities and events in which visitors can participate, its proximity to other vacation attractions and destinations) will draw the most attention from potential visitors.

Based on the attraction or theme park's best attributes, directors then identify the most promising market segments. Today many attractions or theme parks rely on a number of different market segments for visitors: individual travelers, families, international travelers, corporate executives on incentive trips, meetings and convention delegates, tour groups, and other niches.

As the product types and market segments are being determined, directors also must take into account the attraction or theme park's positioning in the marketplace compared to its competitors. For example, should the attraction or theme park focus on serving the mature market or young families? Will it appeal to an upscale or budget audience? Positioning will be critical in deciding what types of promotions and what future services will make the attraction or theme park successful.

Once these basic decisions have been made, directors will begin identifying prospective customers and soliciting their business. For large-volume customers such as travel agencies and tour operators, directors and sales representatives will likely follow up direct-mail letters and telemarketing calls with personal presentations to the groups or selected decision makers. Therefore, directors need to be adept at speaking in front of groups and planning creative presentations to sell the attraction or theme park.

For the most part, however, directors will rely on standard marketing techniques such as advertising, public relations, and direct-mail brochures. Directors must design and plan local advertisements for the attraction or theme park (working in some cases with an outside advertising agency), choose the media involved and make the final placement decisions. Directors usually will coordinate press releases and serve as spokespeople for the company to journalists. Using in-house staffers or an outside firm, directors will design and supervise the production of the park's schedules, brochures, and other printed materials; once these pieces are printed, directors will decide strategies for sending them to prospective visitors.

To gauge the effectiveness of these marketing efforts, directors must research the targeted market segments and track the number of visitors as a result. For example, travelers may be asked to complete evaluation cards at the end of their visit.

Salaries

Salaries of directors vary with the size and popularity of the attraction or theme park. Directors with the smallest companies may earn $25,000 or more, while those working for better-known sites may earn $85,000 or more (plus bonuses).

Employment Prospects

Job openings in this field will be competitive but readily available in coming years, as more attractions and theme parks increase their marketing programs.

Advancement Prospects

The avenues for advancement for directors of sales and marketing include being promoted to vice president of sales and marketing, moving to larger and more prestigious attractions or theme parks, or switching to other areas of the travel industry.

Education and Training

Most attractions or theme parks today require that directors have a college degree. Courses in business management, sales, and travel and tourism will be most helpful, as will additional training in direct sales.

In certain cases, directors who target certain niches may seek specialized designations, such as the Certified Tour Professional (CTP) program of the National Tour Association in Lexington, Kentucky, or the Certified Travel Counselor (CTC) program of the Institute of Certified Travel Agents in Wellesley, Massachusetts.

Additional courses in foreign languages and sales management may be helpful.

Experience, Skills, and Personality Traits

Directors of sales and marketing for attractions or theme parks must demonstrate the direct sales abilities and group presentation skills to discover prospective clients and persuade them to visit. They must have organizational skills and attention to detail to handle questions and requests from different clients.

Increasingly, directors will need computer skills to manage their activities efficiently.

Unions and Associations

As attraction or theme park executives, directors of sales and marketing generally do not belong to a national union, nor do they have a professional association.

The primary national organization for attractions or theme parks is the International Association of Amusement Parks and Attractions (IATPA) in Alexandria, Virginia. IATPA sponsors marketing programs, seminars, publications, and other materials to support attractions or theme parks.

Tips for Entry

1. Strengthen your skills in business management and sales, through courses or direct work experience.
2. Consider whether your interpersonal skills—especially your ability to supervise and relate to your sales representatives—are strong enough for a people-intensive position in attraction or theme park sales.
3. When you apply for attraction or theme park sales jobs, highlight any experience you have had in customer relations and direct sales, from part-time jobs to volunteer assignments.
4. Begin your exposure to the industry by working part time as a park attendant or guide. Most attractions prefer to promote from within; in fact, many directors can trace their careers to a part-time position.
5. Write the major attractions for information about internships and on-the-job management training programs. Many parks offer such tracks for college graduates, so that these new trainees can learn the business from their employers.

SALES REPRESENTATIVE, ATTRACTION/THEME PARK

CAREER PROFILE

Duties: Prepares marketing plans to solicit individual clients; designs advertisements, letters, and proposals for these clients; schedules presentations and makes sales calls on travel companies and other large-volume buyers

Alternate Title(s): Account executive

Salary Range: $15,000 to $85,000

Employment Prospects: Fair

Best Geographic Location: Most regions of the United States will offer job possibilities.

Prerequisites:

Education and Training—High school diploma required, with courses in business management helpful; college degree required, with courses in business management, sales, and hospitality management helpful; additional training in direct sales

Experience—Direct sales; customer relations; work experience in a tour company, travel agency, or travel supplier (e.g., airline, hotel)

Special Skills and Personality Traits—Sales ability; business management skills; strong oral and written communication skills; interpersonal skills; group presentation skills

CAREER LADDER

```
┌─────────────────────────────────────┐
│   Vice President of Sales and        │
│ Marketing, Attraction/Theme Park     │
└─────────────────────────────────────┘

┌─────────────────────────────────────┐
│   Director of Sales and Marketing,   │
│       Attraction/Theme Park          │
└─────────────────────────────────────┘

┌─────────────────────────────────────┐
│      Sales Representative,           │
│       Attraction/Theme Park          │
└─────────────────────────────────────┘

┌─────────────────────────────────────┐
│  Sales Clerk, Attraction/Theme Park  │
└─────────────────────────────────────┘
```

Position Description

Sales representatives perform the bread-and-butter work of contacting prospective clients and persuading them to visit an attraction or theme park. These representatives will write the sales letters, make the telephone calls, and prepare the proposals and presentations for specific clients.

Working from the site's strategic marketing plan, account executives must learn the attraction or theme park's capacity and resources. They must have a first-hand knowledge of the activities and events, the various fares and discounts, and any other background information that may be requested by future visitors.

Under the supervision of the director of sales and marketing, sales representatives will be given specific market segments for which they must be responsible: individual travelers, families, international inbound travelers, travel agencies, meetings and conventions, tour groups, and other niches. In many districts, sales representatives may be given a list of individual accounts rather than an entire segment.

Sales representatives must become very familiar with the dynamics and needs of their accounts. They should know the booking patterns, rates, itineraries, special needs, and other characteristics that distinguish these clients from others. Successful sales representatives round out their knowledge of their accounts by studying the attraction or theme park's files on these travelers, reading their trade publications, establishing a personal rapport with the decision makers at these accounts, and networking with other travel suppliers in the city or state.

Armed with this information, sales representatives will begin identifying prospective customers and soliciting their business. For large-volume customers such as travel agencies and tour operators, sales representatives will follow up direct-mail letters, brochures, and telemarketing calls with personal presentations to the groups or selected decision makers. Sales representatives must be able to speak in front of groups and plan creative presentations to sell the attraction or theme park.

Working together with other sales representatives, they will respond to leads generated by standard marketing techniques such as advertising, public relations, trade shows, and direct-mail campaigns. Sales representatives may help to design and plan advertisements for the attraction or theme park, choose the media involved, and make the final placement decisions. They also may assist in public relations work such as greeting visiting clients and arranging familiarization tours. In some cases, they will staff booths at trade shows.

Sales representatives monitor complaints and questions that may arise. If the clients have arranged special billing procedures, sales representatives may oversee the preparation of those bills.

Given the wide variety of paperwork that the sales representatives handle, strong clerical skills (including data entry, typing, and basic accounting procedures) will be important.

To gauge the effectiveness of these marketing efforts, sales representatives must research the targeted market segments and track the number of their clients who have visited the attraction or theme park.

Salaries

Salaries of sales representatives depend on the size of the attraction or theme park, its position in the marketplace, and other factors. Salaries for new representatives may begin at $15,000, but experienced sales representatives with proven track records of generating business may earn $85,000 or more (including bonuses).

Employment Prospects

Job openings in this field will be competitive but readily available in coming years, as more attractions and theme parks increase their marketing programs.

Advancement Prospects

The avenues for advancement for sales representatives include being promoted to director of sales and marketing, moving to larger and more prestigious attractions or theme parks, or switching to other areas of the travel industry.

Education and Training

Currently there is no continuing education program for professional certification of attraction or theme park sales representatives.

In certain cases, sales representatives who target certain niches may seek specialized designations such as the Certified Tour Professional (CTP) program of the National Tour Association in Lexington, Kentucky, or the Certified Travel Counselor (CTC) program of the Institute of Certified Travel Agents in Wellesley, Massachusetts.

Additional courses in foreign languages and sales management may be helpful.

Experience, Skills, and Personality Traits

Attraction or theme park sales representatives must demonstrate the direct sales abilities and group presentation skills to discover prospective clients and persuade them to book seats. They must have organizational skills and attention to detail to handle service requests from clients.

Increasingly, sales representatives will need computer skills to manage their activities efficiently.

Unions and Associations

As attraction or theme park executives, sales representatives generally do not belong to a national union, nor do they have a professional association.

The primary national organization for attractions or theme parks is the International Association of Amusement Parks and Attractions (IATPA) in Alexandria, Virginia. IATPA sponsors marketing programs, seminars, publications, and other materials to support attractions or theme parks.

Tips for Entry

1. Strengthen your skills in business management and sales, through courses or direct work experience.

2. Consider whether your interpersonal skills are strong enough for a people-intensive position in attraction or theme park sales.

3. When you apply for attraction or theme park sales jobs, highlight any experience you have had in customer relations and direct sales, from part-time jobs to volunteer assignments.

4.   Begin your exposure to the industry by working part time as a park attendant or guide. Most attractions prefer to promote from within; in fact, many directors can trace their careers to a part-time position.

5.   Write the major attractions for information about internships and on-the-job management training programs. Many parks offer such tracks for college graduates, so that these new trainees can learn the business from their employers.

DIRECTOR OF OPERATIONS, ATTRACTION/THEME PARK

CAREER PROFILE

Duties: Manages the overall operations of the attraction or theme park; supervises staffers in various departments of the park; sets rates and guest policies; inspects and maintains facilities and equipment

Alternate Title(s):   None

Salary Range: $21,900 to $86,500

Employment Prospects: Good

Best Geographic Location: Most regions of the United States offer job possibilities.

Prerequisites:

Education and Training—High school diploma required, with courses in business management helpful; college degree usually required, with a major in business management or travel and tourism particularly helpful

Experience—Work experience in a theme park or attraction; work experience in another segment of the travel industry; business management

Special Skills and Personality Traits—Supervisory skills; strong oral and written communication skills; interpersonal skills; financial management skills

CAREER LADDER

```
┌─────────────────────────────────┐
│                                 │
│   General Manager, Attraction/  │
│          Theme Park             │
│                                 │
└─────────────────────────────────┘

┌─────────────────────────────────┐
│                                 │
│     Director of Operations,     │
│      Attraction/Theme Park      │
│                                 │
└─────────────────────────────────┘

┌─────────────────────────────────┐
│                                 │
│  Assistant Director of Operations, │
│      Attraction/Theme Park      │
│                                 │
└─────────────────────────────────┘
```

Position Description

Directors of operations for attractions and theme parks supervise employees and allocate resources so that visitors will be satisfied and the attraction or theme park will realize a profit on its operations.

Directors of operations exert authority over every activity taking place in the attraction or theme park. They approve the different rates charged to visitors (e.g., corporate, tour operator, discount rates such as AAA and AARP) and the procedures by which visitors register or pay admissions.

Working with engineers and the custodial staffers, directors of operations plan the overall look and design of the site's grounds and interiors, from the types of shrubs planted along walkways to the color schemes used in various rooms. They approve the custodial schedules and practices that workers will follow in maintaining the attraction or theme park's appearance.

They inspect facilities and equipment on a regular basis, authorizing repairs and renovations as needed. They observe safety procedures and insure that risks are minimized for visitors.

They work with interpretive specialists and other professionals to install signs and other educational aids, to provide instructions for visitors and to teach them about the attraction or theme park.

If the site includes ancillary operations such as restaurants and gift shops, directors of operations will supervise staffers and coordinate purchases and policies for these facilities.

Salaries

In smaller properties, directors of operations handle many aspects of the site's operations personally, such as design and repairs. Entry-level salaries will begin at $21,000. By progressing to larger properties or to management positions in attraction or these parks companies, directors of operations can boost salary levels to $65,000 and beyond.

Employment Prospects

Job openings in this field will be competitive but readily available in coming years, as more attractions and theme parks increase their marketing programs.

Advancement Prospects

The avenues for advancement for directors of operations include being promoted to general manager, moving to larger and more prestigious attractions or theme parks, or switching to other areas of the travel industry.

Education and Training

Currently there is no continuing education program for professional certification of attraction or theme park directors of operations.

Additional courses in foreign languages and business management may be helpful.

Experience, Skills, and Personality Traits

Directors of operations must demonstrate the interpersonal skills, oral and written communication skills, and supervisory skills to manage large numbers of employees and keep them motivated to do a good job. Because entry-level workers at attractions deal with large amounts of exposure to customers in return for low wages, directors of operations must have the ability to select qualified employees and keep them motivated.

Unions and Associations

As attraction or theme park executives, directors of operations generally do not belong to a national union, nor do they have a professional association.

The primary national organization for attractions or theme parks is the International Association of Amusement Parks and Attractions (IATPA) in Alexandria, Virginia. IATPA sponsors marketing programs, seminars, publications, and other materials to support attractions or theme parks.

Tips for Entry

1. Strengthen your skills in business management and supervision, through courses or direct work experience.

2. Consider whether your interpersonal skills—especially your ability to supervise and relate to entry-level employees—are strong enough for a people-intensive position in attraction or theme park operations.

3. When you apply for attraction or theme park jobs, highlight any experience you have had in customer relations and management, from part-time jobs to volunteer assignments.

4. Begin your exposure to the industry by working part time as a park attendant or guide. Most attractions prefer to promote from within; in fact, many directors can trace their careers to a part-time position.

5. Write the major attractions for information about internships and on-the-job management training programs. Many parks offer such tracks for college graduates, so that these new trainees can learn the business from their employers.

GUEST SERVICES MANAGER, ATTRACTION/THEME PARK

CAREER PROFILE

Duties: Coordinates guest services activities of the attraction or theme park; resolves complaints from visitors and enforces site policies; performs other services for visitors as requested

Alternate Title(s): Guest services representative

Salary Range: $15,000 to $25,000

Employment Prospects: Good

Best Geographic Location: Most regions in the United States offer job possibilities.

Prerequisites:

Education and Training—High school diploma required, with courses in business management helpful; college degree helpful, with courses in business management and travel and tourism

Experience—Work experience in a theme park or attraction; customer relations; work experience in another segment of the travel industry (e.g., travel agency, hotel)

Special Skills and Personality Traits—Courtesy and tact; very strong interpersonal skills; strong oral and written communication skills; organizational skills

CAREER LADDER

```
┌─────────────────────────────────────┐
│                                      │
│   Director of Operations, Theme Park │
│                                      │
└─────────────────────────────────────┘

┌─────────────────────────────────────┐
│                                      │
│        Guest Services Manager,       │
│        Attraction/Theme Park         │
│                                      │
└─────────────────────────────────────┘
```

Position Description

Guest services managers serve as ombudsmen for visitors to theme parks and attractions. They resolve problems and complaints that arise during the visit.

As visitors pay their fees and enter the park or site, they may have questions or concerns about the activities and facilities available to them. Guest services managers will provide maps, offer directions, answer questions about hours and fees, and provide other types of assistance that visitors need to enjoy the park or site.

During the visit, travelers may experience problems or have complaints about many different aspects of the park or site, from their seating arrangements at a show to the availability of certain foods at one of the swimming pools or the prices of souvenirs. Guest services managers will take every opportunity to resolve these complaints. Even in cases where the problem cannot be solved, guest services managers will explain the situation to the visitors and offer redress or compensation if needed.

In extreme cases such as medical emergencies, managers will work with nurses and other staffers to help the visitors.

Salaries

Beginning guest services managers at the smallest attractions will earn starting salaries of $15,000 or more, while experienced representatives at more popular attractions may earn $25,000 or more.

Employment Prospects

Job openings in this field will be competitive but readily available in coming years, as more attractions and theme parks increase their marketing programs due to increasing competition in the industry.

Advancement Prospects

The avenues for advancement for guest services managers include being promoted to director of operations, moving to larger and more prestigious attractions or theme parks, or switching to other areas of the travel industry.

Education and Training

Beyond the high school diploma, guest services managers should earn a college degree in order to remain competitive. Courses in business management and travel and tourism will be most helpful.

Experience, Skills, and Personality Traits

Guest services managers must display the courtesy and tact and strong interpersonal skills to listen to complaints and to resolve them amicably. Organizational skills and strong oral and written communication skills will be helpful in managing many different activities.

Unions and Associations

Guest services managers normally do not belong to a national union or professional association.

The primary national organization for attractions or theme parks is the International Association of Amusement Parks and Attractions (IATPA) in Alexandria, Virginia. IATPA sponsors marketing programs, seminars, publications, and other materials to support attractions or theme parks.

Tips for Entry

1. Strengthen your skills in business management and customer relations, through courses or direct work experience.

2. Consider whether your interpersonal skills—especially your ability to work with other employees to resolve guests' problems—are strong enough for a people-intensive position in attraction or theme park operations.

3. When you apply for attraction or theme park jobs, highlight any experience you have had in customer relations and management, from part-time jobs to volunteer assignments.

4. Begin your exposure to the industry by working part time as a park attendant or guide. Most attractions prefer to promote from within; in fact, many directors can trace their careers to a part-time position.

5. Write the major attractions for information about internships and on-the-job management training programs. Many parks offer such tracks for college graduates, so that these new trainees can learn the business from their employers.

NONPROFIT AND PUBLIC SECTOR ORGANIZATIONS

EXECUTIVE DIRECTOR, CONVENTION AND VISITORS BUREAU

CAREER PROFILE

Duties: Serves as the primary manager in charge of the bureau's activities and staff; recruits and trains staffers; approves marketing programs to attract visitors

Alternate Title(s): President; chief executive officer

Salary Range: $22,000 to $120,000

Employment Prospects: Good

Best Geographic Location: Most regions in the United States offer job opportunities.

Prerequisites:

Education and Training—High school diploma required, with courses in business management helpful; college degree required, with courses in business management and travel and tourism helpful; graduate degree in business management or travel and tourism helpful for advancement

Experience—Work experience in a destination marketing organization or another segment of the travel industry; business management

Special Skills and Personality Traits—Supervisory skills; very strong oral and written communication skills; public speaking skills; organizational skills; interpersonal skills

CAREER LADDER

```
┌─────────────────────────────────┐
│  Executive Director, Convention  │
│       and Visitors Bureau        │
└─────────────────────────────────┘

┌─────────────────────────────────┐
│  Director of Convention Sales or │
│  Director of Tourism Marketing,  │
│    Convention and Visitors       │
│            Bureau                │
└─────────────────────────────────┘

┌─────────────────────────────────┐
│  Assistant Departmental Director,│
│   Convention and Visitors Bureau │
└─────────────────────────────────┘
```

Position Description

Most major cities in the United States and around the world have convention and visitors bureaus—sales and marketing organizations that promote the city as a prime destination for meetings, conventions, and vacations. Executive directors of such bureaus oversee all marketing and promotional activities undertaken on behalf of the city.

For many large and medium-size cities, the primary target market is convention sales and service. Working with the director of convention sales, executive directors identify prospective companies and associations that hold conventions and meetings, determine each group's meeting requirements (e.g., number of hotel rooms, meeting space), and make presentations to the group's decision makers. Executive directors will lead the presentation to the largest clients.

The tourism department works to attract individual and group visitors to the city. Working with the director of tourism marketing, executive directors outline a marketing plan that combines advertising and public relations techniques to target individual travelers. For groups, executive directors will authorize familiarization tours and trade show appearances to reach tour operators and other large-volume travel buyers.

In the bureau's marketing and communications department, executive directors review and authorize general advertising and promotional programs, press releases, newsletters, and other materials. Executive directors will plan and authorize market research programs as well.

As ranking staff officers, executive directors will oversee general administrative functions such as accounting, payroll, and budgeting.

Some bureaus rely on dues from local businesses that hold membership in the bureaus. In these bureaus, executive directors will implement membership campaigns and address member complaints and problems.

Along with the general challenges of running the bureau, executive directors must be prepared to travel for extended periods of time.

Salaries

Salaries in this field vary greatly, depending on the size of the bureau and its funding sources. Executive directors in the smallest cities may earn starting salaries in the low $20,000s, while established executive directors in metropolitan bureaus will earn $120,000 or more.

Employment Prospects

Though the field is very competitive, openings for bureau executive directors will continue to be available in the near future. However, the field is limited in that there are fewer than 1,000 bureaus in the United States.

Advancement Prospects

Once bureau staffers have reached the level of executive director, the primary route for advancement is moving to larger bureaus. They may improve their salaries by switching to another segment of the travel industry.

Education and Training

Working as a bureau professional today requires a college degree, with courses in business management and travel and tourism helpful. Graduate degrees in these fields could prove advantageous in terms of moving to larger bureaus.

Additional training such as in foreign languages may be helpful in some assignments.

Experience, Skills, and Personality Traits

Executive directors of convention and visitors bureaus must have the supervisory skills and organizational skills to coordinate the many diverse projects undertaken at any given time in the bureau, from convention sales to media campaigns.

Increasingly, executive directors will need computer skills to manage their operations effectively.

Unions and Associations

Executive directors of bureaus generally do not belong to a national union.

The primary national trade association for bureau staffers is the International Association of Convention and Visitors Bureaus (IACVB) in Washington, D.C. IACVB organizes seminars, training sessions, publications, research projects, and other aids for executive directors and their bureaus.

Tips for Entry

1.   Gain work experience in several bureau departments, especially both convention sales and tourism marketing, before seeking appointment as executive director.

2.   In this competitive field, you will need distinctive skills to stand out. Try to become fluent in at least one foreign language, improve your computer skills, or extend yourself in other ways.

3.   If you want to advance rapidly, you must be ready to move often in your career and learn about new cities that you must promote with the same fervor as your previous location.

4.   Stay on top of current issues in the travel industry by reading as many different trade publications as possible.

5.   As the leaders of their bureaus, executive directors travel a tremendous amount during their tenures—more so than most other assignments in the industry. Decide if you want to be on the road extensively before you commit to this career.

DIRECTOR OF CONVENTION SALES, CONVENTION AND VISITORS BUREAU

CAREER PROFILE

Duties: Prepares marketing plans to solicit meetings and convention delegates; coordinates advertising, public relations, direct-mail, and other marketing campaigns; schedules presentations and makes sales calls on associations, corporations, meeting planners, and other large-volume buyers

Alternate Title(s): None

Salary Range: $25,000 to $85,000

Employment Prospects: Good

Best Geographic Location: Most regions in the United States offer job possibilities, especially medium-size and large cities.

Prerequisites:

Education and Training—High school diploma required, with courses in business management helpful; college degree required, with courses in business management, sales, and travel and tourism helpful; additional training in direct sales

Experience—Direct sales; customer relations; work experience in a convention bureau, meeting planning firm, or travel supplier (e.g., theme park, hotel)

Special Skills and Personality Traits—Sales ability; business management skills; strong oral and written communication skills; interpersonal skills; group presentation skills

CAREER LADDER

```
┌────────────────────────────────────┐
│     Executive Director, Convention  │
│           and Visitors Bureau       │
└────────────────────────────────────┘

┌────────────────────────────────────┐
│     Director of Convention Sales or │
│     Director of Tourism Marketing,  │
│     Convention and Visitors Bureau  │
└────────────────────────────────────┘

┌────────────────────────────────────┐
│     Assistant Departmental Director,│
│     Convention and Visitors Bureau  │
└────────────────────────────────────┘
```

Position Description

Directors of convention sales manage the primary focus of most large convention and visitors bureaus, because delegates to these meetings spend tremendous amounts of money in a city compared to other types of visitors.

Directors and their staffers identify companies, associations, and other groups that hold regular meetings. Working from this database, they determine each organization's requirements, from the number of hotel rooms to airport shuttle services and auditorium space. Beginning with direct-mail solicitations and telemarket-

ing calls, directors strive to schedule presentations before each group's decision makers to promote the city and its attractions.

If the city is chosen to host a meeting, directors and the bureau will provide follow-up services as the meeting is planned. This effort will range from introducing the group to local travel suppliers to arranging site visits, providing a housing bureau for delegates' reservations, and hiring on-site registration personnel.

One critical function for convention sales directors is keeping in constant touch with hoteliers and other travel suppliers in the city. While directors learn about new additions and services offered by the hotels, the hotel managers keep directors posted on the availability of rooms for potential meetings and conventions.

Directors must be prepared for the pressures of maintaining an extensive travel schedule, which will include trade shows, client presentations, and other industry meetings.

Salaries

Salaries of directors of convention sales depend on the size of the bureau and the city's popularity as a convention destination. Directors with the smallest bureaus may earn $25,000 or more, while those working for more popular sites may earn $85,000 or more.

Employment Prospects

Though the field is very competitive, openings for directors of convention sales will continue to be available in the near future. However, the field is limited in that there are fewer than 1,000 bureaus in the United States.

Advancement Prospects

Once bureau staffers have reached the level of convention sales director, the primary routes for advancement are becoming executive directors or moving to larger bureaus. They may improve their salaries by switching to another segment of the travel industry.

Education and Training

Working as a bureau professional today requires a college degree, with courses in business management and travel and tourism helpful. Graduate degrees in these fields could prove advantageous in terms of moving to larger bureaus.

Additional training such as foreign language classes may be helpful in some assignments.

Experience, Skills, and Personality Traits

Directors of convention sales must demonstrate the direct sales abilities and group presentation skills to discover prospective clients and persuade them to book meetings and conventions in the city. They must have organizational skills and attention to detail to handle questions and requests from many different clients.

Increasingly, directors will need computer skills to manage their activities efficiently.

Unions and Associations

Convention sales directors generally do not belong to a national union.

The primary national trade association for bureau staffers is the International Association of Convention and Visitors Bureaus (IACVB) in Washington, D.C. IACVB organizes seminars, training sessions, publications, research projects, and other aids for executive directors and their bureaus.

Tips for Entry

1. Try to get your foot in the door by working part time in a bureau's convention sales department as a sales trainee or assistant.

2. In this competitive field, you will need distinctive skills to stand out. Try to become fluent in at least one foreign language, improve your computer skills, or extend yourself in other ways.

3. If you want to advance rapidly, you must be ready to move often in your career and learn about new cities that you must promote with the same fervor as your previous location.

4. Stay on top of current issues in the travel industry by reading as many different trade publications as possible.

5. Strengthen your skills in business management and sales, through courses or direct work experience.

6. When you apply for convention sales positions, highlight any experience you have had in customer relations and direct sales, from part-time jobs to volunteer assignments.

DIRECTOR OF TOURISM MARKETING, CONVENTION AND VISITORS BUREAU

CAREER PROFILE

Duties: Prepares marketing plans to solicit individual and group travelers; coordinates advertising, public relations, direct-mail, and other marketing campaigns; schedules presentations and makes sales calls on travel agents, tour operators, and other large-volume buyers

Alternate Title(s): None

Salary Range: $25,000 to $85,000

Employment Prospects: Good

Best Geographic Location: Most regions in the United States offer job possibilities.

Prerequisites:

Education and Training—High school diploma required, with courses in business management helpful; college degree required, with courses in business management, sales, and travel and tourism helpful; additional training in direct sales

Experience—Direct sales; customer relations; work experience in a convention bureau, travel agency, tour operator, or a travel supplier (e.g., theme park, hotel)

Special Skills and Personality Traits—Sales ability; business management skills; strong oral and written communication skills; interpersonal skills; group presentation skills

CAREER LADDER

```
┌─────────────────────────────────────┐
│                                     │
│   Executive Director, Convention and │
│            Visitors Bureau           │
│                                     │
└─────────────────────────────────────┘

┌─────────────────────────────────────┐
│                                     │
│   Director of Convention Sales or    │
│   Director of Tourism Marketing,     │
│   Convention and Visitors Bureau     │
│                                     │
└─────────────────────────────────────┘

┌─────────────────────────────────────┐
│                                     │
│   Assistant Departmental Director,   │
│   Convention and Visitors Bureau     │
│                                     │
└─────────────────────────────────────┘
```

Position Description

Directors of tourism marketing manage the bread-and-butter function of convention and visitors bureaus: targeting and persuading travelers—individuals and groups—to visit the city.

Successfully soliciting these market segments requires two very different approaches. For individuals, directors and other staffers will develop advertising campaigns—on radio and television and in newspapers and magazines—and direct-mail efforts to promote the city. They will prepare press releases and find other ways of generating publicity about the city.

To convince tour operators and other group buyers to visit, directors of tourism marketing will plan familiarization tours, telephone solicitations and mailings, and visits to trade shows. They will provide follow-up service to groups, from offering color slides to use in brochures to writing and printing group tour manuals that help operators to plan their itineraries in the city. In many cases, these duties involve a very heavy travel schedule, so directors must be prepared to work on the road for weeks, and sometimes months, at a time.

Salaries

Salaries of directors of tourism marketing depend on the size of the bureau and the city's popularity as a vacation destination. Directors with the smallest bureaus may earn $25,000 or more, while those working for more popular sites may earn $85,000 or more.

Employment Prospects

Although the field is very competitive, openings for directors of tourism marketing will continue to be available in the near future. However, the field is limited in that there are fewer than 1,000 bureaus in the United States.

Advancement Prospects

Once bureau staffers have reached the level of tourism marketing director, the primary routes for advancement are becoming executive directors or moving to larger bureaus. They may improve their salaries by switching to another segment of the travel industry.

Education and Training

Working as a bureau professional today requires a college degree, with courses in business management and travel and tourism helpful. Graduate degrees in these fields could prove advantageous in terms of moving to larger bureaus.

Additional training such as foreign language classes may be helpful in some assignments.

Experience, Skills, and Personality Traits

Directors of tourism marketing must demonstrate the direct sales abilities and group presentation skills to discover prospective clients and persuade them to visit the city. They must have organizational skills and attention to detail to handle questions and requests from many different clients.

Increasingly, directors will need computer skills to manage their activities efficiently.

Unions and Associations

Tourism marketing directors generally do not belong to a national union.

The primary national trade association for bureau staffers is the International Association of Convention and Visitors Bureaus (IACVB) in Washington, D.C. IACVB organizes seminars, training sessions, publications, research projects, and other aids for executive directors and their bureaus.

Tips for Entry

1. Try to get your foot in the door by working part time in a bureau's tourism marketing department as a sales trainee or assistant.

2. In this competitive field, you will need distinctive skills to stand out. Try to become fluent in at least one foreign language, improve your computer skills, or extend yourself in other ways.

3. If you want to advance rapidly, you must be ready to move often in your career and learn about new cities that you must promote with the same fervor as your previous location.

4. Stay on top of current issues in the travel industry by reading as many different trade publications as possible.

5. Strengthen your skills in business management and sales, through courses or direct work experience.

6. When you apply for tourism marketing positions, highlight any experience you have had in customer relations and direct sales, from part-time jobs to volunteer assignments.

ASSISTANT DIRECTOR, STATE TRAVEL OFFICE

CAREER PROFILE

Duties: Prepares marketing plans to solicit individual and group travelers; coordinates advertising, public relations, direct-mail, and other marketing campaigns; schedules presentations and makes sales calls on travel agents, tour operators, and other large-volume buyers

Alternate Title(s): None

Salary Range: $25,000 to $65,000

Employment Prospects: Poor

Best Geographic Location: Most regions of the United States offer very few job possibilities, given the limited number of state travel offices.

Prerequisites:

Education and Training—High school diploma required, with courses in business management helpful; college degree required, with courses in business management, sales, and travel and tourism helpful; additional training in direct sales

Experience—Direct sales; customer relations; work experience in a convention bureau, travel agency, tour operator, or travel supplier (e.g., theme park, hotel)

Special Skills and Personality Traits—Sales ability; business management skills; strong oral and written communication skills; interpersonal skills; group presentation skills

CAREER LADDER

```
┌─────────────────────────────────────┐
│                                      │
│     Director, State Travel Office    │
│                                      │
└─────────────────────────────────────┘

┌─────────────────────────────────────┐
│                                      │
│ Assistant Director, State Travel Office │
│                                      │
└─────────────────────────────────────┘

┌─────────────────────────────────────┐
│                                      │
│     Manager of Tourism Marketing,    │
│          State Travel Office         │
│                                      │
└─────────────────────────────────────┘
```

Position Description

While most directors of state travel offices around the country are political appointees, assistant directors of those offices are the ranking professionals in the department. Assistant directors manage the staffers and the resources in the office to promote the state as a destination for tourists.

Assistant directors will begin by developing a comprehensive strategic marketing plan for the state. This process begins with an examination of the state's tourism resources, as assistant directors work with other staffers to decide which attractions and cities will draw the most attention from potential visitors.

Based on the state's best attributes, assistant directors then identify the most promising market segments. Today many states rely on a number of different market segments: individual travelers, families, international travelers, corporate travelers, meetings and convention delegates, tour groups, and other niches.

As the product types and market segments are being determined, assistant directors also must take into account the state's positioning in the marketplace, compared to surrounding states. For example, should the state focus on attracting the mature market or young families? Should the state emphasize its professional sports teams over its historic heritage? Positioning will be critical in deciding what types of promotions and what future services will make the state attractive to visitors.

Once these basic decisions have been made, assistant directors will begin identifying prospective customers and soliciting their business. For large-volume customers such as travel agencies and incentive travel specialists, assistant directors will likely follow up direct-mail letters and telemarketing calls with personal presentations to the groups or selected decision makers. Therefore, assistant directors need to be adept at speaking in front of groups and planning creative presentations to sell the state.

For the most part, however, assistant directors will rely on standard marketing techniques such as advertising, public relations, and direct-mail brochures. Assistant directors must design and plan local advertisements for the state (working in some cases with an outside advertising agency), choose the media involved, and make the final placement decisions. Assistant directors usually will coordinate press releases and serve as spokespeople for the state to journalists. Using in-house staffers or an outside firm, assistant directors will design and supervise the production of the state's brochures and other printed materials; once these pieces are printed, assistant directors will decide strategies for sending them to prospective visitors.

To gauge the effectiveness of these marketing efforts, assistant directors must research the targeted market segments and track the number of visitors who decided to come to the state.

Salaries

Salaries of assistant directors depend on the size of the state's budget and its popularity as a vacation destination. Assistant directors in the smallest states may earn $25,000 or more, while those working for more popular states may earn $65,000 or more.

Employment Prospects

Very few openings for assistant directors will be available in the near future. The field is limited in that there are only 50 or so positions in the United States.

Advancement Prospects

Once staffers have reached the level of assistant director, the primary routes for advancement are becoming executive directors of convention and visitors bu-reaus or moving to larger state travel offices. They may improve their salaries by switching to another segment of the travel industry.

Education and Training

Working as an assistant director requires a college degree, with courses in business management and travel and tourism helpful. Graduate degrees in these fields could prove advantageous.

Additional training such as foreign language classes may be helpful in some assignments.

Experience, Skills, and Personality Traits

Assistant directors must demonstrate the direct sales abilities and group presentation skills to discover prospective clients and persuade them to visit the state. They must have organizational skills and attention to detail to handle questions and requests from many different clients.

Increasingly, assistant directors will need computer skills to manage their activities efficiently.

Unions and Associations

Assistant directors of state travel offices generally do not belong to a national union.

Tips for Entry

1.   Try to get your foot in the door by working part time in a bureau's tourism marketing department as a sales trainee or assistant.

2.   In this competitive field, you will need distinctive skills to stand out. Try to become fluent in at least one foreign language, improve your computer skills, or extend yourself in other ways.

3.   If you want to advance rapidly, you must be ready to move often in your career and learn about new cities that you must promote with the same fervor as your previous location.

4.   Stay on top of current issues in the travel industry by reading as many different trade publications as possible.

5.   Strengthen your skills in business management and sales, through courses or direct work experience.

6.   When you apply for tourism marketing positions, highlight any experience you have had in customer relations and direct sales, from part-time jobs to volunteer assignments.

MANAGER OF TOURISM MARKETING, STATE TRAVEL OFFICE

CAREER PROFILE

Duties: Prepares marketing plans to solicit individual clients; designs advertisements, letters, and proposals for these clients; schedules presentations and makes sales calls on travel companies and other large-volume buyers

Alternate Title(s): Director of tourism marketing

Salary Range: $15,000 to $45,000

Employment Prospects: Poor

Best Geographic Location: Most regions in the United States will offer few job possibilities, given the limited number of state travel offices.

Prerequisites:

Education and Training—High school diploma required, with courses in business management helpful; college degree required, with courses in business management, sales, and travel and tourism helpful; additional training in direct sales

Experience—Direct sales; customer relations; work experience in a tour company, travel agency, or travel supplier (e.g., theme park, hotel)

Special Skills and Personality Traits—Sales ability; business management skills; strong oral and written communication skills; interpersonal skills; group presentation skills

CAREER LADDER

Director, State Travel Office

Assistant Director, State Travel Office

Manager of Tourism Marketing, State Travel Office

Position Description

Managers of tourism marketing in state travel offices will execute the marketing plans for encouraging visitors to travel to that state. These managers will write the sales letters, make the telephone calls, attend the trade shows, and prepare the proposals and presentations for specific clients such as tour operators, travel agents, group travel planners, and individual travelers.

Working from the state's strategic marketing plan, managers of tourism marketing must learn the state's tourism strengths and weaknesses. They must have a firsthand knowledge of the attractions and famous sights, the available hotels and transportation links, and other factors that will draw or discourage potential visitors.

Under the supervision of the assistant director, managers of tourism marketing will be given specific market segments for which they must be responsible: individual travelers, families, international inbound travelers, incentive travelers, meetings and convention groups, tour groups, travel agencies, and other niches. Managers of tourism marketing must become very familiar with the dynamics and needs of their assigned niches. They should know the booking patterns, budgets, special needs, and other characteristics that distinguish these clients from others. Successful managers of tourism marketing round out their knowledge of their accounts by studying the state's files on these travelers, reading their trade publications, establishing a personal rapport with the decision makers at these accounts, and networking with other travel suppliers in the city or state.

Armed with this information, managers of tourism marketing will begin identifying prospective customers and soliciting their business. For large-volume customers such as travel agencies and tour operators, managers of tourism marketing will follow up direct-mail letters, brochures, and telemarketing calls with personal presentations to the groups or selected decision makers. In many cases, contact will be made at travel trade shows, when managers staff exhibit booths promoting the state and schedule appointments during the show with clients. Managers of tourism marketing must be able to speak in front of groups and plan creative presentations to sell the state.

Working together with other destination marketers in the state (e.g., convention and visitors bureau staffers), they will respond to leads generated by standard marketing techniques such as advertising, public relations, trade shows, and direct-mail campaigns. Managers of tourism marketing may help to design and plan advertisements for the state, choose the media involved and make the final placement decisions. They also may assist in public relations work such as greeting visiting clients and arranging familiarization tours. Sometimes, these tasks lead to extensive travel schedules, keeping the manager on the road for weeks at a time.

Managers of tourism marketing monitor complaints and questions that may arise. They may intercede with travel suppliers or other professionals to resolve these disputes.

To gauge the effectiveness of these marketing efforts, managers of tourism marketing must research the targeted market segments and track the number of visitors who have traveled to the state as a result of their work.

Salaries

Salaries of managers of tourism marketing depend on the size of the state's budget, its position in the marketplace, and other factors. Salaries for new managers may begin at $15,000, but experienced managers of tourism marketing with proven track records of in-state tourism promotions may earn $55,000 or more.

Employment Prospects

Very few openings for managers of tourism marketing will be available in the near future. The field is limited in that there are only 50 or so offices for states and territories in the United States.

Advancement Prospects

Once staffers have reached the level of managers of tourism marketing, the primary routes for advancement are becoming directors of tourism marketing or executive directors of convention and visitors bureaus or moving to larger state travel offices. They may improve their salaries by switching to another segment of the travel industry.

Education and Training

Working as a manager of tourism marketing requires a college degree, with courses in business management and travel and tourism helpful. Graduate degrees in these fields could prove advantageous in terms of advancement.

Additional training such as foreign language classes may be helpful in some assignments.

Experience, Skills, and Personality Traits

Managers of tourism marketing must demonstrate the direct sales abilities and group presentation skills to discover prospective clients and persuade them to travel to that state. They must have organizational skills and attention to detail to handle questions and requests from different clients.

Increasingly, managers of tourism marketing will need computer skills to manage their activities efficiently.

Unions and Associations

As state employees, managers of tourism marketing generally do not belong to a national union, nor do they have a professional association.

Tips for Entry

1. Strengthen your skills in business management and sales, through courses or direct work experience.

2. When you apply for a position in a state tourism office, highlight any experience you have had in customer relations and direct sales, from part-time jobs to volunteer assignments.

3. Develop a network of contacts by writing state tourism offices for advice on entering the field. Ask about specific requirements in each state, such as civil service exams, that you might have to satisfy before being hired.

ASSISTANT DIRECTOR, NATIONAL TOURISM OFFICE

CAREER PROFILE

Duties: Prepares marketing plans to solicit individual and group travelers; coordinates advertising, public relations, direct-mail, and other marketing campaigns; schedules presentations and makes sales calls on travel agents, tour operators, and other large-volume buyers

Alternate Title(s): None

Salary Range: $25,000 to $65,000

Employment Prospects: Poor

Best Geographic Location: Most jobs in national tourism offices that are based in the United States will be found in major metropolitan areas such as New York City, Los Angeles, Chicago, Atlanta, and Dallas.

Prerequisites:

Education and Training—High school diploma required, with courses in business management helpful; college degree required, with courses in business management, sales, and travel and tourism helpful; additional training in direct sales and marketing

Experience—Direct sales; customer relations; work experience in a convention bureau, travel agency, tour operator, or travel supplier (e.g., theme park, hotel)

Special Skills and Personality Traits—Sales ability; business management skills; strong oral and written communication skills; interpersonal skills; group presentation skills

CAREER LADDER

```
┌─────────────────────────────────────┐
│                                      │
│   Director, National Tourism Office  │
│                                      │
└─────────────────────────────────────┘

┌─────────────────────────────────────┐
│                                      │
│     Assistant Director, National     │
│            Tourism Office            │
│                                      │
└─────────────────────────────────────┘

┌─────────────────────────────────────┐
│                                      │
│    Manager of Tourism Marketing,     │
│         National Tourism Office      │
│                                      │
└─────────────────────────────────────┘
```

Position Description

National tourism offices are the official tourism promotion agencies sponsored by foreign countries to increase travel to those parts of the world. In the United States, each national tourism office normally will be headed by a citizen of that country, while the ranking U.S. citizen in the office will be the assistant director. Assistant directors manage the staffers and the resources in the office to promote that nation as a destination for U.S. tourists.

Working with other staffers, assistant directors will begin by developing a comprehensive strategic marketing plan for the nation. This process begins with an inventory of the nation's tourism resources—famous sights and attractions, transportation routes, hotel accommodations, sightseeing guides, and other factors—to decide what things will draw the most attention from potential visitors.

Based on the resources at hand, assistant directors then identify the most promising market segments for visitors to that country. Today many nations that target U.S. visitors rely on a number of different market segments: individual travelers, families, international travelers, corporate travelers, meetings and convention delegates, tour groups, and other niches.

As the product types and market segments are being determined, assistant directors also must take into account the nation's positioning in the marketplace, compared to its competitors. For example, is the nation known for its resorts or its back-to-nature scenery? Will the prices of accommodations and meals shut out some segments of travelers? Positioning will be critical in deciding what types of promotions and what future services will make the nation attractive to U.S. visitors.

Once these basic decisions have been made, assistant directors will begin identifying prospective customers and soliciting their business. For large-volume customers such as travel agencies and incentive travel specialists, assistant directors will likely follow up direct-mail letters and telemarketing calls with personal presentations to the groups or selected decision makers. Therefore, assistant directors need to be adept at speaking in front of groups and planning creative presentations to sell the nation.

For the most part, however, assistant directors rely on standard marketing techniques such as advertising, public relations, and direct-mail brochures. Assistant directors must design and plan local advertisements for the nation (working in some cases with an outside advertising agency), choose the media involved, and make the final placement decisions. Assistant directors usually will coordinate press releases and serve as spokespeople for the tourism office to journalists. Using in-house staffers or an outside firm, assistant directors will design and supervise the production of the tourism office's brochures and other printed materials; once these pieces are printed, assistant directors will decide strategies for sending them to prospective visitors.

To gauge the effectiveness of these marketing efforts, assistant directors must research the targeted market segments and track the number of visitors who decided to go to the nation as a result of this work.

Salaries

Salaries of assistant directors of national tourism offices depend on the size of the nation's budget, its popularity as a vacation destination, and its policies for paying U.S. nationals. Assistant directors with the smallest countries may earn $25,000 or more, while those working for more popular destinations may earn $65,000 or more.

Employment Prospects

Very few openings for assistant directors will be available in the near future. The field is limited in that fewer than 100 nations operate tourism promotion offices in the United States.

Advancement Prospects

Once U.S. nationals have reached the level of assistant director in another country's tourism promotion office, the primary routes for advancement are becoming executive directors of convention and visitors bureaus or moving to U.S. state travel offices. They may improve their salaries by switching to another segment of the travel industry. In rare instances, assistant directors may be considered for a director's job, if no citizens of that country qualify for the post.

Education and Training

Working as an assistant director of a national tourism office requires a college degree, with courses in business management and travel and tourism helpful. Graduate degrees in these fields could prove advantageous.

In addition, assistant directors must speak the language of the country fluently in order to work successfully with other staffers.

Experience, Skills, and Personality Traits

Assistant directors must demonstrate the direct sales abilities and group presentation skills to discover prospective clients and persuade them to visit the nation. They must have organizational skills and attention to detail to handle questions and requests from many different clients.

Increasingly, assistant directors will need computer skills to manage their activities efficiently.

Unions and Associations

Assistant directors of national tourism offices generally do not belong to a union or trade association.

Tips for Entry

1. Try to get your foot in the door by working part time in the office's tourism marketing department as a sales trainee or assistant.

2. In this competitive field, you will need distinctive skills to stand out. Try to become fluent in at least one foreign language (especially the language spoken in the country you are targeting), improve your computer skills, or extend yourself in other ways.

3. Stay on top of current issues in the travel industry by reading as many different trade publications as possible. You should definitely try to learn as much as you can about the tourism issues affecting the country, as well as the tourism attractions and infrastructure.

4. Strengthen your skills in business management and sales, through courses or direct work experience.

5. When you apply for tourism marketing positions, highlight any experience you have had in customer relations and direct sales, from part-time jobs to volunteer assignments.

MANAGER OF TOURISM MARKETING, NATIONAL TOURISM OFFICE

CAREER PROFILE

Duties: Prepares marketing plans to solicit individual clients; designs advertisements, letters, and proposals for these clients; schedules presentations and makes sales calls on travel companies and other large-volume buyers

Alternate Title(s): Director of tourism marketing

Salary Range: $15,000 to $45,000

Employment Prospects: Poor

Best Geographic Location: Most jobs in national tourism offices that are based in the United States will be found in major metropolitan areas such as New York City, Los Angeles, Chicago, Atlanta, and Dallas.

Prerequisites:

Education and Training—High school diploma required, with courses in business management helpful; college degree required, with courses in business management, sales, and travel and tourism helpful; additional training in direct sales

Experience—Direct sales; customer relations; work experience in a tour company, travel agency, or travel supplier (e.g., theme park, hotel)

Special Skills and Personality Traits—Sales ability; business management skills; strong oral and written communication skills; interpersonal skills; group presentation skills

CAREER LADDER

```
┌─────────────────────────────────────┐
│                                      │
│   Director, National Tourism Office  │
│                                      │
└─────────────────────────────────────┘

┌─────────────────────────────────────┐
│                                      │
│   Assistant Director, National       │
│   Tourism Office                     │
│                                      │
└─────────────────────────────────────┘

┌─────────────────────────────────────┐
│                                      │
│   Manager of Tourism Marketing,      │
│   National Tourism Office            │
│                                      │
└─────────────────────────────────────┘
```

Position Description

Managers of tourism marketing in national tourism offices will execute the marketing plans for encouraging visitors to travel to that country. These managers will write the sales letters, make the telephone calls, attend the trade shows, and prepare the proposals and presentations for specific clients such as tour operators, travel agents, group travel planners, and individual travelers.

Working from the nation's strategic marketing plan, managers of tourism marketing must learn that country's tourism strengths and weaknesses. They must have a firsthand knowledge of the attractions and famous sights, the available hotels and transportation links, and other factors that will draw or discourage potential visitors.

Under the supervision of the assistant director, managers of tourism marketing will be given specific market segments for which they must be responsible: individual travelers, families, international inbound travelers, incentive travelers, meetings and convention groups, tour groups, travel agencies, and other niches. Managers of tourism marketing must become very familiar with the dynamics and needs of their assigned niches. They should know the booking patterns, budgets, special needs, and other characteristics that distinguish these clients from others. Successful managers of tourism marketing round out their knowledge of their accounts by studying the tourism office's files on these travelers, reading their trade publications, establishing a personal rapport with the decision makers at these accounts, and networking with other travel suppliers in that country who are also targeting U.S. visitors. Also, they will investigate the office or national and regional "politics" of dealing with specific clients.

Armed with this information, managers of tourism marketing will begin identifying prospective customers and soliciting their business. For large-volume customers such as travel agencies and tour operators, managers of tourism marketing will follow up direct-mail letters, brochures, and telemarketing calls with personal presentations to the groups or selected decision makers. In many cases, contact will be made at travel trade shows, when managers staff exhibit booths promoting the country and schedule appointments during the show with clients. Managers of tourism marketing must be able to speak in front of groups and plan creative presentations to sell the country. These marketing tasks will involve extensive travel schedules, keeping managers on the road for weeks at a time during certain parts of the year.

Working together with other destination marketers in the country (e.g., convention and visitors bureau staffers), they will respond to leads generated by standard marketing techniques such as advertising, public relations, trade shows, and direct-mail campaigns. Managers of tourism marketing may help to design and plan advertisements for the tourism office, choose the media involved, and make the final placement decisions. They also may assist in public relations work such as greeting visiting clients and arranging familiarization tours.

Managers of tourism marketing monitor complaints and questions that may arise. They may intercede with travel suppliers or other professionals to resolve these disputes.

To gauge the effectiveness of these marketing efforts, managers of tourism marketing must research the targeted market segments and track the number of visitors who have traveled to the country as a result of their work.

Salaries

Salaries of managers of tourism marketing depend on the size of the country's budget, its position in the marketplace, and other factors. Salaries for new managers may begin at $15,000, but experienced managers of tourism marketing with proven track records in generating new business may earn $45,000 or more.

Employment Prospects

Very few openings for managers of tourism marketing will be available in the near future. The field is limited in that fewer than 100 countries maintain tourism promotion offices in the United States.

Advancement Prospects

Once staffers have reached the level of managers of tourism marketing, the primary routes for advancement are becoming assistant director of the office or moving to other national or state tourism offices or into convention and visitors bureaus. They may improve their salaries by switching to another segment of the travel industry.

Education and Training

Working as a manager of tourism marketing requires a college degree, with courses in business management and travel and tourism helpful. Graduate degrees in these fields could prove advantageous in terms of advancement.

In addition, managers of tourism marketing must be fluent in the language of the country that they will be promoting.

Experience, Skills, and Personality Traits

Managers of tourism marketing must demonstrate the direct sales abilities and group presentation skills to discover prospective clients and persuade them to travel to that country. They must have organizational skills and attention to detail to handle questions and requests from different clients.

Increasingly, managers of tourism marketing will need computer skills to manage their activities efficiently.

Unions and Associations

Managers of tourism marketing for national tourism offices generally do not belong to a national union, nor do they have a professional association.

Tips for Entry

1. Strengthen your skills in business management and sales, through courses or direct work experience.

2. Consider whether your interpersonal skills—especially your ability to supervise and relate to different types of visitors—are strong enough for a people-intensive position in national tourism promotion.

3. When you apply for a position in a national tourism office, highlight any experience you have had in customer relations and direct sales, from part-time jobs to volunteer assignments. Also, describe your experiences traveling in or near the country.

4. Develop a network of contacts by writing national tourism offices for advice on entering the field. Ask about specific requirements in each nation, such as civil service exams or citizenship requirements, that you might have to satisfy before being hired.

ASSISTANT MANAGER, AIRPORT

CAREER PROFILE

Duties: Coordinates and directs the construction, maintenance, and operation of the airport; insures compliance with government regulations and airport policies (including security procedures); formulates emergency management policies; supervises airport personnel; inspects airport facilities; manages airport budget

Alternate Title(s): Assistant director; assistant superintendent

Salary Range: $18,000 to $85,000

Employment Prospects: Fair

Best Geographic Location: Most job opportunities in airport management will surface in states with a concentration of airports, such as California, Texas, Florida, Illinois, Ohio, New York, and Pennsylvania.

Prerequisites:

Education and Training—High school diploma required, with courses in business management helpful; college degree required, with a major in aviation, airport management, business management, public administration, or engineering helpful; graduate degree in one of these fields useful for advancement

Experience—Airport operations; business management and regulatory compliance; work experience in another segment of the travel industry

Special Skills and Personality Traits—Supervisory skills; attention to detail; organizational skills; financial management skills; negotiation skills

CAREER LADDER

```
┌─────────────────────────────────────┐
│                                      │
│          Manager, Airport            │
│                                      │
└─────────────────────────────────────┘

┌─────────────────────────────────────┐
│                                      │
│      Assistant Manager, Airport      │
│                                      │
└─────────────────────────────────────┘

┌─────────────────────────────────────┐
│                                      │
│          Engineer, Airport           │
│                                      │
└─────────────────────────────────────┘
```

Position Description

Working under the supervision of airport managers, assistant airport managers direct and coordinate the complex business and operational aspects of an airport, from maintaining safe runways and stocking sufficient airplane fuel to giving VIP tours of the airport and coordinating rescue efforts during an airplane emergency.

Assistant managers will be assigned specific responsibilities in the airport's development and operations, including the design and construction of airport facilities, the formulation of operating rules and regulations, and the establishment of landing, taxi, and takeoff patterns for different types of aircraft. Working with ex-

perts and consultants, assistant managers will make final decisions in these areas or recommend decisions to the airport manager or commission.

Because airports fall under several layers of regulation at the federal, state, and local level, assistant managers must be well versed in these requirements. While insuring that airport staffers comply with these rules, assistant managers also will review the activities and facilities of airlines and other airport tenants to guarantee their compliance as well. Also, assistant managers will negotiate tenant leases and enforce other airport policies as appropriate.

To prepare for potential emergency situations, assistant managers will develop plans of action that would be followed to safeguard airport passengers and property. During an emergency, assistant managers would direct staffers in implementing these plans. After the emergency is contained, assistant managers would coordinate the investigation to determine causes and to enforce airport policies.

Assistant managers will inspect airport facilities and equipment on a regular basis and, if needed, arrange for repairs or replacements.

Depending on the airport's organizational structure, assistant managers will supervise some or all of the airport's employees, setting schedules and reviewing work performance. Assistant managers will prepare and administer the airport's budget, subject to the review of the manager. In some cases, assistant managers will represent the airport before civic groups, boards and commissions, and other groups.

Salaries

Assistant managers of airports will earn starting salaries of $18,000 or more, depending on the size of the airport and the assistant manager's level of experience. Seasoned assistant managers with many supervisory responsibilities at the largest airports may earn $85,000 or more.

Employment Prospects

Although the United States will see an increase in airport construction through the year 2000, openings in this field may continue to be more limited as airports consolidate their staffs and as more airport executives remain actively employed in this field.

Advancement Prospects

Beyond moving into the manager's position at their airport, assistant managers may move laterally to similar jobs at larger airports. Given their experience in regulatory compliance, some assistant managers may join state or federal agencies that oversee airport operations.

Education and Training

Assistant airport managers need a college degree with a major in aviation, airport management, business management, public administration, or engineering. A pilot's license or other flight training would be helpful.

Experience, Skills, and Personality Traits

Assistant airport managers need strong supervisory skills to manage the staffers who operate and control various functions of the airport. They should have organizational skills and a strong attention to detail to track the many different types of regulations governing the airport.

Unions and Associations

Assistant airport managers generally do not belong to a national union.

Their primary trade association is the Airport Operators Council International (AOCI) in Washington, D.C. AOCI offers seminars, publications, government representation, and other assistance to professional airport managers.

Tips for Entry

1. Learn about the operations of an airport by working part time as a clerk, shop attendant, or similar position. While you earn money for school, you can observe the inner workings of the airport.

2. Strengthen your skills in business management and sales, through courses or direct work experience.

3. When you apply for a position in airport management, highlight any experience you have had in flying, customer relations, and management, from part-time jobs to volunteer assignments.

4. Because airport management involves a frustrating amount of paperwork and regulatory oversight, consider whether you would enjoy shouldering these types of responsibility, or whether you would prefer working in another segment of the aviation industry.

DIRECTOR OF COMMUNITY RELATIONS, AIRPORT

CAREER PROFILE

Duties: Prepares press releases and other public relations materials; handles media calls and interview requests; serves as liaison to outside public relations firms; coordinates media relations in emergencies

Alternate Title(s): Director of public relations

Salary Range: $15,000 to $45,000

Employment Prospects: Fair

Best Geographic Location: Most job opportunities in airport management will surface in states with a concentration of airports, such as California, Texas, Florida, Illinois, Ohio, New York, and Pennsylvania.

Prerequisites:

Education and Training—High school diploma required, with courses in journalism and writing helpful; college degree required, with courses in English, journalism, and public relations helpful

Experience—Work experience in a public relations firm or in the field of journalism; work experience in an airport, tour company, travel agency, or travel supplier (e.g., theme park, hotel)

Special Skills and Personality Traits—Writing ability; creativity; organizational skills; attention to detail; very strong oral and written communication skills; interpersonal skills

CAREER LADDER

```
┌─────────────────────────────────────┐
│                                       │
│      Assistant Manager, Airport       │
│                                       │
└─────────────────────────────────────┘

┌─────────────────────────────────────┐
│                                       │
│   Director of Community Relations,    │
│               Airport                 │
│                                       │
└─────────────────────────────────────┘

┌─────────────────────────────────────┐
│                                       │
│    Community Relations Assistant,     │
│               Airport                 │
│                                       │
└─────────────────────────────────────┘
```

Position Description

Directors of community relations for airports create written materials, work with journalists, and serve as the airport's spokespeople. They strive to develop strong ties with the communities surrounding the airport.

Working from the airport's strategic marketing plan, operating policies, and applicable regulations, directors of community relations write press releases, media alerts, briefing papers, and other materials for journalists. Working with other departments, they also may prepare lobbying position papers and other materials for government relations as well as annual reports and other brochures for investor relations. They will write comments and speeches for the airport's managers.

Directors of community relations field calls from journalists who want information or background on a story involving the airport. They will refer some calls and interview requests to other airport executives, briefing them on the situation before comments are made. In many cases, community relations assistants may act as the airport's spokespeople.

If the airport retains an outside public relations firm, directors of community relations will act as liaisons linking the firm with other airport departments. They may review invoices from the firm and forward them to the accounting department for processing.

Directors of community relations will handle community affairs assignments for the airport to strengthen relations with major civic organizations and members of the public. For example, the airport may host events during National Tourism Week in May, or directors of community relations may serve on a citywide task force to develop a public service campaign promoting the benefits of tourism in the region. In these cases, directors of community relations will represent the airport.

In the rare event of an emergency, directors of community relations will serve as the airport's immediate spokespeople. Also, directors will investigate the emergency, relay information to authorities as needed, prepare press releases and media alerts for immediate distribution, and coordinate inquiries from journalists as the emergency is resolved.

Salaries

Salaries of directors of community relations depend on the size of the airport, the complexity of its operations, and other factors. Salaries for directors may begin at $15,000 and progress to $45,000 or more.

Employment Prospects

Job openings in this field are extremely competitive, due to the relatively small number of airports in the United States and the large pool of candidates wanting to enter this field. However, experts predict an expansion in airport construction through the year 2000.

Advancement Prospects

The primary track for promotions in this field is moving to similar positions at larger airports or progressing to become an assistant airport manager. Other directors of community relations can advance in terms of salary by switching to another segment of the travel industry or to a public relations firm that specializes in travel accounts.

Education and Training

Currently there is no continuing education program for professional certification of directors of community relations. However, once they have accrued five years of work experience, they can qualify to take an exam to become accredited (with the "APR" designation) by the Public Relations Society of America.

Additional courses in public relations, journalism, and writing may be helpful.

Experience, Skills, and Personality Traits

Directors of community relations for airports must have strong writing skills to prepare press releases and other written materials that will promote the airport effectively. They must have organizational skills and attention to detail to handle service requests from media and from outside agencies.

Increasingly, directors of community relations will need computer skills to manage their activities efficiently.

Unions and Associations

Directors of community relations generally do not belong to a national union.

Their primary national association is the Public Relations Society of America (PRSA) in New York City. PRSA offers seminars, publications, training materials and videos, and other services to support public relations practitioners.

The primary trade association for airport managerial personnel is the Airport Operators Council International (AOCI) in Washington, D.C. AOCI offers seminars, publications, government representation, and other assistance to professional airport managers.

Tips for Entry

1. When you apply for airport positions, highlight any experience you have had in community relations and journalism, from part-time jobs to volunteer assignments.

2. Strengthen your skills in journalism and public relations, through courses or direct work experience.

3. Consider whether you would prefer working inside the airport, as opposed to an independent public relations firm. Some public relations practitioners like the variety of working for more than one type of client.

4. Write the major airports for information about internships and on-the-job management training programs. Many airports offer such tracks for college graduates, so that these new trainees can learn the business from their employers.

MANAGER OF CULTURAL TOURISM, NONPROFIT ORGANIZATION

CAREER PROFILE

Duties: Prepares marketing plans to solicit leisure travelers; coordinates advertising, public relations, direct-mail, and other marketing campaigns; schedules presentations and makes sales calls on travel agents, tour operators, and other large-volume buyers

Alternate Title(s): Director of cultural tourism

Salary Range: $15,000 to $35,000

Employment Prospects: Fair

Best Geographic Location: Most job openings will be found in areas of the United States that place a premium on historic preservation and cultural tourism, such as New England and the Southwest.

Prerequisites:

Education and Training—High school diploma required, with courses in business management helpful; college degree required, with courses in business management, sales, and travel and tourism helpful; additional training in direct sales

Experience—Direct sales; customer relations; work experience in a tour company, travel agency, or travel supplier (e.g., theme park, hotel)

Special Skills and Personality Traits—Sales ability; business management skills; strong oral and written communication skills; interpersonal skills; group presentation skills

CAREER LADDER

```
┌─────────────────────────────────────┐
│                                      │
│   Executive Director, Nonprofit      │
│            Organization              │
│                                      │
└─────────────────────────────────────┘

┌─────────────────────────────────────┐
│                                      │
│   Assistant Director, Nonprofit      │
│            Organization              │
│                                      │
└─────────────────────────────────────┘

┌─────────────────────────────────────┐
│                                      │
│   Manager of Cultural Tourism,       │
│      Nonprofit Organization          │
│                                      │
└─────────────────────────────────────┘

┌─────────────────────────────────────┐
│                                      │
│    Clerk, Nonprofit Organization     │
│                                      │
└─────────────────────────────────────┘
```

Position Description

Managers of cultural tourism who work for nonprofit organizations—in most cases, historic properties and parks—use all available avenues to plan, coordinate, and execute the sales and marketing activities of the nonprofit group's tourism division.

Managers will begin by developing a comprehensive strategic marketing plan for the nonprofit organization. First, managers will assess the group's tourism resources—the events or sites that would attract visitors. For example, managers at a historic estate might focus on the refurbished great rooms in the main house, the dinner service that is available with reservations, the restored grounds and landscaping, the expert volunteer guides who take groups through the property, and the annual Christmas tree lighting that has become a local tradition.

Based on these features, managers then identify the most promising market segments of travelers. Today, many nonprofit organizations with tourism divisions rely on a number of different market segments: individual travelers, families, international travelers, corporate executives on incentive trips, meetings and convention delegates, tour groups, and other niches.

As the product types and market segments are being determined, managers also must take into account the nonprofit organization's positioning in the marketplace, compared to competing groups. For example, will the estate appeal primarily to history buffs, or does the property contain enough interpretive signs and markers to be appealing to families and groups? Can meal service be rearranged to fit special needs such as corporate groups on retreats? Positioning will be critical in deciding what types of promotions and what future services will make the nonprofit organization's tourism activities successful.

Once these basic decisions have been made, managers begin identifying prospective customers and soliciting their business. For large-volume customers such as travel agencies and incentive travel specialists, managers will likely follow up direct-mail letters and telemarketing calls with personal presentations to the groups or selected decision makers. Therefore, managers need to be adept at speaking in front of groups and planning creative presentations to sell the nonprofit organization.

For the most part, however, managers will rely on standard marketing techniques such as advertising, public relations, and direct-mail brochures. Managers must design and plan advertisements for the nonprofit organization (working in some cases with an outside advertising agency), choose the media involved, and make the final placement decisions. Managers usually will coordinate press releases and serve as spokespeople for the group to journalists. Using in-house staffers or an outside firm, managers will design and supervise the production of the group's schedules, brochures, and other printed materials; once these pieces are printed, managages will decide strategies for sending them to prospective tourists.

To gauge the effectiveness of these marketing efforts, managers must research the targeted market segments and track the number of visitors who come to the nonprofit group's property.

Salaries

Salaries of managers reflect the low wages generally paid to employees of nonprofit groups. Managers with the smallest local nonprofit groups may earn $15,000 or more, while those working for national organizations which operate several tourism properties may earn $35,000.

Employment Prospects

Job openings in this field will be found mostly with local and regional nonprofit groups that want to develop tourism business as a means of supplementing their budgets. Positions with nationally known historic trusts and nonprofit groups will be extremely competitive.

Advancement Prospects

The avenues for advancement for managers of cultural tourism include being promoted to higher manage-

ment positions within their group, moving to larger and more prestigious nonprofit organizations, or switching to other areas of the travel industry.

Education and Training

Most nonprofit organizations today will require a college degree for managers. Courses in business management, sales, and travel and tourism will be most helpful, as will additional training in direct sales.

If the group depends on a specific niche for most of its business, managers may complete a specialized professional certification program such as the Certified Tour Professional (CTP) track offered by the National Tour Association in Lexington, Kentucky.

Experience, Skills, and Personality Traits

Managers of sales and marketing for nonprofit organizations must demonstrate the direct sales abilities and group presentation skills to discover prospective clients and persuade them to visit the group's tourism property. They must have organizational skills and attention to detail to handle questions and requests from different clients.

Increasingly, managers will need computer skills to manage their activities efficiently.

Unions and Associations

As nonprofit executives, managers of sales and marketing generally do not belong to a national union, nor do they have a professional association.

Tips for Entry

1. Strengthen your skills in business management and sales, through courses or direct work experience.

2. Consider whether your interpersonal skills—especially your ability to serve the needs of, and relate to, different types of clients—are strong enough for a people-intensive position in nonprofit organization sales.

3. When you apply for nonprofit organization positions, highlight any experience you have had in customer relations and direct sales, from part-time jobs to volunteer assignments.

4. Visit several historic properties or other tourism attractions operated by nonprofit groups. Talk to the managers about their workload and daily activities. Use these contacts later as you network for internships, part-time employment, or full-time positions.

5. Because these managers work closely with other segments of the travel industry, read as many different travel trade publications as possible to stay abreast of current events in the industry.

ANCILLARY AND SUPPORT SERVICES

SALES REPRESENTATIVE, COMPUTERIZED RESERVATIONS SYSTEM

CAREER PROFILE

Duties: Prepares marketing plans to solicit individual clients; schedules presentations and makes sales calls on travel companies and other buyers; provides after-sale service and training as needed

Alternate Title(s): Account executive

Salary Range: $25,000 to $65,000

Employment Prospects: Fair

Best Geographic Location: Most job openings will be found in major metropolitan areas such as New York City, Los Angeles, Chicago, Dallas and Miami.

Prerequisites:

Education and Training—High school diploma required, with courses in business management helpful; college degree required, with courses in business management, sales, and travel and tourism helpful; additional training in direct sales

Experience—Direct sales; computer operations; customer relations; work experience in a tour company, travel agency, or travel supplier (e.g., theme park, hotel)

Special Skills and Personality Traits—Sales ability; computer operating abilities; strong oral and written communication skills; interpersonal skills; group presentation skills

CAREER LADDER

```
┌─────────────────────────────────┐
│   Vice President of Sales and    │
│   Marketing, Computerized        │
│      Reservations System         │
└─────────────────────────────────┘

┌─────────────────────────────────┐
│   Director of Sales and Marketing,│
│   Computerized Reservations System│
└─────────────────────────────────┘

┌─────────────────────────────────┐
│  Sales Representative, Computerized│
│      Reservations System         │
└─────────────────────────────────┘

┌─────────────────────────────────┐
│     Sales Clerk, Computerized    │
│      Reservations System         │
└─────────────────────────────────┘
```

Position Description

Computerized reservations systems (CRSs) are networks of computer terminals, linked together to a common database that allow travel agents and other sellers of travel services to check schedules and reserve space from a travel supplier such as a hotel, airline, or cruise line. Sales representatives sign up new users for their systems, train them in operating the terminals, and resolve complaints and questions that may arise.

Sales representatives for CRSs will begin their careers with an extensive period of training to learn how to use the terminals in booking travel services. They also must become familiar with the services offered by competing CRSs, since many potential customers already have at least one CRS installed in their offices.

Each sales representative normally will be assigned a geographical territory, ranging in size from a district in one metropolitan area to several states. Sales representatives must research their territories to find prospective customers—mostly travel agents, tour operators, and corporate travel managers with in-house travel agencies—who would be interested in adding CRS services. They will use industry directories and databases, referrals from other customers, travel trade publications, and other sources to locate these potential customers. Working together with other sales representatives, they also will respond to leads generated by standard marketing techniques such as advertising, public relations, trade shows, and direct-mail campaigns.

They will arrange appointments with these prospects, in which they will discuss the merits of their CRS and arrange a demonstration. Sales representatives must be skilled salespeople, with strong presentation abilities, to sign up new users, since many customers already use at least one CRS and the industry is extremely competitive.

When a client agrees to use the CRS, sales representatives will oversee the installation of the computer equipment in the client's office. Then they will train the client in using the various screens and programs of the CRS to book travel services (or arrange for a company trainer to conduct this session).

Sales representatives monitor complaints and questions that may arise from the use of the CRS. They will arrange billing schedules for the client and help with collections if needed.

To gauge the effectiveness of these marketing efforts, sales representatives must research their customers to determine what strategies resulted in the greatest number of new clients.

Salaries

Salaries of CRS sales representatives begin in the low to mid $20,000s, but experienced sales representatives with proven track records of generating business may earn $65,000 or more (including bonuses).

Employment Prospects

Job openings in this field are extremely competitive, due to the relatively small number of CRSs in the United States. Applicants with a track record of sales success—in the travel industry or another business sector—will have the greatest chances of being hired.

Advancement Prospects

The avenues for advancement for sales representatives include being promoted to director of sales and marketing or switching to other areas of the travel industry. Generally, lateral moves to other companies in this competitive industry will not result in major salary increases.

Education and Training

Most CRSs today will require that sales representatives have a college degree. Courses in business management, sales, and travel and tourism will be most helpful, as will additional training in direct sales.

Experience, Skills, and Personality Traits

Sales representatives for computerized reservations systems must demonstrate the direct sales abilities and group presentation skills to discover prospective clients and persuade them to install the CRS. They must have organizational skills and attention to detail to handle questions and requests from different clients. Another valuable asset would be experience working in a travel agency or tour company.

Because their jobs involve selling computer systems, sales representatives will need computer skills to manage their activities efficiently.

Unions and Associations

As CRS employees, sales representatives generally do not belong to a national union, nor do they have a professional association.

Tips for Entry

1.   Strengthen your skills in business management and sales, through courses or direct work experience.

2.   Consider whether your interpersonal skills—especially your ability to prospect for new clients and to handle training new CRS users—are strong enough for a people-intensive position in CRS sales.

3.   When you apply for positions in CRS sales, highlight any experience you have had in customer relations, computer training, and direct sales, from part-time jobs to volunteer assignments.

4.   Because CRS operations require some level of familiarity with computer networks, sign up for online computer networks such as CompuServe and Prodigy. Practice your skills at switching among different levels and screens, especially the travel reservations systems, including EAASY SABRE.

SALES REPRESENTATIVE, TRAVEL RESERVATIONS FIRM/GENERAL SALES AGENT

CAREER PROFILE

Duties: Prepares marketing plans to solicit calls and contacts from travelers on behalf of travel supplier clients; designs advertisements, letters, and telemarketing campaigns to attract travelers; coordinates and confirms reservations for travel supplier clients

Alternate Title(s): Account executive

Salary Range: $15,000 to $70,000

Employment Prospects: Fair

Best Geographic Location: Most job openings will be found in major metropolitan areas such as New York City, Los Angeles, Chicago, Dallas, Miami, and Atlanta.

Prerequisites:

Education and Training—High school diploma required, with courses in business management helpful; college degree required, with courses in business management, sales, and travel and tourism helpful; additional training in direct sales

Experience—Direct sales; customer relations; work experience in a tour company, travel agency, or travel supplier (e.g., theme park, hotel)

Special Skills and Personality Traits—Sales ability; business management skills; strong oral and written communication skills; interpersonal skills; group presentation skills

CAREER LADDER

```
┌─────────────────────────────────┐
│   President, Travel Reservations │
│   Firm/General Sales Agent       │
└─────────────────────────────────┘

┌─────────────────────────────────┐
│   Director of Sales and Marketing,│
│   Travel Reservations Firm/General│
│   Sales Agent                    │
└─────────────────────────────────┘

┌─────────────────────────────────┐
│   Sales Representative, Travel   │
│   Reservations Firm/General Sales Agent│
└─────────────────────────────────┘

┌─────────────────────────────────┐
│   Reservationist or Clerk, Travel│
│   Reservations Firm/General Sales Agent│
└─────────────────────────────────┘
```

Position Description

While many travel suppliers such as hotels and theme parks mount extensive marketing campaigns to attract customers, other travel suppliers—especially small hotels and resorts, or suppliers with extremely specialized niche markets—will appoint a travel reservations firm or general sales agent to solicit customers for them. In return for generating reservations, the firm or agent collects a commission for each client's stay.

To succeed in this field, sales representatives for a travel reservations firm must sign up a sizable base of travel suppliers as clients. The firm must have enough clients to provide an inventory of travel services to sell, without overloading its staffers or marketing resources. Sales representatives must have a firsthand knowledge of the types of travel services, the various fares and discounts, amenities for incentive travelers and tour groups, and any other background information on each client that potential visitors may request. In many cases, sales representatives will conduct a site visit with each client, seeing the property and sampling the travel services firsthand, so that they can sell the client to potential travelers.

Under the supervision of the director of sales and marketing, sales representatives will be given specific market segments for which they must be responsible: individual travelers, families, international inbound travelers, incentive travelers, meetings and convention groups, tour groups, travel agencies, and other niches. In the largest firms, sales representatives may be given a list of individual accounts rather than an entire segment.

Sales representatives must become very familiar with the dynamics and needs of their market segments or accounts. They should know the booking patterns, fares, itineraries, special needs, and other characteristics that distinguish these travelers from others. Successful sales representatives round out their knowledge of their accounts by studying each client's files on these travelers, reading their trade publications, establishing a personal rapport with the decision makers at these accounts, and networking with other travel suppliers in the city or state.

Armed with this information, sales representatives will begin identifying prospective customers and soliciting their business. For large-volume customers such as travel agencies and tour operators, sales representatives will follow up direct-mail letters, brochures, and telemarketing calls with personal presentations to the groups or selected decision makers. Sales representatives must be able to speak in front of groups and plan creative presentations to sell the client's services.

Working together with other sales representatives and the firm's sales clerks, they will respond to leads generated by standard marketing techniques such as advertising, public relations, trade shows, and direct-mail campaigns. (Most of these leads will result from telephone calls from travelers to the sales clerks, in response to ads and articles.) Sales representatives may help to design and plan advertisements for suppliers, choose the media involved, and make the final placement decisions. They also may assist in public relations work such as greeting visiting clients and arranging familiarization tours. In some cases, they will staff booths at trade shows.

Sales representatives will coordinate reservations procedures with their supplier clients. As travelers call the firm to request rates and availability, the clerks will follow these procedures as they book travelers. Sales representatives will insure that the reservations are con-firmed with travelers and forwarded quickly to the clients.

Sales representatives monitor complaints and questions that may arise. If the clients have arranged special billing procedures, sales representatives may oversee the preparation of those bills. Given these responsibilities, the sales representatives must have highly developed clerical skills, including data entry and basic accounting procedures.

To gauge the effectiveness of these marketing efforts, sales representatives must research their targeted market segments, track the number of travelers who have booked services, and present the results of this research to supplier clients as a means of justifying their value as sales agents.

Salaries

Salaries of sales representatives in travel reservations firms depend on the size of the firm, its client list, its position in the marketplace, and other factors. Salaries for new representatives may begin at $15,000, but experienced sales representatives with proven track records of generating travelers' business and securing new clients may earn $70,000 or more (including bonuses).

Employment Prospects

Job openings in this field are fairly competitive and limited to the major metropolitan areas, where sales representatives will be in close proximity to the headquarters or sales offices of many potential supplier clients.

Advancement Prospects

The avenues for advancement for sales representatives include being promoted to director of sales and marketing, starting their own travel reservations firms, or switching to other areas of the travel industry.

Education and Training

Many travel reservations firms today will require a college degree for sales representatives. Courses in business management, sales, and travel and tourism will be most helpful, as will additional training in direct sales.

Experience, Skills, and Personality Traits

Sales representatives for travel reservations firms must demonstrate the direct sales abilities and group presentation skills to discover prospective supplier clients and persuade them to use the firm's services. They must have organizational skills and attention to detail to handle questions and requests from different supplier clients.

Increasingly, sales representatives will need computer skills to manage their activities efficiently.

Unions and Associations

As sales executives, sales representatives for travel reservations firms generally do not belong to a national union, nor do they have a professional association.

Tips for Entry

1.   Strengthen your skills in business management and sales, through courses or direct work experience.

2.   When you apply for positions in travel reservations firms, highlight any experience you have had in customer relations and direct sales, from part-time jobs to volunteer assignments.

3.   Read as many trade publications as possible, to gain a broad understanding of the various sectors of the travel industry and to learn how different types of travel suppliers advertise their services.

4.   Contact travel reservations firms and attempt to set up an internship or part-time job, so that you can learn the business from the inside. In fact, many firms like to promote sales representatives by choosing among their sales clerks and reservationists.

5.   A stint as a general sales agent in a travel agency or tour company could be valuable in terms of teaching you the operations involved in soliciting travelers and tracking reservations.

INSTRUCTOR, TRAVEL ACADEMY

CAREER PROFILE

Duties: Recruits and advises students in travel careers; teaches courses in travel and tourism skills; conducts research in the travel field; participates in faculty and school and industry associations and activities

Alternate Title(s): Travel instructor

Salary Range: $14,000 to $35,000

Employment Prospects: Good

Best Geographic Location: Most regions of the United States will offer job opportunities in travel academies.

Prerequisites:

Education and Training—High school diploma required, with courses in geography and business management helpful; college degree required, with a major in geography, business management, travel and tourism, hospitality management, or a related field helpful; advanced degree usually required, with an emphasis in geography, travel and tourism, business management, or a related field; computer training, especially in the operation of CRSs

Experience—Work experience in a travel agency, tour company, or travel supplier; teaching or training experience

Special Skills and Personality Traits—Teaching skills; interpersonal skills; computer operations abilities (especially CRSs); strong oral and written communication skills; group presentation skills

CAREER LADDER

```
┌─────────────────────────────────────────┐
│                                          │
│   Dean or President, Travel Academy      │
│                                          │
└─────────────────────────────────────────┘

┌─────────────────────────────────────────┐
│                                          │
│     Instructor, Travel Academy           │
│                                          │
└─────────────────────────────────────────┘

┌─────────────────────────────────────────┐
│                                          │
│    Teaching Aide, Travel Academy         │
│                                          │
└─────────────────────────────────────────┘
```

Position Description

Travel academies train students in the skills and techniques needed to work as travel agents, reservationists, escorts, and similar entry-level positions in the travel industry. Instructors at each academy advise students, teach classes, conduct specialized training sessions, carry out research projects, and support the academy's mission and operations in many other ways.

By attending job fairs and similar events sponsored by their school, instructors talk with prospective students and recruit qualified applicants for classes. They advise new students in the proper courses to take and, as students graduate, in the best ways to seek jobs in the travel industry.

They spend the majority of their time conducting classes and training sessions for students. The classes range from geography and travel and tourism principles to sales techniques and the operation of major computerized reservations systems. Instructors use a variety of teaching methods—from lectures and audiovisual presentations to hands-on training labs and presentations by travel professionals—to prepare students for travel careers. They prepare and grade homework assignments, exams, and other coursework for students.

Instructors also may plan and conduct research projects, especially if they want to advance to higher academic positions. Students may be involved in these projects.

Instructors will participate in various faculty and staff assignments for the academy, from choosing library supplies and equipment to planning fund-raising campaigns. They also will be involved in industry activities and national associations as appropriate.

Salaries

Because they work more with entry-level travel employees, salaries for instructors at travel academies will not be commensurate with pay levels at colleges and universities. Beginning instructors (especially those without graduate degrees) will earn salaries from $14,000, while experienced faculty members with graduate degrees may earn $35,000 or more in the largest academies.

Employment Prospects

Job opportunities in travel academies for qualified teachers will continue to expand through the decade, as the industry grows and requires more entry-level employees. Instructors with travel industry work experience and/or graduate degrees will be the ones most in demand.

Advancement Prospects

Instructors who wish to advance may aim for higher academic positions such as dean or director of the academy, transfer to a college or university travel program, or (in a few cases) switch to administer training programs for large travel agencies or travel suppliers.

Education and Training

At the minimum, instructors will need a bachelor's degree with a major in a field related to travel and tourism. To advance in their careers, instructors also should seek at least a master's degree.

Because they will be involved in training front-line employees for travel agents and tour operators, instructors should consider completing a professional continuing education program such as the Certified Travel Counselor (CTC) track offered by the Institute of Certified Travel Agents in Wellesley, Massachusetts.

Additional skills in computer operations, foreign languages, marketing, and geography will be helpful.

Experience, Skills, and Personality Traits

Instructors at travel academies will need strong teaching skills and interpersonal skills to relate to students and to transfer the skills and knowledge needed to function in the travel industry. Strong oral and written communication skills will be helpful as they give lectures and prepare handouts and exam materials.

Because many travel companies rely heavily on databases and computerized reservations systems, instructors should have training in computer operations.

Unions and Associations

Instructors normally do not belong to a national union.

Many instructors are active in the educator categories of the major travel trade associations, notably the American Hotel & Motel Association in Washington, D.C., the American Society of Travel Agents in Alexandria, Virginia, and the National Tour Foundation in Lexington, Kentucky. These groups offer seminars, national conventions, publications, research projects, and other assistance to practicing instructors in travel and tourism.

Tips for Entry

1. Earn a graduate degree in travel and tourism, business management, or a related field, in order to improve your chances at securing an appointment as an instructor.

2. Consider whether you will be happier teaching travel and tourism in an academy as opposed to working directly in the field.

3. Secure part-time employment or an internship in a travel agency, tour company, or travel supplier, so that you can bolster your academic studies with work experience in the field.

4. Read the latest issues of major travel trade magazines and publications, so that you can remain current on the most recent developments in the industry.

5. Take a student membership in a major national travel trade association, or participate in "pro-am" days and similar events that expose prospective travel professionals to people in their chosen field. Network with educators to learn about their careers and about available openings.

PROFESSOR OF TOURISM/HOSPITALITY STUDIES, COLLEGE OR UNIVERSITY

CAREER PROFILE

Duties: Recruits and advises students in travel careers; teaches courses in travel and tourism skills; conducts research in the travel field; participates in faculty and school and industry association and activities

Alternate Title(s): Assistant professor; associate professor

Salary Range: $26,100 to $56,200

Employment Prospects: Good

Best Geographic Location: Most regions of the United States will offer job opportunities in colleges and universities.

Prerequisites:

Education and Training—High school diploma required, with courses in geography and business management helpful; college degree required, with a major in geography, business management, travel and tourism, hospitality management, or a related field helpful; advanced degree required, with an emphasis in geography, travel and tourism, business management, or a related field; computer training helpful

Experience—Work experience in a travel agency, tour company, or travel supplier; teaching or training experience

Special Skills and Personality Traits—Teaching skills; interpersonal skills; research skills; computer operations abilities; strong oral and written communication skills; group presentation skills

CAREER LADDER

```
┌─────────────────────────────────────┐
│  Professor, College or University    │
└─────────────────────────────────────┘

┌─────────────────────────────────────┐
│       Associate Professor,           │
│       College or University          │
└─────────────────────────────────────┘

┌─────────────────────────────────────┐
│       Assistant Professor,           │
│       College or University          │
└─────────────────────────────────────┘

┌─────────────────────────────────────┐
│   Instructor, College or University  │
└─────────────────────────────────────┘
```

Position Description

A growing number of college and universities have established undergraduate and graduate programs in travel and tourism, hospitality management, restaurant management, and related fields to train professionals for the travel industry. Professors in these programs advise students, teach classes, conduct specialized training sessions, carry out research projects, and support the university's mission and operations in many other ways.

By attending job fairs and similar events sponsored by their school, professors talk with prospective students and recruit qualified applicants for classes. They advise new students in the proper courses to take and, as students graduate, in the best ways to seek jobs in the travel industry.

They spend the majority of their time conducting classes and training sessions for students. The classes range from geography and travel and tourism principles to sales techniques and personnel management practices. Professors use a variety of teaching methods—from lectures and audiovisual presentations to hands-on training labs and presentations by leading travel professionals—to prepare students for travel careers. They prepare and grade homework assignments, exams, and other coursework for students.

Professors will plan and conduct research projects, especially if they want to advance to higher academic positions. They will involve students in these projects on many occasions, especially graduate students whom they are advising.

Professors will participate in various faculty and staff assignments for the college or university, from choosing library supplies and equipment to planning fund-raising campaigns. They must spend a portion of their time reading journals and publications to keep up with developments in their specialties. They may serve on academic and administrative committees or serve as advisors for student organizations.

Salaries

Because they work more with budding professionals in travel and tourism, salaries for professors in the travel field will compare favorably with their colleagues' in other liberal arts and applied science departments. Beginning professors at the assistant level will earn salaries from $26,000, while experienced faculty members with doctoral degrees may earn $56,000 or more at the largest universities.

Employment Prospects

Job opportunities in travel and tourism departments at colleges and universities will continue to expand through the decade, as the industry grows and requires more professionals and managers. Professors with travel industry work experience, doctoral degrees, and publishing records will be the ones most in demand.

Advancement Prospects

Professors who wish to advance may aim for higher academic positions such as dean or chairman of the department, transfer into other levels of university administration, or (in a few cases) switch to administer training programs for large travel agencies or travel suppliers. These opportunities will favor professors who have completed a doctoral degree and who have established reputations in the field.

Education and Training

At the minimum, professors will need a master's degree with a major in a field related to travel and tourism. To advance in their careers, professors should plan to seek a doctoral degree.

If they specialize in front-line travel and tourism issues, some professors complete a professional continuing education program such as the Certified Travel Counselor (CTC) track offered by the Institute of Certified Travel Agents in Wellesley, Massachusetts.

Additional skills in computer operations, foreign languages, marketing, and geography will be helpful.

Experience, Skills, and Personality Traits

Professors in university travel and tourism programs will need strong teaching skills and interpersonal skills to relate to students and to transfer the skills and knowledge needed to function in the travel industry. Strong oral and written communication skills will be helpful as they give lectures and prepare handouts and exam materials.

Because many travel companies rely heavily on databases and computerized reservations systems, professors should have training in computer operations.

Unions and Associations

Professors normally do not belong to a national union on most college campuses.

Many professors are active in the educator categories of the major travel trade associations, notably the American Hotel & Motel Association in Washington, D.C., the American Society of Travel Agents in Alexandria, Virginia, and the National Tour Foundation in Lexington, Kentucky. These groups offer seminars, national conventions, publications, research projects, and other assistance to professors in travel and tourism.

Tips for Entry

1. Earn a doctoral degree in travel and tourism, business management, or a related field, in order to improve your chances at securing an appointment at a college or university.

2. Consider whether you will be happier teaching travel and tourism on a college campus, as opposed to working directly in the field.

3. Secure part-time employment or an internship in a travel agency, tour company, or travel supplier, so that you can bolster your academic studies with work experience in the field (while you earn money to pay your graduate tuition).

4. Read the latest issues of major travel trade magazines and publications, so that you can remain current on the most recent developments in the industry.

5. Take a student membership in a major national travel trade association, or participate in "pro-am" days and similar events that expose prospective travel professionals to people in their chosen field. Network with educators to learn about their careers and about available openings.

DIRECTOR, TRAVEL TRADE ASSOCIATION

CAREER PROFILE

Duties: Manages and directs the activities of one or more departments in a trade association (e.g., membership, education, government relations, public relations, marketing, conventions)

Alternate Title(s): Project manager; assistant director

Salary Range: $18,000 to $60,000

Employment Prospects: Fair

Best Geographic Location: Most travel association positions will be located in Washington, D.C., and New York City.

Prerequisites:

Education and Training—High school diploma required; college degree in liberal arts required with coursework in business administration; graduate degree helpful for later advancement; additional training in specific job fields (e.g., public relations, human resources, marketing

Experience—Prior work experience in managing groups of people or serving in public-sector organizations

Special Skills and Personality Traits—Aggressiveness; organization; strong oral and written communication skills; interpersonal skills; computer skills

CAREER LADDER

```
┌─────────────────────────────────┐
│                                 │
│   Executive Director, Travel    │
│       Trade Association         │
│                                 │
└─────────────────────────────────┘

┌─────────────────────────────────┐
│                                 │
│  Director, Travel Trade Association │
│                                 │
└─────────────────────────────────┘

┌─────────────────────────────────┐
│                                 │
│  Project Manager/Assistant Director, │
│       Travel Trade Association  │
│                                 │
└─────────────────────────────────┘

┌─────────────────────────────────┐
│                                 │
│   Administrative Assistant, Travel │
│       Trade Association         │
│                                 │
└─────────────────────────────────┘
```

Position Description

A director for a travel trade association manages one or more departments responsible for programs that benefit association members. While specific job duties will vary, the following areas will be common to most associations.

Conventions: Organizing and managing the group's regular conventions, trade shows, committee meetings, and other sanctioned events.

Education: Preparing seminars, study guides and manuals, audiovisual presentations, and other resources to improve members' understanding of the travel industry.

Foundations: Supervising the organization's scholarship and research programs.

Government relations: Lobbying on behalf of members to effect favorable laws and regulations for the travel industry.

Industry relations: Improving the association's standing within the travel industry and developing cooperative projects with other travel organizations.

International relations: Seeking opportunities for the organization and its members to foster global business ties.

Marketing and public relations: Creating new marketing tools for members and increasing awareness of their services among consumers and other segments of the travel industry through effective relations with consumer and travel trade media.

Member services: Maintaining the association's membership rosters, billing and collecting dues, and providing specific member benefit programs.

Publications: Managing the group's membership magazine, newsletters, and other publications.

In addition, many travel associations employ support personnel in areas such as accounting and legal matters.

Almost every travel association has a headquarters operated by professional managers who report to a volunteer board of directors elected by the members. Thus, successful association directors have the ability to work well within an established organizational structure.

Also, association directors must cope with the strains of working with, and depending on, volunteering members to accomplish the organization's work.

Association directors spend much of their time communicating, among the staff and with volunteers and other members. Also, they spend a great deal of time on the road, so they must be prepared for being away from friends and family for extended periods of time.

Salaries

Pay scales vary according to the organization's size, prestige, and location. Beginning directors normally earn $18,000 to $25,000 annually; mid-level directors, $32,000 to $38,000; and senior directors, $45,000 to $60,000.

Employment Prospects

Since the number of travel associations is limited, prospects for job openings can be described as fair. The best opportunities will be found in the Washington, D.C., and New York City areas, since most national associations are headquartered there.

Advancement Prospects

Directors will have fair prospects of moving to higher posts within their associations, as they complete additional training or degrees and as higher-ranking staffers move on. Although some directors have accepted higher positions within another travel association, such movement is rare. Many more directors leverage their association experience as a springboard to another job or business opportunity within the industry itself (e.g., opening a travel agency, working for a travel supplier).

Education and Training

A college degree will be the basic requirement for almost all director-level positions within travel associations. Helpful areas of study include marketing, public relations, English, journalism, liberal arts, and commu-

nications. To prepare for future advancement, directors should plan to seek a master's degree (especially in business administration or association management).

Advanced training in computers, organizational development, or marketing will help directors develop their skills.

Professional association managers should seek the Certified Association Executive (CAE) designation offered through the American Society of Association Executives (ASAE). This certification course involves a combination of self-study courses, seminars, work experience, and association accomplishments designed to identify professionals who have mastered the basics of association management.

Experience, Skills, and Personality Traits

The primary abilities that an association director needs are well-developed interpersonal communication skills to function in a multilayered association of volunteers and paid staffers and strong organizational habits to track many projects of varying priority. Familiarity with computers and an entrepreneurial mindset will become increasingly important in the 1990s to maximize member benefits with limited resources.

Unions and Associations

Generally, travel association directors do not belong to a union. The American Society of Association Executives (ASAE) is the primary national organization supporting association managers. ASAE offers seminars, regular networking opportunities, government representation, and other services for professional association directors. In addition, many directors belong to national organizations that represent their specific work functions (e.g., Meeting Professionals International for convention planners, Public Relations Society of America for public affairs directors).

Tips for Entry

1. Think about your experiences volunteering for nonprofit organizations. If you have enjoyed working in that environment, your background will serve you well in association management.

2. If you work currently in another segment of the travel industry, consider volunteering for your national association first to determine if you enjoy the routine.

3. Network. Many travel trade associations turn to members of the industry or to others whom they know (e.g., interns) when filling open positions. Contact the staffers whom you know to tell them you have an interest in working for the association.

4. Seek an internship (paid or unpaid) with a travel association, to gain valuable on-the-job training in specific job functions and departments.

5. Review the classified sections of newspapers in major U.S. cities (particularly Washington, D.C., and New York City) for travel association listings. Many associations advertise available positions in association management publications such as Association Management and Association Trends, available in many larger libraries.

6. Read books on association and nonprofit organization management to build a foundation of knowledge as you begin your initial work within a travel association.

7. Consider graduate coursework in association management, offered at several universities around the country. (See the appendixes for listings of degree programs.)

TRAVEL MARKET RESEARCHER

CAREER PROFILE

Duties: Performs statistical tests and conducts surveys to gauge public interest in travel products and services; tabulates results of tests and surveys and analyzes results; recommends strategies to clients

Alternate Title(s): Director of market research

Salary Range: $21,000 to $55,000

Employment Prospects: Fair

Best Geographic Location: While many market researchers who work full time for a company will be based in major metropolitan areas, independent market researchers may be based anywhere in the United States.

Prerequisites:

Education and Training—High school diploma required, with courses in mathematics, economics, and statistics helpful; college degree required, with a major in marketing, market research, statistics, economics or mathematics helpful; graduate degree helpful for advancement

Experience—Work experience in statistical analysis and market research, or in an advertising or marketing firm; work experience in a travel supplier, travel trade association, state or national travel office, or another segment of the travel industry

Special Skills and Personality Traits—Analytical skills; knowledge mathematics and statistical theory; strong oral and written communication skills; computer skills

CAREER LADDER

```
┌──────────────────────────────────┐
│                                  │
│   Director of Market Research     │
│                                  │
└──────────────────────────────────┘

┌──────────────────────────────────┐
│                                  │
│      Market Researcher            │
│                                  │
└──────────────────────────────────┘

┌──────────────────────────────────┐
│                                  │
│   Clerk, Marketing Department     │
│                                  │
└──────────────────────────────────┘
```

Position Description

Given the intangible nature of the types of products and services sold by the travel industry—obviously, if a night in a hotel room or a seat aboard an airline flight is not sold, that "inventory" is lost forever—many companies value accurate and insightful market research as they plan their overall marketing strategies. Market researchers conduct tests and surveys to gauge public interest in specific travel products and services; using that data as a foundation, they make recommendations to their employers or clients.

Market researchers begin this process by clarifying the exact information needs of the employer or client. They analyze what data is being asked for (e.g., the number of people interested in traveling to a particular

state) and probe further to see what information is really needed (e.g., the number of people interested in staying in budget hotels in that state).

With that objective in mind, they then search existing research databases and resources to determine the scope of survey and test results already available. They use this existing data to refine their research plans.

To gather brand-new data, market researchers employ a number of methods. After selecting a sample of consumers, they may mail questionnaires, call the consumers to ask the questions over the telephone, or send field workers out to question consumers "on the street." Other options include reply cards distributed in hotel rooms or through various means, comments from field workers who secretly observe consumers, and "mystery shoppers" who sample a travel product or service and report their findings. All of these methods would be devised and supervised by market researchers in charge of the project.

Once the data have been gathered, the results would be coded and tabulated into a readable form, such as graphs or charts. Market researchers studying the results would formulate opinions and recommendations for the director of marketing. For example, if a survey revealed that most families with children under 10 years of age prefer budget hotels in a particular state, then researchers might recommend spending advertising dollars targeted to these families and focusing on trips to that state.

In a related vein, market researchers may be asked to study the effects of travel advertising. They can pretest commercials and new products or services on carefully selected focus groups of consumers and analyze the impact of certain forms of media on the buying patterns of consumers.

Because these operations require heavy use of computers, market researchers should be well versed in statistical computer programs and software.

Salaries

Salaries of market researchers will depend on the size and prominence of their employers. Beginning market researchers working in trade associations or other non-profit groups may earn $21,000 or more, while independent market researchers who consult for clients could earn $55,000 or more.

Employment Prospects

Job opportunities in the field of market research will continue to be stable in coming years, as more firms and organizations recognize the value of market research. However, positions will remain fairly competitive. Applicants with advanced degrees or experience in the field will continue to have an advantage.

Advancement Prospects

Promotions in this field tend to come slowly, compared to other aspects of marketing. Market researchers can work to advance to director of market research or director of marketing, if they have the requisite management abilities. Other options include becoming an independent consultant or transferring to a larger organization.

Education and Training

A college degree with a major in market research, marketing, economics, statistics, or mathematics will be required in almost every entry-level position. Master's degrees in business management or marketing will be crucial for higher management positions.

Experience, Skills, and Personality Traits

Market researchers need well-developed analytical skills and an understanding of statistical theory to handle the "grunt work" of market research projects and to form conclusions based on the findings. They should have strong oral and written communication skills to work with other marketers in implementing their findings.

Unions and Associations

Market researchers generally do not belong to a national union.

Their primary national associations are the American Marketing Association (AMA) and the Marketing Research Association (MRA), both located in Chicago. AMA and MRA offer seminars, publications, training programs, and other assistance to professional market researchers.

Tips for Entry

1.   Strengthen your skills in mathematics, marketing, and computer operations, through courses or direct work experience.

2.   Network by writing market researchers in travel companies and associations for career advice. Ask them questions about colleges, course selections, and possible part-time employment or internship opportunities within their firms or groups.

3.   Review the classified sections of newspapers in major U.S. cities (particularly Washington, D.C., and New York City) for market research listings.

4.   Read books and trade publications in the travel and market research industries, to learn the latest trends in these fields.

5.   Consider completing your graduate degree while you are still in school, so that you will have an advantage when you begin applying for full-time jobs.

TRAVEL LAWYER

CAREER PROFILE

Duties: Interprets laws and regulations as they apply to clients; researches laws and cases and formulates opinions for clients; represents clients in court and before other agencies

Alternate Title(s): Travel attorney

Salary Range: $25,000 to $120,000+

Employment Prospects: Very good

Best Geographic Location: Most job opportunities in travel law will be found in major metropolitan areas, especially for lawyers who specialize in this area full time. Other attorneys who handle different types of cases may be located anywhere in the United States.

Prerequisites:

Education and Training—High school diploma required, with courses in English and writing helpful; college degree required, with courses in English, writing, and business management helpful; law degree from an accredited law school required, with courses in commercial law, antitrust law, and labor law helpful

Experience—Writing and research; work experience in a travel agency, tour company, or another segment of the travel industry

Special Skills and Personality Traits—Strong oral and written communication skills; analytical skills; research skills; public speaking abilities; interpersonal skills

CAREER LADDER

```
┌─────────────────────────────────┐
│                                 │
│         Travel Lawyer           │
│                                 │
└─────────────────────────────────┘

┌─────────────────────────────────┐
│                                 │
│    Travel Law Clerk/Paralegal   │
│                                 │
└─────────────────────────────────┘
```

Position Description

Many companies and individuals in the travel industry find themselves in need of legal advice from time to time, like other entrepreneurs and professionals in similar industries. Travel lawyers represent their interests and interpret laws and regulations, with a specialization in legal issues commonly arising in travel businesses.

First, they interpret existing and new laws, statutes, and regulations that apply to their travel industry clients. These laws may range from nondiscriminating employment procedures enforced on all employers to licensing and bonding rules for travel agents and companies in a certain state. Travel lawyers must stay abreast of the latest legal developments in their regions and areas of specialty; then they must determine how those developments affect their clients.

In specific matters brought to them by clients, travel lawyers must research the laws and cases that apply and render an opinion to the client. For example, if a travel agent is being sued by a traveler for a problem that occurred on a cruise, a travel lawyer must find the applicable laws and cases involved, decide whether the travel agent bears legal responsibility for the incident, and advise the client how to proceed with defending him- or herself against possible legal action by the traveler.

If the incident proceeds to court, the travel lawyer will represent the client in court, prepare the best possible defending case, and (if needed) initiate appeals in the case of an unfavorable verdict.

Many incidents that arise during an average travel lawyer's practice involve questions of commercial law (the various responsibilities of travel suppliers, travel agents, and consumers during the course of a trip), antitrust law (the competitive practices that may pit travel suppliers and agents against each other), and labor law (the employment practices of a travel company).

While many lawyers handle a few travel-related cases as part of their general commercial practice, some lawyers in larger cities have devoted their entire practices to representing travel companies. In some cases, they become in-house counsel for major travel companies such as airlines and hotel companies.

Salaries

As with other types of lawyers, travel lawyers with established client bases can earn significant salaries. Beginning lawyers in a firm may make $25,000 or more as they begin their practices, but well-known travel lawyers who represent the largest travel suppliers may earn $120,000 or more in a given year.

Employment Prospects

While the overall demand for lawyers may be slowing somewhat in the United States, attorneys who specialize in travel issues will continue to find good opportunities, since the specialty of travel law has only begun to establish itself. Attorneys with graduate degrees or expertise in business management or taxation, or those with significant industry contacts, will stand the greatest chances of establishing a travel-only practice. Fluency in foreign languages may be helpful, especially if attorneys want to develop clients in other countries who do business in the United States.

Advancement Prospects

Travel lawyers may advance themselves by adding clients and subordinate lawyers to their firms or, in some cases, by becoming in-house counsel for major travel companies.

Education and Training

Travel lawyers must have a college degree and a law degree from an accredited law school. Also, they must pass the bar exam in the state or states in which they want to practice. Some lawyers who want to specialize in taxation or other advanced topics will seek a "masters of law" degree beyond the standard law degree.

Experience, Skills, and Personality Traits

Travel lawyers need strong oral and written communication skills to interview clients and to negotiate solutions to their problems. Research and analytical abilities will help them as they prepare cases and recommend actions.

Computer skills will grow more important in coming years, as legal research begins to depend more on computerized databases and online computer networks.

Unions and Associations

Travel lawyers generally do not belong to a national union.

Their primary national trade organization is the American Bar Association (ABA) in Chicago, Illinois. ABA offers seminars, national meetings, publications, research studies, and other assistance for practicing attorneys.

Tips for Entry

1. Consider working part time for a lawyer, not necessarily one who focuses on travel cases. You will learn firsthand whether you like this line of work.

2. Write letters to well-known travel attorneys, asking for advice on law school and course selections and for leads on internships and clerkships while in law school.

3. Read trade magazines and other publications in the legal profession and the travel industry, to keep up-to-date on the latest developments. Read the classified advertising sections in these magazines for job leads.

4. Improve your writing and research skills, through courses or direct work experience.

5. Gain work experience in some aspect of the travel industry, so that you can display this common background as you work in the future with clients.

TRAVEL PHOTOGRAPHER

CAREER PROFILE

Duties: Takes photographs to illustrate articles, advertisements, and other printed materials; arranges logistics for photography sessions; secures permissions for the use of photographs; compiles and maintains a photography library

Alternate Title(s): Photojournalist

Salary Range: $12,000 to $45,000

Employment Prospects: Fair

Best Geographic Location: While most salaried job opportunities will be found in major metropolitan areas such as New York City and Los Angeles, travel photographers who operate as free-lancers may be found in any part of the country.

Prerequisites:

Education and Training—High school diploma required, with courses in art and business management helpful; college degree helpful, with courses in photography, art, graphic arts, and business management helpful; professional courses or an apprenticeship in photography

Experience—Work experience as a photographer; art direction; graphic arts; printing production

Special Skills and Personality Traits—Creativity; photography skills; graphic arts and design skills; business management skills

CAREER LADDER

```
┌─────────────────────────────────────┐
│  Director of Photography/Photo Editor │
└─────────────────────────────────────┘

┌─────────────────────────────────────┐
│            Photographer              │
└─────────────────────────────────────┘

┌─────────────────────────────────────┐
│        Photographer's Assistant       │
└─────────────────────────────────────┘
```

Position Description

While the working life of the average travel photographer or photojournalist has been overly glamourized, these professionals do provide essential services for the production of newspapers, magazines, travel guides, and other printed products. They select, coordinate, produce, and stock photographs that illustrate these materials, with the primary goal of enticing travelers to visit a destination.

They begin their work on most projects by scouting potential photographs that capture the spirit of the event or destination. They will use existing travel guides, destination brochures, and other resources to research possible locations for photography; they also will interview the clients to gauge their impressions of these locations.

With this list of potential photographs in hand, travel photographers will journey to the locations to scout the photographs firsthand. They will check the availability of the actual sites, reserve the space if needed, coordinate the borrowing or rental of props in the shots, secure models or volunteers if needed, and make any other advance arrangements before the photographs are taken.

On the day of the photo shoot, travel photographers will check existing conditions for photography, such as the weather and lighting conditions. Also, photographers will stage each shot by assembling props and models as needed.

In other cases, travel photographers do not have the luxury of setting up each shot perfectly. Instead, they will tour a destination (alone or with a guide) and take photographs on an impromptu basis, trying to capture images and settings as they appear. Photographers may take many shots of a single image or setting, in order to select the best print afterward.

When they return from the trip, travel photographers will process the film themselves in most cases, developing the shots by hand using sophisticated processing equipment. They will take special steps in developing certain shots, such as cropping a picture to fit the desired space in a book or magazine.

They will maintain a comprehensive library of the photographs they have taken during their career, so that they can develop additional photographs as needed if a client needs pictures from a previous photo shoot. These files will be kept mostly as negatives (thin strips of film with reversed images, from which photographs can be developed), which can be damaged easily, so they must take great care to see that the files are cataloged and stored in optimum conditions.

Many travel photographers serve on the staff of a magazine, newspaper, or book publisher, taking assignments as made by their supervising editors. On the other hand, some photographers choose to work independently as free-lancers, proposing ideas to publishers and accepting temporary assignments from many different clients.

In any case, travel photographers must be prepared for the rigors of being constantly on the road, away from home for weeks or even months at a time.

Salaries

Salaries for travel photographers vary widely, depending on their work arrangements (free-lance or employee) and the size and prestige of their clients. Free-lance travel photographers who work for regional or local publishers may earn as little as $12,000 each year, while travel photographers on the staff of a major national travel magazine may earn $45,000 or more.

Employment Prospects

Job opportunities in this field are very competitive, so the prospects for new entrants will remain fair at best through the next decade. While free-lancing offers a travel photographer freedom to take different assignments, the most stable opportunities will come from the staffs of established publishers.

Advancement Prospects

Photojournalists employed by a publisher may advance into management positions such as art director or photography editor, switch to larger publishers, or open their own photography business. Free-lance travel photographers must add additional clients or expand into larger markets if they want to advance on an independent basis.

Education and Training

A college degree will be required for many positions with major publishers, but a high school diploma is the basic requirement. One essential requirement will be training in photographic skills, through courses at community college or universities or an apprenticeship with an established photographer.

Additional training in graphic arts and business management will be helpful, especially for free-lancers.

Experience, Skills, and Personality Traits

Travel photographers must have the creativity to plan and execute attractive photographs that will give readers a positive impression of the destination or event being featured. They need well-developed photography skills to take pictures in a variety of conditions, in different parts of the world.

If they operate as free-lancers, they should have business management skills to handle the billing and accounting demands of their firm.

Unions and Associations

Travel photographers generally do not belong to a national union.

Their primary national association is the Professional Photographers of America (PPA) in Des Plaines, Illinois. PPA offers seminars, training courses, publications, contests, and other assistance to professional travel photographers.

Tips for Entry

1. Develop a portfolio of your best travel photographs, so that you can use to show potential employers and clients your expertise in the field.

2. Arrange to work part time in the photography department of your local newspaper, a travel magazine, or a professional photographer. Try to set up an apprentice agreement, so that you will be given small assignments that will strengthen your skills as a photographer.

3. Consider getting a college degree in photography, art, graphic arts, or business management, especially if you want to advance into higher management positions within a major publisher.

4. Network in this field by writing travel photographers or the photography editors of travel magazines for career advice or by attending photography conferences and trade shows.

5. Send ideas for articles and photographs to travel magazines and newspapers, offering your services for the photography or the entire package. Several free-lance assignments will generate materials for your portfolio, while giving you a firsthand look at the life of a free-lance photojournalist.

TRAVEL WRITER

CAREER PROFILE

Duties: Researches and outlines a travel article; conducts interviews and assembles supporting materials; writes the article; edits the article for clarity and journalistic style

Alternate Title(s):   Travel journalist

Salary Range: $12,000 to $55,000

Employment Prospects: Fair

Best Geographic Location: While most salaried job opportunities will be found in major metropolitan areas such as New York City and Los Angeles, travel writers who operate as free-lancers may be found in any part of the country.

Prerequisites:

Education and Training—High school diploma required, with courses in English, journalism, and business management helpful; college degree helpful, with courses in English, writing, journalism, geography, and business management helpful; additional courses and seminars in travel writing

Experience—Work experience as a writer (newspapers, magazines and books); editing experience; computer operations

Special Skills and Personality Traits—Creativity; writing skills; business management skills

CAREER LADDER

```
┌─────────────────────────────┐
│                             │
│      Managing Editor        │
│                             │
└─────────────────────────────┘

┌─────────────────────────────┐
│                             │
│           Editor            │
│                             │
└─────────────────────────────┘

┌─────────────────────────────┐
│                             │
│      Assistant Editor       │
│                             │
└─────────────────────────────┘

┌─────────────────────────────┐
│                             │
│       Senior Writer         │
│                             │
└─────────────────────────────┘

┌─────────────────────────────┐
│                             │
│           Writer            │
│                             │
└─────────────────────────────┘
```

Position Description

Working on the staff of a publisher or in a free-lance capacity, travel writers plan, research, write, and edit the articles for newspapers, magazines, and other periodicals as well as travel guides and other books.

They generate ideas for new articles and books, working from an established editorial calendar or from current developments in the travel industry. As they come up with these ideas, they use available library materials and industry sources to gauge the demand for

the destinations being covered, the appeal of the trip to readers, and the logistics involved in preparing the article or book. With this information in hand, they seek approval for the article or book from the publisher or supervising editor.

Once the project has been approved, travel writers proceed with the actual research. They track down other reference sources containing information on the destinations, vessels, and travel companies involved in the trip. They conduct interviews with guides, travel company executives, front-line employees such as desk clerks and drivers, and actual travelers to generate quotes and comments for the project.

In many cases, this phase also commits travel writers to journeying to the destination for a firsthand look at the experiences that the trip offers. Travel writers visit the same sites and engage in the same activities that their readers might attempt so that they can offer comments and suggestions based on their own experiences.

When they return from the trip and complete their research, travel writers begin outlining and writing the article or book. This phase can range from a day or two for very short articles to a year or more for extensive travel guides. They may redraft the project one or more times before arriving at a final draft.

After this self-editing phase, the writers will submit their work to a supervising editor who also will review it. The writers may be asked to make additional changes or corrections before the project is judged complete. In some cases, the writers will be asked to take photographs or to secure slides from travel companies and destination marketing organizations to illustrate the article or book.

While many writers serve as employees on the staffs of publishers, other travel writers prefer to operate as free-lancers, proposing ideas to and accepting assignments from different publishers. In any case, they must be prepared to operate on the road, shouldering heavy travel schedules that will keep them away from home for extended periods of time.

Salaries

Salaries for travel writers vary widely, depending on their work arrangements (free-lance or employee) and the size and prestige of their clients. Free-lance travel writers who work for regional or local publishers may earn as little as $12,000 each year, while travel writers on the staff of a major national travel magazine may earn $55,000 or more.

Employment Prospects

Job opportunities in this field are very competitive, so the prospects for new entrants will remain fair at best through the next decade. While free-lancing offers a travel writer freedom to take different assignments, the most stable opportunities will come from the staffs of established publishers.

Advancement Prospects

Travel writers employed by a publisher may advance into management positions such as assistant editor, editor, or managing editor; switch to larger publishers; or establish their own magazines or free-lance writing

businesses. Free-lance travel writers must add additional clients or expand into larger markets if they want to advance on an independent basis.

Education and Training

A college degree will be required for many positions with major publishers, but a high school diploma is the basic requirement. Travel writers who can exhibit some training in journalism or writing, through courses or direct work experience, will have the greatest chances of being hired.

Additional training in business management will be helpful, especially for free-lancers.

Experience, Skills, and Personality Traits

Travel writers must have the writing skills to handle many different types of assignments quickly and efficiently. Computer skills will help, as many publishers convert their operations to desktop publishing and expect their writers to use these software programs as they prepare their articles or books.

If they operate as free-lancers, they should have business management skills to handle the billing and accounting demands of their firm.

Unions and Associations

Travel writers may belong to the National Writers Union (NWU) in New York City. NWU offers sample contracts and conducts negotiations with major publishers on behalf of writers in all specialties.

Their primary national association is the Society of American Travel Writers (SATW) in Washington, D.C. SATW provides publications, directories, seminars, regional and national meetings, and other assistance to professional travel writers.

Some writers may belong to the American Society of Journalists and Authors (ASJA) in New York City. ASJA represents writers of all specialties in providing sample contracts, national meetings, publications, and other assistance to its members.

Tips for Entry

1. Develop a portfolio of your best magazine articles and other written projects—even in areas other than travel—that you can use to show potential employers and clients your expertise in writing and editing.

2. Arrange to work part time in the editorial department of your local newspaper, a travel magazine, or a book publisher. Volunteer for any assignment that will strengthen your writing skills and generate materials for your portfolio.

3. Consider getting a college degree in English, writing, journalism, or business management, especially if you want to advance into higher management positions within a major publisher.

4. Network in this field by writing travel writers or the editors of travel magazines for career advice or by attending writers' conferences and meetings.

5. Send ideas for articles and photographs to travel magazines and newspapers, offering your services for the article or the entire package. Several free-lance assignments will generate materials for your portfolio, while giving you a firsthand look at the life of a free-lance travel writer.

APPENDIXES

APPENDIX I
College Programs in Travel and Tourism

A. CERTIFICATES, DIPLOMAS, AND ASSOCIATE DEGREES

The following schools grant certificates, diplomas, and associate degrees in travel and tourism, travel agency operations, hotel or restaurant administration, and related fields. The courses offered in these programs range from using computerized reservations systems to planning tours. The schools have been grouped by state.

Because additional schools introduce travel and tourism programs every year, and the following schools expand their courses, consult the latest copy of college guides such as *Lovejoy's* and *Peterson's* (found in the reference sections of libraries or in guidance counseling centers) for the most up-to-date information.

ALABAMA

Auburn University
Auburn, AL 36849-5605
205/844-3264

ALASKA

University of Alaska—Anchorage
3211 Providence Drive
Anchorage, AK 88508
907/786-1401

ARIZONA

Chaparral Career College
4585 E. Speedway Boulevard
Tucson, AZ 85712
602/327-6866

Mundus Institute
4745 N. 7th Street
Phoenix, AZ 85014
800/835-3727

Pima County Community College District
1255 N. Stone Avenue, P.O. Box 5027
Tucson, AZ 85703-0027
602/884-6541

CALIFORNIA

California Culinary Academy
625 Polk Street
San Francisco, CA 94103
415/771-3536 or 800/BAY-CHEF

City College of San Francisco
50 Phelan Avenue
San Francisco, CA 94112
415/239-3152

Columbia College
P.O. Box 1849
Columbia, CA 95310
209/533-5100

Cosumnes River College
8401 Center Parkway
Sacramento, CA 95823
916/688-7334

Grossmont College
8800 Grossmont College Drive
El Cajon, CA 92020
619/465-1700

Management College of San Francisco
1255 Post Street, Suite 450
San Francisco, CA 94109
415/776-7244

Mission College
3000 Mission College Boulevard
Santa Clara, CA 95054-1897
408/748-2753

Oxnard College
4000 S. Rose Avenue
Oxnard, CA 93033
805/488-0911

Santa Barbara City College
721 Cliff Drive
Santa Barbara, CA 93109
805/965-0581

COLORADO

Colorado Mountain College
P.O. Box 10001
Glenwood Springs, CO 81602
800/621-8559

CONNECTICUT

Briarwood College
2279 Mount Vernon Road
Southington, CT 06489
203/628-4751

Gateway Community-Technical College
60 Sargent Drive
New Haven, CT 06511
203/789-7067

Manchester Community College
60 Bidwell Street
Manchester, CT 06040
203/647-6121

Naugatuck Valley Community-Technical College
750 Chase Parkway
Waterbury, CT 06708
203/575-8175

Norwalk Community-Technical College
188 Richards Avenue
Norwalk, CT 06854-1655
203/855-6638

DELAWARE

Delaware Technical and Community College
P.O. Box 610
Georgetown, DE 19947
302/856-5400

FLORIDA

Broward Community College
3501 S.W. Davie Road
Ft. Lauderdale, FL 33314
305/475-6889

Daytona Beach Community College
P.O. Box 2811
Daytona Beach, FL 32115
904/254-3051

Edison Community College
8099 College Parkway, SW
Ft. Myers, FL 33906-6210
813/489-9260

Florida Community College at
Jacksonville
3939 Roosevelt Boulevard
Jacksonville, FL 32205
904/381-3555

ITT Technical Institute
2600 Lake Lucien Drive, Suite 140
Maitland, FL 32751
407/660-2900

National Career Institute
3910 U.S. Highway 301 North, Suite 200
Tampa, FL 33619
813/620-1446

North Technical Educational
Center
7071 Garden Road
Riviera Beach, FL 33404
407/881-4626

Pinellas Technical Education
Center—Clearwater
6100 154th Avenue North
Clearwater, FL 34620
813/531-3531

GEORGIA

Gwinnett Technical Institute
1250 Atkinson Road, Box 1505
Lawrenceville, GA 30246
404/962-7580

HAWAII

Kapiolani Community College
4303 Diamond Head Road
Honolulu, HI 96816
808/734-9485

IDAHO

College of Southern Idaho
P.O. Box 1238
Twin Falls, ID 83303-1238
208/733-9554

ILLINOIS

Belleville Area College
4950 Maryville Road
Granite City, IL 62040
618/931-0600

The Cooking and Hospitality
Institute of Chicago
361 W. Chestnut
Chicago, IL 60610
312/944-0882

Echols International Travel &
Hotel Schools, Inc.
676 N. St. Clair, Suite 1950
Chicago, IL 60611
312/943-5500

Educational Foundation of the
National Restaurant Association
250 S. Wacker Drive, Suite 1400
Chicago, IL 60606
312/715-1010

Joliet Junior College
214 N. Ottawa Street
Joliet, IL 60431

Kendall College
2408 Orrington Avenue
Evanston, IL 60201
708/866-1304

Lexington Institute of
Hospitality Careers
10840 S. Western Avenue
Chicago, IL 60643-3294

Moraine Valley Community College
10900 S. 88th Avenue
Palos Hills, IL 60465
708/974-5320

INDIANA

Indiana University—Purdue
University at Fort Wayne
2101 Coliseum Boulevard East
Neff Hall 330-G
Fort Wayne, IN 46805-1499
219/481-6562

Indiana Vocational Technical
College
1440 E. 35th Avenue
Gary, IN 46409
219/981-1111

Indiana Vocational Technical
College—Central Indiana
1 W. 26th Street
Indianapolis, IN 46208
317/921-4882

Purdue University
1266 Stone Hall
West Lafayette, IN 47907-1266
317/494-4643

Purdue University—North Central
1401 S. U.S. 421
Westville, IN 46391
219/785-5326

IOWA

American Institute of Commerce
1801 E. Kimberly Road
Davenport, IA 52807
319/355-3500

KANSAS

Cloud County Community College
2221 Campus Drive, P.O. Box 1002
Concordia, KS 66901-1002
800/729-5101

Johnson County Community
College
12345 College Boulevard
Overland Park, KS 66210
913/469-8500

KENTUCKY

Sullivan College
3101 Bardstown Road
P.O. Box 33-308
Louisville, KY 40232
502/456-6504

LOUISIANA

The Culinary Arts Institute of
Louisiana
427 Lafayette Street
Baton Rouge, LA 70802
504/343-6233

MAINE

Southern Maine Technical College
Fort Road
South Portland, ME 04106
207/767-9520

MARYLAND

Anne Arundel Community College
101 College Parkway
Arnold, MD 21012
410/541-2390

Baltimore International
Culinary College
25 S. Calvert St.
Baltimore, MD 21202
410/752-4710

Essex Community College
Baltimore County, MD 21237
410/780-6556

Montgomery College
51 Mannakee Street
Rockville, MD 20850
301/279-5176

MASSACHUSETTS

Bay State College
122 Commonwealth Avenue
Boston, MA 02116
617/236-8035

Cape Cod Community College
Route 132
West Barnstable, MA 02668
508/362-2131

Holyoke Community College
303 Homestead Avenue
Holyoke, MA 01040
413/538-7000

Massachusetts Bay Community College
19 Flagg Drive
Framingham, MA 01701-5914
508/875-5300

Newbury College
129 Fisher Avenue
Brookline, MA 02146
617/730-7084

MICHIGAN

Educational Institute of the American Hotel & Motel Association
1407 S. Harrison Road
P.O. Box 1240
East Lansing, MI 48826
800/344-4381

Ferris State University
West Commons
Big Rapids, MI 49307
616/592-2383

Gogebic Community College
E4946 Jackson Road
Ironwood, MI 49938
906/932-4231

Grand Rapids Community College
151 Fountain, NE
Grand Rapids, MI 49503
616/771-3690

Jackson Community College
2111 Emmons Road
Jackson, MI 49201
517/787-0800

Northern Michigan University
Marquette, MI 49855
906/227-2365

Northwestern Michigan College
Traverse City, MI 49684
616/922-1197

Oakland Community College
27055 Orchard Lake Road
Farmington Hills, MI 48334
313/471-7786

Washtenaw Community College
4800 E. Huron River Drive
Ann Arbor, MI 48106
313/973-3584

MINNESOTA

Normandale Community College
9700 France Avenue South
Bloomington, MN 55431
612/832-6375

University of Minnesota— Crookston
Crookston, MN 56716-5001
218/281-6510

MISSOURI

St. Louis Community College at Forest Park
5600 Oakland Avenue
St. Louis, MO 63110
314/644-9751

NEBRASKA

Central Community College
P.O. Box 1024
Hastings, NE 68902
402/461-2458

Southeast Community College
8800 O Street
Lincoln, NE 68520
402/437-2465

NEW JERSEY

Atlantic Community College
5100 Black Horse Pike
Mays Landing, NJ 08330-2699
609/343-4922

Bergen Community College
400 Paramus Road
Paramus, NJ 07652
201/447-7192

Burlington County College
Route 530
Pemberton, NJ 08068
609/894-9311

County College of Morris
214 Center Grove Road
Randolph, NJ 07869-2086
201/328-5000

Hudson County Community College
161 Newkirk Street
Jersey City, NJ 07306
201/714-2193

Middlesex County College
P.O. Box 3050
Edison, NJ 08818-3050
908/906-2538

NEW YORK

Broome Community College
Front Street, P.O. Box 1017
Binghamton, NY 13905
607/778-5008

The Culinary Institute of America
433 Albany Post Road
Hyde Park, NY 12538-1499
914/452-9430

Erie Community College
6205 Main Street
Williamsville, NY 14221
716/851-1393

Finger Lakes Community College
4355 Lakeshore Dirve
Canandaigua, NY 14424
716/394-3500

Jefferson Community College
Watertown, NY 13601
315/786-2278

Mohawk Valley Community College
Upper Floyd Avenue
Rome, NY 13440
315/339-3470

Monroe Community College
1000 E. Henrietta Road
Rochester, NY 14623
716/292-2000

Nassau Community College
Garden City, NY 11530
516/222-7344

New York Institute of Technology
Carleton Avenue
Central Islip, NY 11722
516/348-3290

Paul Smith's College of Arts and Sciences
Paul Smiths, NY 12970
518/327-6218

Rockland Community College
145 College Road
Suffern, NY 10901
914/574-4486

Schenectady County Community College
78 Washington Avenue
Schenectady, NY 12305
518/346-6211

State University of New York at Cobleskill
Cobleskill, NY 12043
518/234-5425

State University of New York, College of Agriculture and Technology at Morrisville
Morrisville, NY 13408
315/684-6016

Sullivan County Community College
P.O. Box 269
Loch Sheldrake, NY 12759
914/434-5750

Tompkins Cortland Community College
Dryden, NY 13053

Westchester Community College
75 Grasslands Road
Valhalla, NY 10595-1698
914/285-6551

NORTH CAROLINA

Asheville-Buncombe Technical Community College
340 Victoria Road
Asheville, NC 28801
704/254-1921

Southwestern Community College
275 Webster Road
Sylva, NC 28779
704/586-4091

OHIO

The University of Akron
200 E. Exchange Street, #102
Akron, OH 44325
216/972-6601

Cincinnati Technical College
3520 Central Parkway
Cincinnati, OH 45223
513/569-1662

Columbus State Community College
550 E. Spring Street
Columbus, OH 43215
800/621-6407 or 614/227-2579

Cuyahoga Community College
2900 Community College Avenue
Cleveland, OH 44115
216/987-4081

OREGON

Chemeketa Community College
P.O. Box 14007
Salem, OR 97309
503/399-5091

Mt. Hood Community College
26000 SE Stark Street
Gresham, OR 97030
503/667-7486

PENNSYLVANIA

Bucks County Community College
Swamp Road
Newtown, PA 18940
215/968-8378

Central Pennsylvania Business School
College Hill Road
Summerdale, PA 17093-0309
717/732-0702 or 800/759-2727

Delaware County Community College
Route 252
Media, PA 19063
215/359-5267

Harcum Junior College
Morris and Montgomery Avenue
Bryn Mawr, PA 19010
215/526-6073

Harrisburg Area Community College
1 HACC Drive
Harrisburg, PA 17110
717/780-2495

IUP Academy of Culinary Arts
Reschini Building
Indiana, PA 15705
800/727-0997

Keystone Junior College
La Plume, PA 18440

Luzerne County Community College
Prospect Street and Middle Road
Nanticoke, PA 18634
717/821-1514

Mount Aloysius College
Cresson, PA 16630
814/886-4131

Northampton Community College
3835 Green Pond Road
Bethlehem, PA 18017
215/861-5593

Pennsylvania Institute of Culinary Arts
717 Liberty Avenue
Pittsburgh, PA 15222
800/432-2433

The Pennsylvania State University—Beaver Campus
Brodhead Road
Monaca, PA 15068-1798
412/773-3762

Pennsylvania State University—Berks Campus
P.O. Box 7009
Reading, PA 19610-6009
215/320-4813

The Restaurant School
4207 Walnut Street
Philadelphia, PA 19104
215/222-4200

RHODE ISLAND

Johnson & Wales University
8 Abbott Park Place
Providence, RI 02903

SOUTH CAROLINA

Greenville Technical College
P.O. Box 5616, Station B
Greenville, SC 29606-5616
803/250-8404

Horry Georgetown Community and Technical College
Myrtle Beach, SC 29577
803/448-8506

Johnson & Wales University at Charleston
701 E. Bay Street
Charleston, SC 29403
800/868-1522 or 803/723-4638

Trident Technical College
P.O. Box 10367
Charleston, SC 29411
803/722-5542

TEXAS

The Art Institute of Houston
1900 Yorktown
Houston, TX 77056
713/623-2040

Del Mar College
Baldwin at Ayers
Corpus Christi, TX 78404
512/886-1734

El Centro College
Main and Lamar
Dallas, TX 75202-3604
214/746-2202

El Paso Community College
P.O. Box 20500
El Paso, TX 79998
915/594-2056

Houston Community College
1300 Holman, Room 302
Houston, TX 77044
713/630-1191

St. Philip's College
1801 Martin Luther King Drive
San Antonio, TX 78203
210/531-3315

UTAH

Utah Valley Community College
800 W. 1200 South
Orem, UT 84058
801/222-8000

VERMONT

New England Culinary Institute
RR #1, 250 Main Street
Montpelier, VT 05602
802/223-6324

VIRGINIA

Commonwealth College
4160 Virginia Beach Boulevard
Virginia Beach, VA 23452
804/340-0222

Northern Virginia Community College
8333 Little River Turnpike
Annandale, VA 22003
703/323-3457

WASHINGTON

Olympic College
1600 Chester
Bremerton, WA 98310-1699
206/478-4709

Renton Technical College
3000 NE 4th Street
Renton, WA 98056
206/235-7863

WISCONSIN

Mid–State Technical College
500 32nd Street North
Wisconsin Rapids, WI 54494
715/422-5476

Nicolet Area Technical College
P.O. Box 518
Rhinelander, WI 54501
715/369-4410

Waukesha County Technical College
800 Main Street
Pewaukee, WI 53072
414/691-5254

SCHOOLS IN OTHER COUNTRIES

ARGENTINA

Ateneo de Estudios Terciarios
Las Heras 2191
(1127) Buenos Aires, Argentina
(54-1) 804-4723

AUSTRALIA

Australian Capital Territory Canberra Institute of Technology
P.O. Box 826
Canberra City 2601 Australia
(06) 273125

Box Hill College
465 Elgar Road
Box Hill, Victoria, Australia 3128
03/895-1229

College of Tourism and Hospitality
Merivale and Tribune Streets
South Brisbane, Queensland, Australia 4101
07/840-2911

William Angliss College
555 La Trobe Street
Melbourne 3000, Australia
03/606-2111

BERMUDA

Bermuda College
P.O. Box DV356
Devonshire DV BX Bermuda
809/236-9000

CANADA

Algonquin College
1385 Woodroffe Avenue
Nepean, ON K2G 1V8 Canada
613/727-4723

Camosun College
3100 Foul Bay Road
Victoria, BC V8P 5J2 Canada
604/370-3146

Canadore College of Applied Arts and Technology
100 College Drive, P.O. Box 5001
North Bay, ON P1B 8K9 Canada
705/474-7600

Centennial College of Applied Arts and Technology
P.O. Box 631, Station A
Scarborough, ON M1K 5E9 Canada
416/698-4157

Constellation College of Hospitality
900 Dixon Road
Etobicoke, ON M9W 1J7 Canada
416/675-2175

George Brown College
300 Adelaide Street East
Toronto, ON M5A 1N1 Canada
416/867-2231

Georgian College of Applied Arts and Technology
One Georgian Drive
Barrie, ON L4M 3X9 Canada
705/722-1592

Holland College, Culinary Institute of Canada Division
305 Kent Street
Charlottetown, Prince Edward Island
C1A 1P5 Canada
902/566-9550

Humber College
205 Humber College Boulevard
Rexdale, ON M9W 5L7 Canada
416/675-3111

New Brunswick Community College—St. Andrews
P.O. Box 427
St. Andrews, NB E0G 2X0 Canada
506/529-8801

Niagara College of Applied Arts and Technology
5881 Dunn Street
Niagara Falls, ON L2G 2N9 Canada
416/374-7454

Nova Scotia Community College
21 Woodlawn Road
Dartmouth, NS B2W 2R7 Canada
902/434-2020

Saskatchewan Institute of Applied Science and Technology-Kelsey Institute
P.O. Box 1520
Saskatoon, Saskatchewan S7K 3R5 Canada
306/933-6730

Sir Sandford Fleming College of Applied Arts and Technology
Brealey Drive
Peterborough, ON K9J 7B1 Canada
705/743-5610

Southern Alberta Institute of Technology
1301-16th Avenue, NW
Calgary, AB T2M 0L4 Canada
403/284-8366

University College of The Cariboo
P.O. Box 3010
900 College Way
Kamloops, BC V2C 5N3
Canada

FRANCE

Le Cordon Bleu
8 rue Leon Delhomme
75015 Paris, France
33-1/48 56 06 06

GREECE

The Alpine Center
37-39 Pat. Ioakim Street
P.O. Box 17082
GR-100 24 Kolonaki Athens, Greece
01/7213 700

NEW ZEALAND

Central Institute of Technology
Private Bag 39807
Wellington Mail Centre
Wellington, New Zealand
04/527-7089

SWITZERLAND

Alpina School of Hotel Management
CH-7076 Parpan, Switzerland
081/35 11 91

Glion International Center
CH 1823 Glion/Montreux
Switzerland
21/963 48 41

Hotel and Tourism School (Hosta)
1854 Leysin, Switzerland
25/34 26 11

Hotel Institute Montreux
15 Avenue des Alpes
1820 Montreux, Switzerland
021/963 74 04

THAILAND

International Hotel and Tourism —Industry Management School
79 Soi Ramkhamhaeng 50, Bangapi
Bangkok 10240 Thailand
66-2-3751880

TURKEY

Bilkent University
06533 Ankara, Turkey
90-4/266-4297

UNITED KINGDOM

Institute of Hospitality Management and English Studies, Isle of Man, British Isles
Windsor House
Port Erin, Isle of Man United Kingdom
0624/832836

B. BACCALAUREATE DEGREES

The following schools grant bachelor's degrees in travel and tourism, hotel administration, restaurant management, and related fields. The courses offered in these programs range from operating computerized reservations systems to planning tours. The schools have been grouped by state.

Because additional schools introduce travel and tourism programs every year, and the following schools expand their courses, consult the latest copy of college guides such as *Lovejoy's* and *Peterson's* (found in the reference sections of libraries or in guidance counseling centers) for the most up-to-date information.

ALABAMA

Auburn University
Auburn, AL 36849-5605
205/844-3264

Tuskegee University
Tuskegee, AL 36088
205/727-8331

University of Alabama
P.O. Box 870158
Tuscaloosa, AL 35487-0158

ALASKA

University of Alaska—Fairbanks
Fairbanks, AK 99775-1070
907/474-6528

ARIZONA

Northern Arizona University
P.O. Box 5638
Flagstaff, AZ 86011-5638

ARKANSAS

Arkansas Tech University
Russellville, AR 72801
501/968-0607

CALIFORNIA

California State Polytechnic University
3801 W. Temple Avenue
Pomona, CA 91768
909/869-2275

Golden Gate University
536 Mission Street
San Francisco, CA 94105
415/904-6718

San Francisco State University
San Francisco, CA 94132
415/338-6087

San Jose State University
San Jose, CA 95192-0058
408/924-3106

United States International University
10455 Pomerado Road
San Diego, CA 92131
619/693-4627

University of San Francisco
San Francisco, CA 94117

COLORADO

Colorado State University
Fort Collins, CO 80523
303/491-5093

Fort Lewis College
1000 Rim Drive
Durango, CO 81301
303/247-7162

University of Colorado at Boulder
Campus Box 419
Boulder, CO 80309

University of Denver
Denver, CO 80208
303/871-4268

CONNECTICUT

Teikyo Post University
800 Country Club Road
Waterbury, CT 06723-2540
203/596–4683

University of New Haven
300 Orange Avenue
West Haven, CT 06516
203/932-7362

DELAWARE

Delaware State College
1200 N. DuPont Highway
Dover, DE 19901
302/739-4971

University of Delaware
Rextrew House
Newark, DE 19716
302/831-6077

DISTRICT OF COLUMBIA

Howard University
2600 Sixth Street, NW
Washington, DC 20059
202/806-1514

FLORIDA

Bethune-Cookman College
640 Second Avenue
Daytona Beach, FL 32115
904/255-1401

Florida International University
North Miami Campus
North Miami, FL 33181
305/948-4500

Lynn University
3601 N. Military Trail
Boca Raton, FL 33431-5598
407/994-0770

Saint Leo College
P.O. Box 2067
Saint Leo College, FL 33574
904/588-8309

Saint Thomas University
16400 NW 32nd Avenue
Miami, FL 33054

University of Central Florida
Orlando, FL 32816
407/823-2188

Webber College
P.O. Box 96
Babson Park, FL 33827
813/638-1431

GEORGIA

Georgia Southern University
LB8034
Statesboro, GA 30460-8034
912/681-5345

Georgia State University
P.O. Box 4018
Atlanta, GA 30302
404/651-3512

HAWAII

Brigham Young University— Hawaii
Laie, HI 96762
808/293-3586

Hawaii Pacific University
1188 Fort Street.
Honolulu, HI 96813
808/544-0229

University of Hawaii at Manoa
2560 Campus Road
Honolulu, HI 96822

ILLINOIS

Chicago State University
95th Street at King Drive
Chicago, IL 60628-1598
312/995-3978

Eastern Illinois University
Klehm Hall
Charleston, IL 61920
217/581-6076

Kendall College
2408 Orrington Avenue
Evanston, IL 60201
708/866-1304

Northern Illinois University
DeKalb, IL 60115
815/753-6333

Southern Illinois University at Carbondale
209 Quigley Hall
Carbondale, IL 62901
618/453-5193

University of Illinois at Urbana-Champaign
905 S. Goodwin Avenue
Urbana, IL 61801
217/333-2024

Western Illinois University
Macomb, IL 61455
309/298-1085

INDIANA

Ball State University
Muncie, IN 47306
317/285-5931

Purdue University
1266 Stone Hall
West Lafayette, IN 47907-1266
317/494-4643

IOWA

Iowa State University
11 MacKay Hall
Ames, IA 50011
515/294-1730

KANSAS

Kansas State University
104 Justin Hall
Manhattan, KS 66506
913/532-5521

KENTUCKY

Morehead State University
Morehead, KY 40351
606/783-2966

Transylvania University
Lexington, KY 40508
606/233-8249

University of Kentucky
122 Erikson Hall
Lexington, KY 40506-0050
606/257-4965

Western Kentucky University
Bowling Green, KY 42101
502/745-4352

LOUISIANA

Grambling State University
P.O. Box 4299
Grambling, LA 71245
318/274-2249

University of New Orleans
New Orleans, LA 70148
504/286-6385

MARYLAND

**University of Maryland, Eastern
  Shore**
Princess Anne, MD 21853
410/651-6567

MASSACHUSETTS

Boston University
808 Commonwealth Avenue
Boston, MA 02215
617/353-3261

Endicott College
376 Hale Street
Beverly, MA 01915
508/927-0585

Lasell College
1844 Commonwealth Avenue
Newton, MA 02166
617/243-2172

Mount Ida College
777 Dedham Street
Newton Centre, MA 02159
617/969-7000

**University of Massachusetts/
  Amherst**
Flint 107
Amherst, MA 01003
413/545-2535

MICHIGAN

Central Michigan University
Smith 100
Mt. Pleasant, MI 48859
517/774-3701

Davenport College
415 E. Fulton
Grand Rapids, MI 49503
616/451-3511

Eastern Michigan University
06H Roosevelt Hall
Ypsilanti, MI 48197
313/487-2490

Ferris State University
West Commons
Big Rapids, MI 49307
616/592-2383

Michigan State University
424 Eppley Center
East Lansing, MI 48824-1121
517/355–5080

MINNESOTA

Moorhead State University
Moorhead, MN 56560
218/236-2486

Southwest State University
Marshall, MN 56258
507/537-7179

MISSISSIPPI

Central Missouri State University
Warrensburg, MO 64093
816/543-4362

**Southwest Missouri State
  University**
901 South National
Springfield, MO 65804
417/836-4908

University of Missouri-Columbia
122 Eckles Hall
Columbia, MO 65211
314/882-4115

NEBRASKA

University of Nebraska
Lincoln, NE 68583-0806
402/472-1582

NEVADA

**Sierra Nevada College-
  Lake Tahoe**
800 College Drive, P.O. Box 4269
Incline Village, NV 89450-4269
702/831-1314

University of Nevada, Las Vegas
4505 Maryland Parkway
Las Vegas, NV 89154-6013
702/895-3161

NEW HAMPSHIRE

New Hampshire College
2500 N. River Road
Manchester, NH 03106-1045
603/644-3128

University of New Hampshire
McConnell Hall
Durham, NH 03824
603/862-3303

NEW JERSEY

Fairleigh Dickinson University
Hesslein Building
Rutherford, NJ 07070
201/460-5362

Montclair State College
Upper Montclair, NJ 07866
201/893-7073

NEW MEXICO

New Mexico State University
P.O. Box 30003
Las Cruces, NM 88003
505/646-5995

NEW YORK

Cornell University
Statler Hall
Ithaca, NY 14853
607/255-6376

Keuka College
Keuka Park, NY 14478
315/536-5324

Mercy College
555 Broadway
Dobbs Ferry, NY 10522
914/693-4500

New York City Technical College
300 Jay Street, Namm 220
Brooklyn, NY 11201
718/260-5630

New York Institute of Technology
Carleton Avenue
Central Islip, NY 11722
516/348-3290

New York University
35 W. Fourth Street, 10th Floor
New York, NY 10003
212/998-5588

Niagara University
Niagara University, NY 14109
716/286-8272

Rochester Institute of Technology
School of Food, Hotel and Travel
    Management
Rochester, NY 14623
716/475-5576

State University of New York at Buffalo
1300 Elmwood Avenue
Buffalo, NY 14222
716/878-5913

State University of New York at Plattsburgh
Plattsburgh, NY 12901
518/564-2164

Syracuse University
034 Slocum Hall
Syracuse, NY 13244-1250

NORTH CAROLINA

Appalachian State University
Boone, NC 28608
704/262-6222

Barber-Scotia College
Concord, NC 28025
704/786-5171

East Carolina University
School of Human Environmental Sciences
Greenville, NC 27858-4353
919/757-6817

Western Caroline University
Cullowhee, NC 28723

NORTH DAKOTA

North Dakota State University
Fargo, ND 58105
701/237-7356

OHIO

Ashland University
Ashland, OH 44805
419/289-5698

Bowling Green State University
Bowling Green, OH 43403
419/372-8713

Ohio University
Athens, OH 45701-2979
614/593-2880

Tiffin University
155 Miami Street
Tiffin, OH 44883
419/447-6485

OKLAHOMA

Langston University
P.O. Box 339
Langston, OK 73050

Northeastern State University
Tahlequah, OK 74464-2399
918/456-5511

Oklahoma State University
210 Human Environmental Sciences West
Stillwater, OK 74078
405/744-8486

OREGON

Southern Oregon State College
Ashland, OR 97520
503/552-6718

PENNSYLVANIA

Cheyney University
Cheyney, PA 19319
215/399-2252

Drexel University
Nesbitt College of Design Arts, 13-503
Philadelphia, PA 19104
215/895-2411

East Stroudsburg University
East Stroudsburg, PA 18301
717/424-3511

Indiana University of Pennsylvania
Ackerman Hall
Indiana, PA 15705
412/357-4440

Marywood College
2300 Adams Avenue
Scranton, PA 18509-1598
717/348-6277

Mercyhurst College
Glenwood Hills
Erie, PA 16546
814/824-2333

Pennsylvania State University
203 S. Henderson
University Park, PA 16802
814/863-0009

Widener University
One University Place
Chester, PA 19013
215/499-1101

RHODE ISLAND

Johnson & Wales University
8 Abbott Park Place
Providence, RI 02903
800/343-2565

SOUTH CAROLINA

University of South Carolina
Columbia, SC 29208
803/777-6665

SOUTH DAKOTA

Black Hills State University
USB 9007
Spearfish, SD 57799-9007
605/642-6212

TENNESSEE

Tennessee State University
Nashville, TN 37209
615/320-3354

University of Tennessee, Knoxville
Knoxville, TN 37996-1900
615/974-5445

TEXAS

Stephen F. Austin State University
Nacogdoches, TX 75962-3014
409/568-2171

Texas Tech University
P.O. Box 41162
Lubbock, TX 79409
806/742-3068

University of Houston
Houston, TX 77204-3902
713/743-2600

University of North Texas
P.O. Box 5248
Denton, TX 76201-5248
817/565–2436

University of Texas at San Antonio
San Antonio, TX 78249-0631
210/691-5778

VIRGINIA

James Madison University
Harrisonburg, VA 22807
703/568-3225

**Virginia Polytechnic Institute and
State University**
362 Wallace Hall
Blacksburg, VA 24061-0429
703/231-5515

Virginia State University
P.O. Box 9211
Petersburg, VA 23806
804/524-5048

WASHINGTON

Washington State University
Pullman, WA 99164-4742
509/335-5766

WEST VIRGINIA

Concord College
Athens, WV 24712
304/384-5218

Shepherd College
Shepherdstown, WV 25443
304/876-2511

West Virginia University
P.O. Box 6124
Morgantown, WV 26506-6124
304/293-3402

WISCONSIN

Mount Mary College
2900 N. Menomonee River Parkway
Milwaukee, WI 53222
414/258-4810

University of Wisconsin—Stout
Menomonie, WI 54751
715/232-2088

SCHOOLS IN OTHER COUNTRIES

AUSTRALIA

Bond University
Gold Coast
Queensland 4229, Australia
61/075 95 2258

University of New South Wales
P.O. Box 1
Kensington 2033, Australia
02/3995294

CANADA

Mount Saint Vincent University
166 Bedford Highway
Halifax, NS B3M 2J6
Canada
902/457-6398

Ryerson Polytechnical Institute
350 Victoria Street
Toronto, ON M5B 2K3
Canada
416/979-5041

University of Calgary
Calgary, AB T2N 1N4
Canada
403/220-8310

University of Guelph
Guelph, ON N1G 2W1
Canada
519/824-4120

HONG KONG

Hong Kong Polytechnic
Hung Hom, Kowloon
Hong Kong
852/7666383

THE NETHERLANDS

Hoge Hotelschool Maastricht
Bethlehemweg 2
P.O. Box 3900
6202 NX Maastricht
The Netherlands
31/43 687272

**Hotel Management School
Leeuwarden**
P.O. Box 1298
8900 CG Leeuwarden
The Netherlands
58/33 03 30

**Hotelschool the Hague, Institute of
Hospitality Management**
2 Brusselselaan
2587 AH The Hague
The Netherlands
31/70-3512481

SWITZERLAND

**International Hotel and Tourism
Training Institutes, Ltd.**
P.O. Box 4006
Basel, Switzerland
061/312 30 94

TURKEY

Bilkent University
06533 Ankara, Turkey
90-4/266-4297

UNITED KINGDOM

**Birmingham College of Food,
Tourism and Creative Studies**
Summer Row
Birmingham B3 1JB
England
021/235–2774

**Manchester Metropolitan
University**
Old Hall Lane
Manchester, England
061/224 2717

Queen Margaret College
Clerwood Terrace
Edinburgh, Scotland EH12 8TS

University of Huddersfield
Queensgate, Huddersfield HD1 3DH
England
0484 422288

University of Surrey
Guildford, Surrey GU2 5XH
England
0483/300800

C. GRADUATE DEGREES

The following schools grant master's and doctoral degrees in travel and tourism, hotel administration, restaurant management, and related fields. The courses offered in these programs range from operating computerized reservations systems to planning tours. The schools have been grouped by state.

Because additional schools introduce travel and tourism programs every year, and the following schools expand their courses, consult the latest copy of college guides such as *Lovejoy's* and *Peterson's* (found in the reference sections of libraries or in guidance counseling centers) for the most up-to-date information.

CALIFORNIA

Golden Gate University
536 Mission Street
San Francisco, CA 94105
415/904-6718

COLORADO

University of Denver
Denver, CO 80208
303/871-4268

DISTRICT OF COLUMBIA

George Washington University
817 23rd Street, NW
Washington, DC 20052
202/994-6280

FLORIDA

Florida International University
North Miami Campus
North Miami, FL 33181
305/948-4500

Lynn University
3601 N. Military Trail
Boca Raton, FL 33431
407/994-0770

HAWAII

University of Hawaii at Manoa
2560 Campus Road
Honolulu, HI 96822
808/956-8946

INDIANA

Purdue University
1266 Stone Hall
West Lafayette, IN 47907-1266
317/494-4643

IOWA

Iowa State University
11 MacKay Hall
Ames, IA 50011-1120
515/294-8474

KANSAS

Kansas State University
104 Justin Hall
Manhattan, KS 66506-1404
913/532-5521

MASSACHUSETTS

**University of Massachusetts—
   Amherst**
Amherst, MA 01003
413/545-4046

MICHIGAN

Eastern Michigan University
206H Roosevelt Hall
Ypsilanti, MI 48197
313/487-2490

Michigan State University
424 Eppley Center
East Lansing, MI 48824-1121
517/355–5080

NEVADA

University of Nevada, Las Vegas
4505 Maryland Parkway
Las Vegas, NV 89154-6014
702/895–3903

NEW YORK

Cornell University
Statler Hall
Ithaca, NY 14853-6902
607/255-7246

New York University
35 W. Fourth Street, 10th Floor
New York, NY 10003
212/998-5588

Niagara University
Niagara University, NY 14109
716/286-8271

Rochester Institute of Technology
Rochester, NY 14623
716/475-6017

PENNSYLVANIA

The Pennsylvania State University
20 Henderson Building
University Park, PA 16802
814/863-4847

RHODE ISLAND

Johnson & Wales University
8 Abbott Park Place
Providence, RI 02903
401/456-4738

SOUTH CAROLINA

University of South Carolina
Columbia, SC 29208
803/777-6665

TENNESSEE

University of Tennessee, Knoxville
1215 Cumberland Avenue
Knoxville, TN 37996-1900
615/974-5445

TEXAS

Texas Tech University
P.O. Box 41162
Lubbock, TX 79409-1162

University of Houston
Houston, TX 77204-3902
713/743-2428

University of North Texas
P.O. Box 5248
Denton, TX 76201-5248
817/565-2436

VIRGINIA

**Virginia Polytechnic Institute and
   State University**
362 Wallace Hall
Blacksburg, VA 24061-0429
703/231-5515

WISCONSIN

University of Wisconsin—Stout
Menomonie, WI 54751
715/232-2364

SCHOOLS IN OTHER COUNTRIES

AUSTRALIA

Bond University
Gold Coast
Queensland 4229, Australia
61/075 95 2293

CANADA

University of Calgary
Calgary, AB T2N 1N4
Canada
403/220-8310

University of Guelph
Guelph, ON N1G 2W1
Canada
519/824-4120

FRANCE

Institut de Management Hotelier International
95021 Cergy-Pontoise Cedex
France
33-1/3443 3172

APPENDIX II
Trade Associations and Unions

The following trade associations and unions involve as members the professionals mentioned in this book. Contact the applicable groups for the latest information on position requirements, education and training, salaries, and other information regarding these career fields.

Air Line Employees Association, International
5600 S. Central Avenue
Chicago, IL 60638
312/767-3333

Air Line Pilots Association, International
1625 Massachusetts Avenue, NW
Washington, DC 20036
703/689-2270 or 202/328-5400

Air Transport Association
1301 Pennsylvania Avenue, NW, Suite 1100
Washington, DC 20004-1707
202/626-4000

Airport Consultants Council
421 King Street, Suite 200
Alexandria, VA 22314
703/683-5908

Airport Ground Transportation Association
901 Scenic Drive
Knoxville, TN 37919
615/525-1108

Airports Council International
1775 K Street, NW, Suite 500
Washington, DC 20006
202/293-8500

American Association of Airport Executives
4212 King Street
Alexandria, VA 22302
703/824-0500

American Bar Association
750 N. Lake Shore Drive
Chicago, IL 60611
312/988-5000

American Bed and Breakfast Association
10800 Midlothian Turnpike, Suite 254
Richmond, VA 23235-4700
804/379-2222

American Bus Association
1100 New York Avenue, NW, Suite 1050
Washington, DC 20005-3934
202/842-1645

American Car Rental Association
1225 Eye Street, NW, Suite 1000
Washington, DC 20005
202/682-4770

American Hotel and Motel Association
1201 New York Avenue, NW, Suite 600
Washington, DC 20005-3931
202/289-3100

American Marketing Association
250 S. Wacker Drive, Suite 200
Chicago, IL 60606
312/648-0536

American Society of Association Executives
1575 I Street, NW
Washington, DC 20005-1168
202/626-2723

American Society of Travel Agents
1101 King Street
Alexandria, VA 22314-2944
703/739-2782

American Spa and Health Resort Association
P.O. Box 585
Lake Forest, IL 60045
708/234-8851

Assembly of National Tourist Office Representatives
347 Fifth Avenue, Suite 610
New York, NY 10016
212/447-0027

Association of Corporate Travel Executives
66 Morris Avenue
Springfield, NJ 07801
201/467-2850

Association of Flight Attendants
1625 Massachusetts Avenue, NW
Washington, DC 20036
202/328-5400

Association of Group Travel Executives
c/o The Light Group, Inc.
424 Madison Avenue, Suite 705
New York, NY 10017
212/486-4300

Association of Physical Fitness Centers
600 Jefferson Street, Suite 203
Rockville, MD 20852
301/424-7744

Association of Retail Travel Agents
845 Sir Thomas Court, Suite 3
Harrisburg, PA 17109
717/545-9548

Association of Travel Marketing Executives
257 Park Avenue South, 17th Floor
New York, NY 10010
212/598-2472

Center for Hospitality Research and Service
c/o Department of Hotel, Restaurant and Institutional Management
Virginia Polytechnic Institute and State University
Blacksburg, VA 24061
703/231-5515

Computerized Airline Sales and Marketing Association
c/o Swissair Building 15, JFK Airport
Jamaica, NY 11430
718/481-4505

Council on Hotel, Restaurant, and Institutional Education
1200 17th Street, NW
Washington, DC 20036-3097
202/331-5990

Cruise Lines International Association
500 Fifth Avenue, Suite 1407
New York, NY 10110
212/921-0066

Educational Foundation of the National Restaurant Association
250 S. Wacker Drive, No. 1400
Chicago, IL 60606
312/715-1010

Hospitality Lodging and Travel Research Foundation
c/o AHMA
1201 New York Avenue, Suite 600
Washington, DC 20005-3931
202/289-3117

Hospitality Sales and Marketing Association International
1300 L Street, NW, Suite 800
Washington, DC 20005
202/789-0089

Hotel Employees and Restaurant Employees International Union
1219 28th Street, NW
Washington, DC 20007
202/393-4373

Independent Innkeepers Association
P.O. Box 150
Marshall, MI 49068
616/789-0393

Institute of Certified Travel Agents
148 Linden Street, P.O. Box 812059
Wellesley, MA 02181-0012
617/237-0280

International Association of Amusement Parks and Attractions
1448 Duke Street
Alexandria, VA 22314
703/836-4800

International Association of Conference Centers
243 N. Lindbergh Boulevard, Suite 315
St. Louis, MO 63141
314/993-8575

International Association of Convention and Visitors Bureaus
2000 L Street, NW, Suite 702
Washington, DC 20036-4990
202/296-7888

International Association of Tour Managers—North American Region
65 Charnes Drive
East Haven, CT 06513-1225
203/466-0425

International Association of Travel Journalists
P.O. Box D
Hurleyville, NY 12747
914/434-1529

International Federation of Festival Organizations
4230 Stansbury Avenue, No. 105
Sherman Oaks, CA 91423
818/789-7596

International Federation of Flight Attendants
630 Third Avenue, 5th Floor
New York, NY 10017
212/818-1130

International Federation of Women's Travel Organizations
13901 N. 73rd Street, Suite 201B
Scottsdale, AZ 85260-3125
602/596-6640

International Festivals Association
1034 Caroline, P.O. Box 2950
Port Angeles, WA 98362-0336
206/457-3141

International Flight Attendants Association
2314 Old New Windsor Pike
New Windsor, MD 21776

International Food, Wine, and Travel Writers Association
P.O. Box 13110
Long Beach, CA 90803
310/433-5969

International Institute of Convention Management
9200 Bayard Place
Fairfax, VA 22032
703/978-6287

International Society of Women Airline Pilots
P.O. Box 66268
Chicago, IL 60666-0268

International Spa and Fitness Association
1300 L Street, NW, Suite 1050
Washington, DC 20005-4107
202/789-5920

International Special Events Society
8335 Allison Pointe Trail, Suite 100
Indianapolis, In 46250
317/577-1910

Les Clefs d'Or USA (concierges)
c/o John Neary
The Carlyle Hotel
35 E. 76th Street
New York, NY 10021
212/744-1600

Marketing Research Association
2189 Silas Deane Highway, Suite 5
Rocky Hill, CT 06067
203/257-4008

Meeting Professionals International
1950 Stemmons Freeway
Infomart Building, Suite 5018
Dallas, TX 75207-3109
214/712-7700

National Bed-and-Breakfast Association
P.O.Box 332
Norwalk, CT 06852
203/847-6196

National Business Travel Association
1650 King Street, No. 301
Alexandria, VA 22314-2747
703/684-0836

National Coalition of Black Meeting Planners
10320 Little Patuxent Parkway, Suite 1106
Columbia, MD 21044
202/628-3952

National Council of State Travel Directors
1100 New York Avenue, NW
Washington, DC 20005-3934
202/408-8422

National Motorcoach Network
Patriot Square, 10527C Braddock Road
Fairfax, VA 22032
703/250-7897

National Press Photographers Association
3200 Croasdaile Drive, Suite 306
Durham, NC 27705
919/383-7246

National Restaurant Association
1200 17th Street, NW
Washington, DC 20036
202/331-5900

National Tour Association
546 E. Main Street
Lexington, KY 40508
606/226-4444

National Trust for Historic Preservation
1785 Massachusetts Avenue, NW
Washington, DC 20036
202/673-4000

North American Ski Journalists Association
P.O. Box 5334
Takoma Park, MD 20913
301/864-8428

Outdoor Writers Association of America
2017 Cato Avenue, Suite 101
State College, PA 16801
814/234-1011

Professional Convention Management Association
100 Vestavia Office Park, Suite 220
Birmingham, AL 35216
205/823-7262

Professional Guides Association of America
2416 S. Eads Street
Arlington, VA 22202-2532
703/892-5757

Professional Photographers of America
1090 Executive Way
Des Plaines, IL 60018
708/299-8161

Professional Travelogue Sponsors
19403 R. H. Johnson Boulevard
Sun City West, AZ 85375

Receptive Services Association
2 Greentree Center, Suite 225
Marlton, NJ 08053
609/985-2878

Regional Airline Association
1200 19th Street, NW, Suite 300
Washington, DC 20036-2401
202/857-1170

Resort and Commercial Recreation Association
P.O. Box 1208
New Port Richey, FL 34656
813/845-7373

Society for the Advancement of Travel for the Handicapped
347 Fifth Avenue, Suite 610
New York, NY 10016
212/447-7284

Society of American Travel Writers
4101 Lake Boone Trail, Suite 201
Raleigh, NC 27607
919/787-5181

Society of Corporate Meeting Professionals
2600 Garden Road, No. 208
Monterey, CA 93940
408/649-6544

Society of Government Meeting Planners
219 E. Main Street
Mechanicsburg, PA 17055
717/795-7467

Society of Incentive Travel Executives
21 W. 38th Street, 10th Floor
New York, NY 10018-5584
212/575-0910

Society of Travel and Tourism Educators
19364 Woodcrest
Harper Woods, MI 48225
313/526-0710

Travel and Tourism Research Association
10200 W. 44th Avenue, Suite 304
Wheat Ridge, CO 80033
303/940-6557

Travel Industry Association of America
1100 New York Avenue, NW
Washington, DC 20005-3934
202/408-8422

Travel Journalists Guild
P.O. Box 10643
Chicago, IL 60610
312/664-9279

Union of Flight Attendants
5621 Bower Court
Commerce City, CO 80022
303/289-1689

United Bus Owners of America
1300 L Street, NW, Suite 1050
Washington, DC 20005
202/484-5623

U.S. Tour Operators Association
211 E. 51st Street, Suite 12-B
New York, NY 10022
212/750-7371

U.S. Travel Data Center
1100 New York Avenue, NW
Washington, DC 20005-3934
202/408-1832

APPENDIX III
Major National Travel Employers

The following companies are the premier employers in their segments of the travel industry. You can research them further by consulting the reference departments of local libraries for directories and articles in magazines and newspapers.

Use this list when applying for internships, summer jobs, or permanent positions.

TRAVEL AGENCIES

While the best opportunities can be found in your local travel agencies—most of America's travel agents work in small mom-and-pop agencies grossing less than $5 million annually—these large national agencies may offer employment to qualified agents with experience.

Carlson Travel Group, Inc.
701 Carlson Parkway
Minneapolis, MN 55459
612/449-2199

Fugazy Executive Travel Service, Inc.
260 Franklin Street
Boston, MA 02110
617/261-7700

Garber's Travel Service, Inc.
1047 Commonwealth Avenue
Boston, MA 02215
617/787-0600

Omega World Travel Inc.
3102 Omega Office Park
Fairfax, VA 22031
703/359-0200

Rosenbluth International, Inc.
1650 Market Liberty Place
Philadelphia, PA 19107
215/981-1700

Travel & Transport Inc.
2120 S. 72nd Street
Omaha, NE 68124
402/592-4100

Travel Services Network, Inc.
147 Charter Oak Avenue
Hartford, CT 06106
203/541-6829

USTravel Affiliates
70 E. Lake Street, Suite 1100
Chicago, IL 60601-5905
312/782-6870

Wright Travel Agency Inc.
1 Burton Hills Boulevard
Nashville, TN 37215
615/665-1111

TOUR OPERATORS

Abercrombie & Kent International
1520 Kensington Road
Oak Brook, IL 60521
708/954-2944

Americantours International, Inc.
9800 S. Sepulveda Boulevard
Los Angeles, CA 90045
213/641-9953

Apple Vacations
7 Campus Boulevard
Newtown Square, PA
215/359-6500

Brendan Tours, Inc.
15137 Califa Street
Van Nuys, CA 91411
818/785-9696

Collette Travel Services, Inc.
162 Middle Street
Pawtucket, RI 02860
401/728-3805

DER Tours, Inc.
11933 Wilshire Boulevard
Los Angeles, CA 90025
310/479-4411

GoGo Tours Inc.
69 Spring Street
Ramsey, NJ 07446
201/934-3500

Jetset Tours
1775 Broadway
New York, NY 10019
212/474-8740

Maritz Inc.
1375 N. Highway Drive
Fenton, MO 63099
314/827-4000

Maupintour
1515 St. Andrews Drive
Lawrence, KS 66047
913/843-1211

Mayflower Tours
1225 Warren St.
Downers Grove, IL 60515
708/960-3430

MTI Vacations Inc.
1220 Kensington Road
Oak Brook, IL 60521
708/990-6340

Perillo Tours
577 Chestnut Ridge Road
Woodcliff Lake, NJ 07675
201/307-1234

Tauck Tours
11 Wilton Road
Westport, CT 06880
203/226-6911

Travcoa
2350 SE Bristol Street
Newport Beach, CA 92660
714/476-2800

Travel Impressions Limited, Inc.
465 Smith Street
Farmingdale, NY 11735
516/845-8000

AIRLINES

Air Wisconsin Inc.
203 Challenger Drive
Appleton, WI 54915
414/739-1325

Alaska Airlines Inc.
19300 Pacific Highway South
Seattle, WA 98188
206/433-3100

Aloha Airlines Inc.
Honolulu International Airport
Honolulu, HI 96819
808/836-4101

America West Airlines Inc.
4000 E. Sky Harbor Boulevard
Phoenix, AZ 85034
602/693-0800

American Airlines Inc.
P.O. Box 619616 DFW Airport
Dallas, TX 75261
817/967-2640

American Trans Air Inc.
7337 W. Washington St.
Indianapolis, IN 46231
317/247-4000

Atlantic Southeast Airlines Inc.
100 Hartsfield Center Parkway
Atlanta, GA 30354
404/766-1400

Carnival Airlines Inc.
1815 Griffin Road, Suite 205
Dania, FL 33004
305/923-8672

Comair Inc.
P.O. Box 75021
Cincinnati, OH 45275
606/525-2550

Continental Airlines Inc.
2929 Allen Parkway, Suite 1100
Houston, TX 77019
713/834-5000

Delta Air Lines Inc.
1030 Delta Boulevard
Atlanta, GA 30320
404/715-2600

Hawaiian Airlines Inc.
531 Ohohia Street
Honolulu, HI 96820
808/835-3700

Kiwi International Air Lines Inc.
Hemisphere Plaza
Newark, NJ 07114
201/645-1133

MGM Grand Air
1500 Rosencrans Avenue, Suite 350
Manhattan Beach, CA 90266
310/536-7500

Markair Inc.
P.O. Box 196769
Anchorage, AK 99519-6769
907/243-1414

Midwest Express Airlines Inc.
4915 S. Howell Avenue
Milwaukee, WI 53207
414/747-4000

Northwest Airlines Inc.
5101 Northwest Drive
St. Paul, MN 55111-3034
612/726-2111

Reno Air Inc.
220 Edison Way
Reno, NV 89502
702/686-3835

Southwest Airlines
P.O. Box 36611
Dallas, TX 75235-1661
214/263-1717

Trans World Airlines Inc.
515 N. Sixth Street
St. Louis, MO 63101
314/589-3000

United Airlines Inc.
P.O. Box 66100
Chicago, IL 60666
708/952-4000

USAir Inc.
2345 Crystal Drive
Arlington, VA 22227
703/418-7000

WestAir Commuter Airlines Inc.
5588 Air Terminal Drive
Fresno, CA 93727
209/294-6915

CAR RENTAL COMPANIES

Alamo Rent-A-Car Inc.
110 SE Sixth Street
Fort Lauderdale, FL 33301
305/522-0000

Avis Rent-A-Car System Inc.
900 Old Country Road
Garden City, NY 11530
516/222-3000

Budget Rent-A-Car Systems Inc.
4225 Naperville Road
Lisle, IL 60532
708/955-1900

Dollar Rent-A-Car Systems Inc.
P.O. Box 33167
Tulsa, OK 74135-1167
918/669-3000

Hertz Corp.
225 Brae Boulevard
Park Ridge, NJ 07656-0713
201/307-2866

Kemwel Group Inc.
106 Calvert Street
Harrison, NY 10528-3199
914/835-5555

National Car Rental System Inc.
7700 France Avenue South
Minneapolis, MN 55435
612/830-2121

Thrifty Rent-A-Car System Inc.
5330 E. 31st Street, Suite 100
Tulsa, OK 74135
918/665-3930

Value Rent-A-Car Inc.
2500 N. Military Trail, Suite 300
Boca Raton, FL 33431
407/998-7200

CRUISE LINES AND RIVERBOATS

Alaska Sightseeing/Cruise West
4th and Battery Building., Suite 700
Seattle, WA 98121
206/441-8687

American Hawaii Cruises
Two N. Riverside Plaza
Chicago, IL 60606
312/466-6000

Bergen Line
405 Park Avenue
New York, NY 10022
212/319-1300

Carnival Cruise Lines
3655 NW 87th Avenue
Miami, FL 33178-2428
305/599-2600

Celebrity Cruises
5200 Blue Lagoon Drive
Miami, FL 33126
305/262-6677

Clipper Cruise Line
7711 Bonhomme Avenue
St. Louis, MO 63105
314/727-2929

Costa Cruise Lines
80 SW Eighth Street
Miami, FL 33130-3097
305/358-7325

Crystal Cruises
2121 Avenue of the Stars
Los Angeles, CA 90067
310/785-9300

Cunard Line
555 Fifth Avenue
New York, NY 10017
212/880-7500

Delta Queen Steamboat Co.
30 Robinson Street Wharf
New Orleans, LA 70130-1890
504/586-0631

Dolphin Cruise Line
P.O. Box 025420
Miami, FL 33102-5420
305/358-5122

Holland America Line—Westours
300 Elliott Avenue West
Seattle, WA 98119
206/281-3535

Memphis Queen Co.
Foot of Monroe Avenue
Memphis, TN 38103
901/527-5694

Mississippi Belle II
311 Riverview Drive
Clinton, IA 52732
319/243-9000

Norwegian Cruise Line
95 Merrick Way
Coral Gables, FL 33134
305/447-9660

Orient Lines
1510 SE 17th Street
Ft. Lauderdale, FL 33316
305/527-6660

Pearl Cruises
6301 NW 5th Way
Ft. Lauderdale, FL 33309
305/772-8600

Premier Cruise Lines
400 Challenger Road
Cape Canaveral, FL 32920
407/783-5061

President Riverboat Casino Missouri
802 N. 1st Street
St. Louis, MO 63102
314/622-1800

President Riverboat Casinos
130 W. River Drive
Davenport, IA 52801
319/322-2578

Princess Cruises
10100 Santa Monica Boulevard
Los Angeles, CA 90067
310/553-1770

Radisson Diamond Cruises
600 Corporation Drive, Suite 410
Ft. Lauderdale, FL 33344
305/776-6123

Regency Cruises
260 Madison Avenue
New York, NY 10016
212/972-4774

Renaissance Cruises
1800 Eller Drive, Suite 300
P.O. Box 350307
Ft. Lauderdale, FL 33335-0307
305/463-0982

Royal Caribbean Cruise Line
1050 Caribbean Way
Miami, FL 33132-2096
305/539-6000

Royal Cruise Lines
1 Maritime Plaza
San Francisco, CA 94111
415/788-0610

Seabourn Cruise Line
55 Francisco Street
San Francisco, CA 94133
415/391-7444

Special Expeditions
720 Fifth Avenue
New York, NY 10019
212/765-7740

THEME PARKS

Busch Entertainment Corp.
1 Busch Place
St. Louis, MO 63118
314/577-2000

Fiesta Texas Theme Park
17000 I-10 West
San Antonio, TX 78257
210/697-5000

Knott's Berry Farm
8039 Beach Boulevard
Buena Park, CA 90620
714/827-1776

Marine World Foundation
Marine World Parkway
Vallejo, CA 94589
707/644-4000

Old Tucson Co.
201 S. Kinney Road
Tucson, AZ 85746
602/883-0100

Opryland USA
2802 Opryland Drive
Nashville, TN 37214
615/889-6600

Paramount Parks
8720 Red Oak Boulevard, Suite 315
Charlotte, NC 28217
704/525-5250

Santa Claus Land
Highway 162
Santa Claus, IN 47579
812/937-4401

Sea World of Florida
7007 Seaworld Drive
Orlando, FL 32821
407/351-3600

Six Flags Entertainment Corp.
400 Interplace Parkway
Parsippany, NJ 07054
201/402-8100

Universal City Studios—California
100 Universal City Plaza
Universal City, CA 91608
818/777-1000

Universal City Studios—Florida
1000 Universal Studios Place
Orlando, FL 32819
407/363-8100

Walt Disney Co.
500 S. Buena Vista Street
Burbank, CA 91521
818/560-1000

Walt Disney World Co.
1375 N. Buena Vista Avenue
Orlando, FL 32818

HOTELS

Best Western International
6201 North 24th Parkway
Phoenix, AZ 85016-2023
602/957-4200

Choice Hotels International
10750 Columbia Pike
Silver Spring, MD 20901
301/593-5600

Days Inns of America
339 Jefferson Road
Parsippany, NJ 07054
201/428-9700

Doral Hotels & Resorts
122 E. 42nd Street, Suite 1601
New York, NY 10168

Doubletree Hotels Corp.
410 N. 44th Street, Suite 700
Phoenix, AZ 85008
602/220-6666

Embassy Suites/Hampton Inns/Promus Hotels
6800 Poplar Avenue, Suite 200
Memphis, TN 38138
901/758-3100

Helmsley Hotels
36 Central Park South
New York, NY 10019
212/371-4000

Hilton Hotels Corp.
9336 Civic Center Drive
Beverly Hills, CA 90210
310/278-4321

Holiday Inn Worldwide
3 Ravinia Drive
Atlanta, GA 30346-2149
404/604-2000

Howard Johnson Franchise Systems
339 Jefferson Road
Parsippany, NJ 07054
201/428-9700

Hyatt Hotels & Resorts Corp.
200 W. Madison Street
Chicago, IL 60606
312/750-1234

ITT Sheraton Corp.
60 State Street
Boston, MA 02109
617/367-3600

La Quinta Inns
112 Pecan Street
San Antonio, TX 78205
210/302-6000

Marriott Hotels, Resorts & Suites
1 Marriott Drive
Washington, DC 20058
301/380-9000

Motel 6
14651 Dallas Parkway, Suite 500
Dallas, TX 75240
214/386-6161

Radisson Hotels International
Carlson Parkway, P.O. Box 59159
Minneapolis, MN 55459-8204
612/540-5526

Ramada Franchise Systems, Inc.
339 Jefferson Road
Parsippany, NJ 07054
201/428-9700

Red Lion Hotels & Inns
4001 Main Street, P.O. Box 1027
Vancouver, WA 98666
206/696-0001

Red Roof Inns
4355 Davidson Road
Hilliard, OH 43026-2491
614/876-3200

Ritz/Carlton Hotel Co.
3414 Peachtree Road NE, Suite 300
Atlanta, GA 30326
404/237-5500

Stouffer & Renaissance Hotels
2655 Le Jeune Road, Suite 800
Coral Gables, FL 33134
305/460-1900

Travelodge/Thriftlodge
1973 Friendship Drive
El Cajon, CA 92020
619/448-1884

APPENDIX IV
Travel Recruiting Firms

The following firms recruit entry–level employees and executives for all types and sizes of travel companies around the United States and in other countries. While these agencies operate on a national or regional basis, you may find other recruiters in local telephone directories or newspaper classified advertising sections.

When you begin searching for employment, you should send your resume and other application materials to these recruiters. However, the author does not endorse these agencies, and you should consider any offers from a recruiter—such as representing you to travel employers for a fee— very carefully before signing any agreement.

America's Travel Employment Agency
7334 Topanga Canyon Boulevard, Suite 216
Canoga Park, CA 91303
818/347-8841

Passport Placement
Box 1117
Fairfax, CA 94930
415/258-0900

Pratt Personnel
Box 1506
Sausalito, CA 94966
415/332-7761

Provelle Associates
16800 Devonshire Street, Suite 315
Granada Hills, CA 92134
818/360-7589

The Randolph Agency
30 E. 42nd Street
New York, NY 10017
212/599-0310

Temporary Travel Personnel
93 South S Street, #E
Livermore, CA 94550
415/455-0501

Temps for Travel
116A Park Avenue South
Winter Park, FL 32789
407/629-2290

Travel Career Network
303 Congress Street, Suite 600
Boston, MA 02210
617/951-0974

Travel Executive Search
5 Rose Avenue.
Great Neck, NY 11021
516/829-8829

Travel Industry Consultants
404 East Street
Hingham, MA 02043
617/749-8344

Travel Industry Placement Service
26711 N. Western Highway, Suite 420
Southfield, MI 48034
313/352-8496

Travel People Personnel
20 Park Plaza, Suite 606
Boston, MA 02116
800/242-3020
617/542-0070

Travel Personnel
9515 E. Valley Ranch Parkway, Suite 1054
Irving, TX 75063
214/638-0118

Travel Placement Service
1640 E. 78th Street
Minneapolis, MN 55423
800/328-5541 612/866-9754

The Travel Recruiter
5202 Washington Street, #8
Downers Grove, IL 60515
708/852-8862

TravelSearch Network
12860 Hillcrest Road, Suite 201
Dallas, TX 75280
214/458-1145

Travel Temps
7390 Twin Branches Road
Atlanta, GA 30328
404/399-9350

Travel Temps
7720 Wisconsin Avenue, Suite 217
Bethesda, MD 20814
301/654-5556

Yours in Travel Personnel Agency
12 W. 37th Street
New York, NY 10018
212/697-7855

APPENDIX V
Bibliography

A. BOOKS

Thousands of books have been written about the many facets of the global travel and tourism industry. While the following books have been divided into general categories, the content of a book in one area may apply equally well to other categories.

Begin your search for these books in your local library or bookstores. If the library does not have the specific titles you want to read, ask the librarian to order them for you through the interlibrary loan system.

This short list is only a beginning. To find other books on these subjects, check the business and travel sections in your library or local bookstores. You also can check *Books in Print* (found in the reference section of most libraries) to locate other titles.

TRAVEL AGENTS

Boyd, Wilma. *Travel Agent*. New York: Prentice-Hall, 1989.

Dominitz, Ben, and Dominitz, Nancy D. *Travel Free! How to Start & Succeed in Your Own Travel Consultant Business*. Roseville, Calif.: Prima Publishing, 1984.

Ford-Woodcock, Jean. *Introduction to Airline & Travel Agency Operations*. Glen Ellyn, Ill.: Bridgewater Publishing Co., 1986.

Fremont, Pamela. *How to Open & Run a Money-Making Travel Agency*. New York: John Wiley & Sons, 1983.

Friedheim, Eric. *Travel Agents: From Caravans & Clippers to the Concorde*. New York: Eric Friedheim, 1992.

Goldsmith, Carol, and Waigand, Ann. *Building Profits with Group Travel*. San Francisco: Dendrobium Books, 1990.

Gregory, Aryear. *The Travel Agent: Dealer in Dreams*. New York: Prentice-Hall, 1992.

Lehmann, Armin D. *Travel & Tourism: An Introduction to Travel Agency Operations*. New York: Macmillan, 1978.

Rosenbluth, Hal. *The Customer Comes Second, And Other Secrets*. New York: William Morrow, 1992.

Thompson, Douglas. *How to Open Your Own Travel Agency*. San Francisco: Dendrobium Books, 1992.

Todd, Ginger, and Rice, Susan. *Travel Perspectives: A Guide to Becoming a Travel Agent (Update Two)*. Albany, N.Y.: Delmar, 1992.

BUSINESS TRAVEL

Cummings, Jack. *Business Travel Survival Guide*. New York: John Wiley & Sons, 1991.

DeKieffer, Donald E. *The International Business Traveler's Companion*. Yarmouth, Me.: Intercultural Press, 1992.

Jenkins, Darryl. *Managing Business Travel: Improving the Bottom Line Through Effective Travel Management*. Homewood, Ill.: Business One Irwin, 1992.

Jenkins, Darryl. *Savvy Business Travel: Management Tips from the Pros*. Homewood, Ill.: Business One Irwin, 1992.

TOUR OPERATORS

Gleasner, Diana. *Touring by Bus at Home and Abroad*. Washington, D.C.: American Association of Retired Persons, 1989.

Grinder, Alison L., and McCoy, E. Sue. *The Good Guide: A Sourcebook for Interpreters, Docents, & Tour Guides*. Scottsdale, Ariz.: Ironwood Publishing, 1985.

Mitchell, Gerald E. *How to Design & Package Tours*. Englewood, Fla.: G.E. Mitchell & Associates, 1992.

Mitchell, Gerald E. *How to Be a Tour Guide*. Englewood, Fla.: G.E. Mitchell & Associates, 1992.

Poynter, James M. *Tour Design, Marketing, & Management*. New York: Prentice-Hall, 1992.

Reilly, Robert T. *Handbook of Professional Tour Management*. Albany, N.Y.: Delmar, 1990.

Warren, Stuart. *Bus Touring: A Guide to Charter Vacations, USA*. Santa Fe, N.M.: John Muir, 1989.

CONVENTION AND MEETING PLANNING

Burleson, Clyde W. *Effective Meetings: The Complete Guide*. New York: John Wiley & Sons, 1990.

Devney, Darcy C. *Organizing Special Events & Conferences*. Sarasota, Fla.: Pineapple Press, 1990.

Dodson, Dorian. *How to Put on a Great Conference: A Straightforward, Friendly and Practical Guide*. Santa Fe, N.M.: Adolfo Street, 1992.

Ernst & Young Staff. *The Complete Guide to Special Event Management: Business Insights, Financial Advice, & Successful Strategies from Ernst & Young*. New York: John Wiley & Sons, 1992.

Lord, Robert W. *Running Conventions, Conferences, and Meetings*. Ann Arbor, Mich.: Books on Demand.

Penner, Richard H. *Conference Center Planning & Design*. New York: Watson-Guptill, 1991.

Petersen, David C. *Convention Centers, Stadiums, & Arenas*. Washington, D.C.: Urban Land, 1989.

Seekings, David. *How to Organize Effective Conferences and Meetings*. East Brunswick, N.J.: Nichols Publishing, 1992.

Shaw, Margaret, ed. *Convention Sales: A Book of Readings*. East Lansing, Mich.: Educational Institute of the American Hotel & Motel Association, 1990.

Weirich, Marguerite L. *Meetings and Convention Management*. Albany, N.Y.: Delmar, 1992.

HOTELS AND INNS

Baker, Sue, et al. *Principles of Hotel Front Office Operations: A Study Guide*. New York: Cassell, 1994.

Bardi, James. *Front Office Management*. New York: Van Nostrand Reinhold, 1990.

Bryson, McDowell, and Ziminski, Adele. *The Concierge: Key to Hospitality*. New York: John Wiley & Sons, 1992.

Craig, Stephen R. *Housekeeping Management in the Hospitality Industry*. New York: Prentice-Hall, 1988.

Fewell, Arnold V., and Wills, Neville. *Marketing in the Hospitality Industry*. Stoneham, Mass.: Butterworth-Heinemann, 1992.

Gray, William S., and Liguori, Salvatore. *Hotel & Motel Management & Operations*. New York: Prentice-Hall, 1990.

Hart, Christopher W., and Troy, David A. *Strategic Hotel-Motel Marketing*. East Lansing, Mich.: Educational Institute of the American Hotel & Motel Association, 1986.

Hotch, Ripley, and Glassman, Carol. *How to Start & Run Your Own Bed & Breakfast Inn*. Mechanicsburg, Pa.: Stackpole, 1992.

Hoyle, Leonard H., et al. *Managing Conventions & Group Business*. East Lansing, Mich.: Educational Institute of the American Hotel & Motel Association, 1989.

Kasavana, Michael L., and Brooks, Richard M. *Managing Front Office Operations*. East Lansing, Mich.: Educational Institute of the American Hotel & Motel Association, 1991.

Lattin, Gerald W. *The Lodging & Food Service Industry*. East Lansing, Mich.: Educational Institute of the American Hotel & Motel Association, 1989.

Martin, Robert J., and Jones, Tom. *Professional Management of Housekeeping Operations*. New York: John Wiley & Sons, 1992.

Nebel, Ed. *Managing Hotels Effectively*. New York: Van Nostrand Reinhold, 1991.

Nykiel, Ronald A. *Marketing in the Hospitaglity Industry*. New York: Van Nostrand Reinhold, 1988.

Powers, Tom. *Marketing Hospitality*. New York: John Wiley & Sons, 1990.

Reid, Robert. *Hospitality Marketing Management*. New York: Van Nostrand Reinhold, 1988.

Renner, Peter F. *Basic Hotel Front Office Procedures*. New York: Van Nostrand Reinhold, 1988.

Rey, Anthony M., and Wieland, Ferdinand. *Managing Service in Food & Beverage Operations*. East Lansing, Mich.: Educational Institute of the American Hotel & Motel Association, 1985.

Rundback, Betty. *Bed & Breakfast U.S.A. 1993*. New York: NAL-Dutton, 1993.

Schneider & Tucker. *The Professional Housekeeper*. New York: Van Nostrand Reinhold, 1989.

Shortt, C. Vincent. *How to Open & Successfully Operate a Country Inn: Completely Revised, Updated for the 90's*. Stockbridge, Mass.: Berkshire House, 1993.

Stankus, Jan. *How to Open & Operate a Bed & Breakfast Home*. Old Saybrook, Conn.: Globe Pequot, 1992.

Stiel, Holly, and Collins, Delta. *Ultimate Service: Complete Handbook to the World of the Concierge*. New York: Prentice-Hall, 1994.

Taylor, Monica, and Taylor, Richard. *Start & Run a Profitable Bed & Breakfast: Your Step-by-Step Business Plan*. Bellingham, Wash.: ISC Press, 1992.

Witteman, Ad. *Hotel Bell Captain*. Las Vegas: Camelot Consulting, 1987.

Witteman, Ad. *Hotel Housekeeper*. Las Vegas: Camelot Consulting, 1986.

Witzky, Herbert K. *Modern Hotel-Motel Management Methods*. Jenks, Okla.: Williams Book Co., 1987.

Witzman, Joseph E., and Block, Jack. *Front! A Complete Guide to Hotel Front Office Procedures*. San Diego, Calif.: Educational Publications, 1989.

Zander, Mary L. *How to Start Your Own Bed & Breakfast: A Guide to Hosting Paying Guests in Your House or Apartment*. Spencertown, N.Y.: Golden Hill Press, 1985.

CASINOS

Bain, Joseph H., and Dror, Eli. *Casinos: The International Casino Guide*. Port Washington, N.Y.: Bain Dror, 1991.

Johnston, David. *Temples of Chance*. New York: Doubleday, 1992.

Tegtmeier, Ralph. *Casinos*. New York: Vendome, 1989.

RESTAURANTS

Brown, Douglas R. *The Restaurant Manager's Handbook: How to Set Up, Operate, & Manage a Financially Successful Restaurant*. Ocala, Fla.: Atlantic, 1989.

Campbell, Monty, and Gruppioni, Fabrizio. *So, You Want to Own a Restaurant? The Dream, The Steps, The Reality*. Ventura, Calif.: Archangel Press, 1989.

Chavez-Irvin, Dixie L., and O'Malley, Thomas. *Secrets of Service (How to Make Money in the Restaurant Business)*. Santa Monica, Calif.: Institute Press of Santa Monica, 1978.

Coltman, Michael M. *Start & Run a Profitable Restaurant: A Step-by-Step Business Plan*. Bellingham, Wash.: ISC Press, 1991.

Drewes, Jack C. *The Restaurant Owner's Handbook: Success Through Management Awareness*. Albuquerque, N.M.: Posh Publishing, 1988.

Egerton-Thomas, Christopher. *How to Open & Run a Successful Restaurant*. New York: John Wiley & Sons, 1989.

Gordon, Robert T. *Restaurant Management Guide*. New York: Prentice-Hall, 1984.

Green, Eric, et al. *Profitable Food & Beverage Management: Planning*. New York: Van Nostrand Reinhold, 1990.

Green, Eric, et al. *Profitable Food & Beverage Management: Operations*. New York: Van Nostrand Reinhold, 1987.

Herbert, Jack. *Creating a Successful Restaurant: An Expert's Fact-Filled Handbook for Anyone Going into (or Even Thinking About Going into) the Restaurant Business*. New York: St. Martin's Press, 1985.

Lawrence, Elizabeth. *The Complete Restaurateur: A Practical Guide to the Craft & Business of Restaurant Ownership*. New York: NAL-Dutton, 1992.

Lundberg, Donald A. *The Restaurant: From Concept to Operation*. New York: John Wiley & Sons, 1993.

Lundberg, Donald A. *The Hotel & Restaurant Business*. New York: Van Nostrand Reinhold, 1988.

Lundberg, Donald E., and Armatas, James. *The Management of People in Hotels & Restaurants*. Madison, Wisc.: Brown & Benchmark, 1992.

McHugh, Donald. *Table Attendant Training*. Garden City, N.Y.: Bergwall, 1983.

Martin, William B. *Quality Service: The Restaurant Manager's Bible*. Ithaca, N.Y.: Cornell University School of Hotel Administration, 1986.

Martin, William B. *Restaurant Server's Guide*. Menlo Park, Calif.: Crisp Publications, 1987.

Schiavi, Lynn. *The Whole Waitress Handbook*. Sterling, N.J.: Midnight Oil Press, 1985.

The Waitresses Handbook: A Guide to the Legal Rights of Waitresses & Other Restaurant Workers. Washington, D.C.: Women's Legal Defense, 1986.

Ware, Richard, and Rudnick, James. *How to Open Your Own Restaurant*. New York: Viking Penguin, 1991.

Wilson, Jack. *The Nuts and Bolts of Operating a Successful Restaurant: Making Money in the Food Business*. Dunedin, Fla.: CMN Press, 1992.

AIRLINES AND AIRPORTS

Airport Landside Planning & Operations. Washington, D.C.: Transportation Research Board, 1993.

Banfe, Charles. *Airline Management*. Englewood Cliffs, N.J.: Prentice-Hall, 1991.

Carpenter, Sylvia. *How to Get a Job in the Airlines*. Santa Barbara, Calif.: Broughton Hall, 1986.

Doganis, Rigas. *The Airport Business*. New York: Routledge, 1992.

Dunlop, Reginald. *Come Fly with Me: Your Nineties Guide to Becoming a Professional Flight Attendant*. Chicago: Maxamillian, 1992.

Gesell, Laurence E. *The Administration of Public Airports*. Chandler, Ariz.: Coast Aire, 1992.

Leary, William M. *The Airline Industry*. New York: Facts On File, 1992.

March, Carol. *Choosing an Airline Career: In-Depth Descriptions of Entry-Level Positions, Travel Benefits, How to Apply & Interview*. New York: Capri Publishing, 1992.

Paradis, Adrian A. *Opportunities in Airline Careers*. Lincolnwood, Ill.: NTC Publishing Co., 1983.

Rabalais, Ken J. *The Flight Attendant Interview Handbook: How to Get a Job with the Airlines*. Denver, Co.: Plane Sense, 1992.

Rudman, Jack. *Airport Supervisor*. Syosset, N.Y.: National Learning, 1991.

Shearer, Debby, and Ross, Jim. *How You Too Can Become a Flight Attendant! A Step by Step Guide*. Slippery Rock, Pa.: Ross Publishing Co., 1987.

Wells, Alexander T. *Airport Planning and Management*. Blue Ridge Summit, Pa.: TAB Books, 1992.

CRUISE LINES

Braynard, Frank O., and Miller, William H. *Fifty Famous Liners, Vol. 3*. New York: Norton, 1988.

Fodor Staff. *Fodor's Cruises & Ports of Call '93: Choosing the Perfect Ship & Enjoying Your Time Ashore*. New York: Fodors Travel, 1992.

Fricker, Phillip J. *Ocean Liners*. Boston: T. Reed Publications, 1992.

Kennedy, Don. *How to Get a Job on a Cruise Ship*. Atlanta: Career South Publications, 1991.

Miller, Mary F. *How to Get a Job with a Cruise Line*. St. Petersburg, Fla.: Ticket Adventure, 1992.

Reilly, George. *Guide to Cruise Ship Jobs*. Babylon, N.Y.: Pilot Books, 1993.

THEME PARKS

Adams, Judith A., and Perkins, Edwin J. *The American Amusement Park Industry: A History of Technology & Thrills*. New York: Macmillan, 1991.

American Automobile Association Staff. *AAA Guide to North America's Theme Parks*. New York: Macmillan, 1992.

ASSOCIATIONS

Drucker, Peter F. *Managing the Non-Profit Organization: Principles and Practices*. New York: HarperCollins, 1990.

Encyclopedia of Associations. Detroit: Gale Research, 1994.

Ernstthal, Henry, and Jefferson, Vivian, ed. *Principles of Association Management*. Washington, D.C.: American Society of Association Executives, 1988.

MARKETING AND MARKET RESEARCH

Aaker, David A., and Day, George S. *Marketing Research*. New York: John Wiley & Sons, 1990.

Butters, John P., and Lew, Roberta A., eds. *Travel Industry Marketing*. Wellesley, Mass.: Institute of Certified Travel Agents, 1990.

Dillon, William R. *Essentials of Marketing Research*. Homewood, Ill.: Irwin, 1992.

Fry, R. *Marketing & Sales Career Directory*. Detroit: Visible Ink Press, 1992.

Holbert, Neil. *Careers in Marketing*. Ann Arbor, Mich.: Books on Demand.

Steinberg, Margery. *Opportunities in Marketing Careers*. Lincolnwood, Ill.: NTC Publishing Group, 1988.

TRAVEL JOURNALISM AND PHOTOGRAPHY

Burgett, Gordon. *The Travel Writer's Guide: How to Earn at Least Twice What You Spend on Travel by Writing Newspaper & Magazine Articles*. Roseville, Calif.: Prima Publishing, 1991.

Casewit, Curtis. *How to Make Money from Travel Writing*. Old Saybrook, Conn.: Globe Pequot, 1988.

Darling, Dennis C. *Chameleon with Camera: A Unique Primer on Travel Photography & How to Survive the Trip*. Austin, Tex.: Dorsoduro Press, 1989.

Levoy, Gregg. *This Business of Writing*. Cincinnati: Writer's Digest Books, 1992.

McCartney, Susan. *Travel Photography: A Complete Guide to How to Shoot & Sell*. New York: Allworth Press, 1992.

Purcell, Ann, and Purcell, Carl. *A Guide to Travel Writing & Photography*. Cincinnati: Writer's Digest Books, 1991.

Weir, Nevada. *Adventure Travel Photography: How to Shoot Great Pictures off the Beaten Track*. New York: Watson-Guptill, 1992.

Zobel, Louise Purwin. *The Travel Writer's Handbook*. Chicago: Surrey Books, 1992.

B. MAGAZINES AND PERIODICALS

Trade magazines and periodicals can help you in several ways as you begin considering a career in travel and tourism. Reading them during the initial stages of your educational program or job search will keep you abreast of the latest developments in the industry, from new companies which have formed to current travel trends among consumers. Many publications feature classified or display advertising sections which will alert you to openings in your field. They also publicize the activities of trade associations, such as seminars and training programs, that you may want to investigate.

Check the periodicals department of your local libraries for these publications. If you want to subscribe to a magazine, send a postcard to the proper address requesting prices and terms. (Some travel periodicals circulate free of charge, while others require a subscription fee.)

TRAVEL INDUSTRY (GENERAL)

Airliners
P.O. Box 52-1238
Miami, FL 33152

Business Travel Management
488 Madison Ave.
New York, NY 10022

Business Travel News
600 Community Drive
Manhasset, NY 11030

Bus Tours Magazine
9698 W. Judson Road
Polo, IL 61064

Frequent Flyer
1775 Broadway
New York, NY 10019

Jax Fax Travel Marketing Magazine
397 Post Road
Darien, CT 06820

Tour & Travel News
600 Community Drive
Manhasset, NY 11030

Travel Agent Magazine
801 Second Avenue
New York, NY 10017

Travel Management Daily
1775 Broadway, 19th Floor
New York, NY 10019

Travel Trade
15 W. 44th Street, Sixth Floor
New York, NY 10036

Travel Weekly
500 Plaza Drive
Secaucus, NJ 07094

TravelAge Caribbean
1775 Broadway, 19th Floor
New York, NY 10019

TravelAge East
1775 Broadway
New York, NY 10019

TravelAge Europe
1775 Broadway, 19th Floor
New York, NY 10019

TravelAge West
49 Stevenson
San Francisco, CA 94105

AIRLINES

Air Transport World
1350 Connecticut Avenue, NW, Suite 902
Washington, DC 20036

Air Line Pilot
535 Herndon Parkway, P.O. Box 1169
Herndon, VA 22070

Airfair
6401 Congress Avenue, Suite 100
Boca Raton, FL 33487

Airline Executive
6255 Barfield Road
Atlanta, GA 30328

Airports
1156 15th Street, NW
Washington, DC 20005

Professional Pilot
3014 Colvin Street
Alexandria, VA 22314

AMUSEMENT PARKS, CASINOS, AND THEME PARKS

Amusement Business
49 Music Square West
Nashville, TN 37203

Gaming & Wagering Business
Seven Penn Plaza
New York, NY 10001

Tourist Attractions and Parks
7000 Terminal Square, #210
Upper Darby, PA 19082

HOTELS, MOTELS, RESORTS, AND SPAS

Club Management
8730 Big Bend Boulevard
St. Louis, MO 63119

Florida Hotel & Motel Journal
200 W. College Avenue
Tallahassee, FL 32301

Hotel & Motel Management
7500 Old Oak Boulevard
Cleveland, OH 44130

Hotel-Motel Management
120 Second Street
Duluth, MN 55810

Hotels
1350 E. Touhy Avenue
Des Plaines, IL 60018

Lodging Hospitality
1100 Superior Avenue
Cleveland, OH 44114

Lodging Magazine
1201 New York Avenue, NW
Washington, DC 20005

RESTAURANTS AND CATERING

Airline, Ship & Catering Onboard Services Magazine
665 La Villa Drive
Miami, FL 33166

Chef/Institutional
134 Main Street
New Canaan, CT 06840

The Florida Restaurant, Hotel & Motel Journal
P.O. Box 1228
Pensacola, FL 32596

Food & Service
2401 South I-35
Austin, TX 78741

Food Arts
387 Park Avenue
New York, NY 10016

Food Management
270 Madison Avenue, Fifth Floor
New York, NY 10016

Food Service Director
633 Third Avenue
New York, NY 10017

Food Service East
545 Boylston Street, Suite 605
Boston, MA 02116

Foodservice Equipment & Supplies
  Specialist
1350 E. Touhy Avenue
Des Plaines, IL 60018

Foodservice Product News
104 Fifth Ave.
New York, NY 10011

The Kansas Restaurant
359 S. Hydraulic
Wichita, KS 67211

Midsouthwest Restaurant Magazine
3800 N. Portland
Oklahoma City, OK 73112

The Missouri Restaurant
4049 Pennsylvania, Suite 201
Kansas City, MO 64111

Nation's Restaurant News
425 Park Avenue
New York, NY 10022

Restaurant Business
633 Third Avenue
New York, NY 10017

Restaurant Hospitality
1100 Superior Avenue
Cleveland, OH 44114

Restaurant Management Insider
1541 Morris Avenue
Bronx, NY 10457

Restaurants & Institutions
1350 E. Touhy Avenue
Des Plaines, IL 60018

Restaurants USA
1200 17th Street, NW
Washington, DC 20036

Restaurateur
7926 Jones Brance Drive, #530
McLean, VA 22102

Southeast Food Service News
3678 A-1 Steward Drive
Doraville, GA 30340

Wisconsin Restaurateur
125 W. Doty
Madison, WI 53703

ALLIED SUBJECTS

Advertising Age
740 N. Rush Street
Chicago, IL 60611

Adweek
49 E. 21st Street
New York, NY 10010

Editor & Publisher
11 W. 19th Street
New York, NY 10011

Folio: The Magazine for Magazine
  Management
6 River Bend
Stamford, CT 06907

Journal of Applied Nutrition
P.O. Box 18433
Asheville, NC 28814

Journal of the American Dietetic
  Association
216 W. Jackson, Suite 800
Chicago, IL 60606

O'Dwyer's PR Services Report
271 Madison Avenue, #600
New York, NY 10016

Passenger Train Journal
923 Friedman Drive
Waukesha, WI 53186

PR Reporter
The Dudley House, 14 Front Street
Exeter, NH 03833

Public Relations Journal
33 Irving Place
New York, NY 10003

Public Relations News
127 E. 80th Street
New York, NY 10021

The Public Relations Quarterly
44 W. Market Street
Rhinebeck, NY 12572

Writer's Digest
1507 Dana Avenue
Cincinnati, OH 45207

CONSUMER TRAVEL
MAGAZINES

AAA Going Places Magazine
1515 N. Westshore Boulevard
Tampa, FL 33607

AAA Motorist
1020 Hamilton Street, P.O. Box 1910
Allentown, PA 18105

AAA Motorist of N.E. Pennsylvania
1035 N. Washington Avenue
Scranton, PA 18509

AAA Today
95 S. Hanover Street
Pottstown, PA 19464

AAA Today
1380 Dublin Road, Suite 109
Columbus, OH 43215

AAA Traveler
118 E. Market Street
York, PA 17401

AAA World
1000 AAA Drive
Lake Mary, FL 32746

AAA World Magazine
8030 Excelsior Drive
Madison, WI 53717

Accent Magazine
1720 Washington Boulevard,
P.O. Box 10010
Ogden, UT 84404

Adventure Road
641 Lexington Avenue, 2nd Floor
New York, NY 10022

American Way
4333 Amon Carter Boulevard, MD 5598
Fort Worth, TX 76155

Arizona Highways Magazine
2039 W. Lewis Avenue
Phoenix, AZ 85009

Asia Pacific Travel
1540 Gilbreth Road
Burlingame, CA 94010

ASU Travel Guide
1525 E. Francisco Blvd.
San Rafael, CA 94901

Away
888 Worcester Street
Wellesley, MA 02181

Bank Travel Management
130 N. Broadway
Lexington, KY 40507

Country Inns—Bed & Breakfast
P.O. Box 182
South Orange, NJ 07079

Courier
546 E. Main Street
Lexington, KY 40508

Cruises & Tours
1502 Augusta, Suite 415
Houston, TX 77057

Cruise Travel
990 Grove Street
Evanston, IL 60201

Diversion
60 E. 42nd Street
New York, NY 10165

Go
720 E. Morehead Street
Charlotte, NC 28202

The Group Travel Leader
130 N. Broadway
Lexington, KY 40507

Hartford Automobiler
815 Farmington Avenue
W. Hartford, CT 06119

Home & Away
3750 Guion Road
Indianapolis, IN 46222

Home & Away Magazine
910 N. 96th Street
Omaha, NE 68114

Keystone AAA Motorist
2040 Market Street
Philadelphia, PA 19103

The Maryland Motorist
1401 Mt. Royal Avenue
Baltimore, MD 21217

The Mature Traveler Newsletter
P.O. Box 50820
Reno, NV 89513

Mexico Today!
2388 Champlain Street, NW, #12
Washington, DC 20009

Michigan Living
1 Auto Club Drive
Dearborn, MI 48126

The Midwest Motorist
12901 N. Forty Drive
St. Louis, MO 63141

Motor Club News
484 Central Avenue
Newark, NJ 07107

The Motorist
P.O. Box 186
Johnstown, PA 15907

Motorland
150 Van Ness Avenue
San Francisco, CA 94102

Motor News
201 Kings Highway South
Cherry Hill, NJ 08034

National Motorist
188 The Embarcadero
San Francisco, CA 94105

New York Motorist
1415 Kellum Place
Garden City, NY 11530

Northwest Travel
P.O. Box 18000
Florence, OR 97439

Odyssey
1027 N. 7th Street
Milwaukee, WI 53233

The Ohio Motorist
6000 S. Marginal Road
Cleveland, OH 44103

The Oregon Motorist
600 SW Market Street
Portland, OR 97201

Out West
10522 Brunswick Road
Grass Valley, CA 95945

Recommend Magazine
5979 NW 151st Street, Suite 120
Hialeah, FL 33014

Rocky Mountain Motorist
4100 E. Arkansas Avenue
Denver, CO 80222

See Magazines
3675 Clark Road
Sarasota, FL 34233

Sky
12955 Biscayne Boulevard
Miami, FL 33181

Southern Accents
2100 Lakeshore Drive
Birmingham, AL 35209

Sun Scene/Voyager
2001 Killebrew Drive, Suite 105
Minneapolis, MN 55425

Touring America
P.O. Box 583
Mount Morris, IL 61054

Travel & Leisure
1120 Avenue of the Americas
New York, NY 10036

Travel 50 & Beyond
1502 Augusta, Suite 415
Houston, TX 77057

Travel/Holiday
28 W. 23rd Street
New York, NY 10010

Travel Smart
40 Beechdale Road
Dobbs Ferry, NY 10522

Travel South
2100 Lakeshore Drive
Birmingham, AL 35209

USAir Magazine
1301 Carolina Street
Greensboro, NC 27401

The Valley Motorist
100 Hazel Street
Wilkes Barre, PA 18702

The Washington Motorist
330 Sixth Avenue
Seattle, WA 98109

The Western New York Motorist
100 International Drive
Williamsville, NY 14221

Westways
2601 S. Figueroa Street
Los Angeles, CA 90007

INDEX

Boldface page numbers indicate main topics.